Sloppy, not focused analytically blunt.
Proppity!

HATE THY NEIGHBOR

Hate Thy Neighbor

Move-In Violence and the Persistence of Racial Segregation in American Housing

Jeannine Bell

NEW YORK UNIVERSITY PRESS

New York and London

NEW YORK UNIVERSITY PRESS
New York and London
www.nyupress.org

References to Internet websites (URLs) were accurate at the time of writing.
Neither the author nor New York University Press is responsible for URLs that
may have expired or changed since the manuscript was prepared.

LIBRARY OF CONGRESS CATALOGING-IN-PUBLICATION DATA

Bell, Jeannine, 1969-
Hate thy neighbor : move-in violence and the persistence of racial segregation in American
housing / Jeannine Bell.
pages cm
Includes bibliographical references and index.
ISBN 978-0-8147-9144-8 (cl : alk. paper)
1. Discrimination in housing—United States. 2. Minorities—Housing—United States. 3.
Racism—United States. I. Title.
HD7288.76.U5B45 2013
363.5'1—dc23
                                  2012050530

New York University Press books are printed on acid-free paper, and their binding materials
are chosen for strength and durability. We strive to use environmentally responsible
suppliers and materials to the greatest extent possible in publishing our books.
Manufactured in the United States of America
10 9 8 7 6 5 4 3 2 1

For Ella Serena, my daughter

CONTENTS

ACKNOWLEDGMENTS

I am so grateful to the many people who, though they were lucky enough to have lives very different from those of the people whose experiences I chronicle here, nevertheless supported this book.

Some of the first to hear about the project provided critical support, from beginning to end. Early funding for the research project that became this book came from Indiana University's Faculty Research Support Program. The O'Byrne Fund at the Indiana University Maurer School of Law supported the hiring of research assistants and the writing of the book over multiple summers. In this regard, one of the project's biggest supporters was my dean, Lauren Robel, who has continuously supported the project from its very beginning.

Earlier versions of the project were presented at the American Bar Foundation, where I spent a year as a fellow. I'm grateful to several colleagues who provided guidance while I was doing research in Chicago. The book was also presented at the Critical Race Theory and Empirical Methods workshop in Irvine, California, and I'm indebted to workshop participants who offered important comments. I have presented this work at many annual meetings of the Law and Society Association and was gratified by feedback offered by meeting participants.

Part of this book was written while I was a fellow at the Law and Public Affairs Program at Princeton University. At Princeton, my life (and consequently my writing and research) was made far easier by Kim Lane Scheppele, Leslie Gerwin, Jennifer Bolton, and Judi Rivkin. Over the year, I discussed the project with many Princeton colleagues and want to especially thank Paul Frymer, Dirk Hartog, Stanley Katz, Kevin Kruse, Imani Perry, Ralf Michaels, and Eli Salzberger.

I'm especially beholden to those who provided important work "behind the scenes." Indiana University Maurer School of Law librarians retrieved countless volumes from far-flung libraries for me. Many

Indiana University law students—and one criminal justice graduate student (Cindy Stewart)—worked on the project. I am particularly indebted to one Indiana University undergraduate, Brittany Francis, who spent four years working as my research assistant and contributed to the book immeasurably. Thanks as well to Keisha Blain, a history graduate student at Princeton, who tirelessly combed through archival materials. Rita Eads, at Indiana University Maurer School of Law, transcribed interviews, read seemingly endless drafts, and provided moral support whenever it was needed.

A number of Indiana University colleagues attended conferences and colloquia where I presented parts of the book, read drafts, and offered valuable feedback. In this regard, I'm especially thankful to Aviva Orenstein, Florence Roisman, Gene Shreve, Susan Williams, Ajay Mehrotra, Kevin Brown, Jody Madeira, and Seth Lahn. Special thanks go to my former colleague in the Indiana University History Department, Khalil Muhammad, who provided important advice about Chicago.

Sometimes one's help comes from the most unlikely places. In that regard, I cannot thank Leonard Rubinowitz enough. He has generously provided the best of advice and assistance on the project at every stage. I would also like to thank George Lovell, who read countless drafts and offered critical advice, often on short notice.

I am very much in the debt of the anonymous respondents who talked with me at great length about their lives living in and integrating neighborhoods.

Very sincere and deep thanks go to my editor at New York University Press, Deborah Gershenowitz, who expressed interest in the project from an early stage and whose substantive feedback contributed tremendously to the final project. Rosalie Morales Kearns at the press was an absolutely stellar copyeditor.

I want to express my deepest gratitude to my parents, John and Jeanette Bell, who sacrificed so that, as children, my sister Jerilyn and I always had the best that white neighborhoods could offer. This changed my life and I am forever in their debt.

Finally, this book is dedicated to my precious daughter, Ella Serena, who makes it all worthwhile.

Introduction

Violence and the Neighborhood Color Line

> The night after members of a black family moved into their new house in a predominately Italian neighborhood, a mob of roughly a thousand whites, who had been rioting in a nearby park, surrounded the family's house and began to throw stones, breaking windows. The following evening, two hundred teenagers gathered close to the family's home shouting, "We want blood."[1]

late 1950s

> Soon after Reginald Doster purchased a home for his family in a white neighborhood in Taylor, Michigan, two white men plotted to burn down the Dosters' house. They and several other men broke a window in the house, poured gasoline inside, and ignited the gasoline.[2]

2002

How can we make sense of these two incidents? Though they are similar in that they both involve blacks who have moved into all-white neighborhoods, what is perhaps most interesting is that more than fifty years separate these events. The first occurred in the late 1950s, the second in 2002. Though many assume that violence directed at racial and ethnic minorities who have moved to white neighborhoods is a relic of this country's long-dead history, such behavior is not uncommon. In fact, scenarios like the ones described above, targeting racial and ethnic minorities who integrate white neighborhoods, are so common that scholars have coined the term "move-in violence" to describe such acts of violence and intimidation.[3]

The harassment of the Doster family, which occurred in the twenty-first century and not in the Jim Crow era, is disquieting. As the latest census data show, racial and ethnic minorities constitute an increasingly large portion of the US population.④Moreover, survey research reveals that this increasing racial and ethnic diversity has correlated with increases in tolerance.[5] Perhaps surprisingly, the experience of the Dosters and other minorities like them is not rooted in changes in the number of minorities; nor is it rooted in increases in acceptance for interracial marriage. After describing the history of anti-integrationist violence and its contemporary effects in chapters 1 and 2, I will address in chapter 3 the paradox of the phenomenon of increased tolerance alongside violence directed at minorities who live in white neighborhoods.

A more nuanced look at present-day race relations in the United States reveals the existence of anti-integrationist violence to be far less surprising. First, such crimes occur in entrenched white neighborhoods. Over the past thirty years, the overall level of racial segregation in housing has changed little. Many communities are nearly as segregated today as they were in the 1980s. Data from the 2010 census indicate that the "average" white person lives in a neighborhood that is 75 percent white.[6] The racial composition of the residential neighborhoods where African Americans live is very different. Despite tolerance scores indicating that African Americans prefer to live in racially integrated communities, combined with the fact that predominately white neighborhoods are safer and generally offer greater access to valuable amenities like parks, stores, libraries, and good schools, data from the 2010 census indicate that the typical African American lives in a neighborhood that is only 35 percent white.[7] In other words, despite significant progress in race relations, there are still wide gaps in the housing experiences of African Americans and whites.

With the exception of chapter 4, which focuses on Latino/black neighborhoods, *Hate Thy Neighbor* focuses primarily on the integration into white neighborhoods of African Americans, the nation's most segregated racial minority group. Census data show that Asian Americans and Hispanics are simply not as segregated as African Americans. This is not because these groups never face discrimination in housing or incidents of move-in violence. Rather, as I detail in chapter 3, survey research suggests that Asian American and Hispanic moves to white neighborhoods are much more palatable to whites than is African American integration.

There are thus simply many more incidents of violence directed at African Americans moving to white neighborhoods.

African Americans and other people of color who are victims upon moving to white neighborhoods are often motivated to move to improve their life chances. When they experience violence in the form of cross burning, assault, vandalism, and arson, these incidents exact a terrible emotional and financial toll on their targets, who are more inclined to return to black neighborhoods than risk exposing themselves and their families to another white neighborhood. Any incentive for African Americans to remain in majority-black neighborhoods is a terrible outcome for housing segregation, which has particularly troubling consequences for the poorest blacks. Those African Americans limited to segregated neighborhoods tend to live in the worst housing, partake of the fewest public resources, and have the least access to employment.[8] Poor black neighborhoods often have high crime rates as well. The cycle repeats as the children of blacks living in segregated neighborhoods tend to attend the worst schools, which affects their life chances and the neighborhoods to which they will have access as adults. Even if blacks do not live in poor housing, in segregated neighborhoods their houses tend to be valued less than those in integrated neighborhoods. Plenty of reasons exist for blacks to prefer living in integrated white neighborhoods, so the segregation cannot be explained by black preference to live in all-black or predominately black communities.

Beyond the issue of failing to honor individual choice, housing segregation exacerbates the danger and harm of move-in violence. The intense level of black-white segregation leads to spaces that are ripe for move-in violence. All-white neighborhoods provide the settings for acts of intimidation like that directed at the Dosters. One of the most commonly understood explanations for such harassment is that perpetrators desire to preserve the white neighborhood and prevent "white flight," the phenomenon in which large numbers of middle- and upper-class white people leave neighborhoods in search of new spaces that are predominately white. White flight has occurred in large cities across the country when minorities, particularly African Americans seeking better housing, move to white neighborhoods. Rather than being an inevitable consequence of housing integration, historically, white flight was exacerbated by unscrupulous "blockbusters," real estate speculators

intent on exploiting—for profit—the "deep-seated fears of white home-owners who dreaded Black encroachment on their turf."⁹

Hate Thy Neighbor is an attempt to move the conversation about housing integration beyond the discussion of white flight by focusing on the fact that some number of white residents, from the beginning of housing integration through the current day, elected to remain in their neighborhoods. Throughout the book, in neighborhoods in cities as diverse as Detroit, Los Angeles, Philadelphia, Portland, and Atlanta, I profile individuals who made the decision to fight neighborhood integration. Confronted with their neighborhoods' changing racial dynamics, whites in such neighborhoods "blocked the penetration as if defending against a foreign enemy, using any means at their disposal to deter the migration."¹⁰ White flight and violence are not the only two responses to minority integration. From managed integration to solutions crafted by those who are intent on creating diverse neighborhoods, I discuss several racially inclusive approaches to neighborhood creation that might serve as alternatives to the more typical paths of flight or resistance.

When "Home" Is Where the Violence Is

Even today, minorities moving to, and in some cases living in, neighborhoods around the country have faced harassment, vandalism, and assault perpetrated by white neighbors who wished them to live elsewhere. I use the term "anti-integrationist violence" to describe two phenomena: (1) extralegal acts of terrorism, or crimes directed at minorities immediately upon moving to white neighborhoods; and (2) crimes targeted at African Americans and other racial and ethnic minorities while residing in majority-white neighborhoods that are designed to drive them out. This definition reflects the full range of experiences of those racial and ethnic minorities whose integrating presences are rejected by their white neighbors. As chapter 6 details, such violence is illegal. If acts of anti-integrationist violence come to the attention of law enforcement, they may be investigated and prosecuted as hate crimes. Such incidents also violate state and federal fair housing legislation. However, as chapter 6 also discusses, many of these crimes may fall through the cracks in the police and prosecutorial systems.

As chapters 4 and 5 demonstrate, the problem of anti-integrationist violence is more complex than the term "hate crime" or "bias crime" can capture. Anti-integrationist violence is special, and has a distinctive place among other bias crimes because it occurs in and around individuals' homes. Whether one is renting or owns one's residence, one's home has special significance, both culturally and legally. Culturally, Americans are fond of considering "a man's home his castle." In this view, the home is seen as both a place of security and the location of individual freedom from outside pressures.

Since the founding of the United States, American legal doctrine has enshrined this cultural understanding of the home as a place that is specially protected. Most Americans are familiar with the common law right to use deadly force to defend oneself when one is attacked in one's home. Legal protection for the home goes far deeper than the right to self-defense, however. So concerned with the sanctity of the home were the framers of the US Constitution that the Third Amendment forbids the quartering of soldiers in individuals' homes without the homeowners' consent. This is in keeping with the cultural idea that the home is a place of personal freedom; common law has recognized the home as a locale where individuals are freer from restrictions on behavior and may thus avoid government scrutiny. Though exceptions exist, the Fourth Amendment generally prohibits the government from searching homes without a warrant.[11] The Supreme Court has been quite diligent in forbidding any intrusion into the home without appropriate justification.[12] Even private possession of obscene materials inside one's home is constitutionally protected.[13]

By attacking the homes of minorities who move to white neighborhoods, perpetrators violate entrenched cultural and legal understandings about the home. For targets of anti-integrationist violence, home is not a place of security. For these individuals, unlike most Americans, home may be where the heart is, but home is also where the violence is.

The Political Nature of Anti-Integrationist Violence

Like racially motivated crimes in general, a minority of acts of anti-integrationist violence are committed by ideological extremists—members of the Ku Klux Klan, skinhead organizations, or other hate groups. That being said, acts of anti-integrationist violence are nonetheless fiercely political. Those men—in my research I have found the vast majority of perpetrators to be male—deciding to burn a cross on their new black neighbor's lawn have strong ideas about what they want their community to look like, who belongs in that community, and who does not. At the most basic level, acts of anti-integrationist violence are strong statements about what residential communities should look like and who the perpetrator wants to see as part of his private, neighborhood life. Though offenders may claim to be motivated by the abstract notions of protecting property values or other nonracial motivation, as the term "anti-integrationist" suggests, perpetrators of such acts are explicitly discriminating and rejecting notions of a racially inclusive community. Not wanting minorities to live in their neighborhood renders perpetrators and those who support them segregationists, even though they claim not to be racists.

Fair housing statutes try to limit the extent to which individuals can control the complexion of their neighborhood. Extralegal behavior—acts of vandalism or harassment aimed at minorities who are able to enter white neighborhoods—subvert statutory protections. Move-in violence will have its intended effect if the person of color is "crimed out" and ends up leaving the neighborhood. If perpetrators are able to force racial minorities out of white neighborhoods, their actions have devastating and far-reaching implications. In committing acts of anti-integrationist violence, perpetrators reinforce notions of racial hierarchy that place whites at the apex and mandate separation of the races.

The incidents that constitute anti-integrationist violence are not what we traditionally think of as "hate crimes," crimes motivated by prejudice on the basis of race, religion, or sexual orientation. The animus may not specifically arise from racial hatred—perpetrators would not seek out minorities outside their community to harass. Nevertheless, such incidents clearly fit into the paradigm created for hate crimes, particularly when motivated by underlying racial prejudice. In conforming to this picture, such incidents represent a more nuanced and compelling frontier in this recently created category of crime. This book argues that anti-integrationist violence constitutes a little-explored, separate category of hate crime that has the power to significantly affect minorities' decisions to move to white neighborhoods.

Because the term "victim" has a number of negative connotations, I do not use it to describe those minorities who are attacked in this context. In the anti-integrationist violence context, individuals are *targeted*. The perpetrator intentionally selects someone because of their race. One who is attacked is a target, not someone who has been unlucky enough to stumble into some unfortunate circumstance.

Police departments reported 3,135 racially motivated bias incidents to the FBI in 2010.[14] This is a small percentage of the roughly 10.3 million violent and property crimes that were reported to the FBI that same year.[15] Though the overall number of incidents is comparatively small, legal scholars and policy makers should pay much more attention to racially motivated bias crimes that constitute anti-integrationist violence. As I describe at several points in this book, our society has evinced an inability to address anti-integrationist violence, both socially and legally. Despite a number of penalties associated with bias-motivated violence, the legal system does not provide sufficient remedy for the phenomenon of anti-integrationist violence. For instance, the arson of the Dosters' house was eventually attributed to two white men, Wayland Mullins and Michael Richardson.[16] Mullins's mother lived across the street from the home the Dosters had purchased. Mullins and Richardson were charged with, among other things, violating the Dosters' housing rights, because the purpose of the arson was to frighten the family and prevent the Dosters from moving into their home.

There is little social support for targets of anti-integrationist violence. Neighbors rarely reach out to let the targets of this violence know that they are indeed welcome in the neighborhood. As a result, when this type of violence or harassment is targeted at minorities who have made the courageous choice to move to white neighborhoods, those minorities often choose to leave. In the Dosters' case, the harassment that drove the family to leave included dead cats and dogs being thrown into the family's yard and on their doorstep. In addition, trash was dumped in their yard and their cars were vandalized. "You name it, they did it," said Lori Doster when interviewed several years after the family had left the neighborhood.[17]

After a second trial resulted in Mullins's conviction, though Doster told a reporter she was happy to see justice done, she recognized that the harassment the family endured had a lasting effect. Doster noted that three years of harassment had destroyed their daughter's child-hood.[18] As chapter 2 describes, in the contemporary period, incidents like the harassment directed at the Dosters are all too common. Such incidents serve as a clear disincentive to families unwilling to pay the long-lasting emotional toll that such harassment causes. As the following chapters suggest, if we want to fully address the causes of racial segregation in housing, we must pay more attention to anti-integrationist violence.

The book's organization is as follows. The first two chapters, organized chronologically, present a history of anti-integrationist violence, from its beginnings until 2010. In chapter 1, which covers the period from 1865 to 1968, the year the Fair Housing Act was passed, I describe relatively uncontroversial interracial neighborhoods in both the North and the South before and after the Civil War. The postbellum period was followed, as I describe in the chapter, by an increase in violence soon after the turn of the twentieth century, when large numbers of blacks crossed the color line to obtain housing in white neighborhoods.

Chapter 2 begins where the previous chapter ended, in the early 1970s, evaluating the occurrence of violence associated with housing integration even in the wake of the passage of major legislation designed to address it. In this chapter, I set forth changes both in the form that violence takes and in its characterization under the new "bias crime" label. In the section that addresses the current manifestation of anti-integrationist violence, I describe its wide diffusion throughout the United States and also address the emotionally disabling impact of the harassment on many of the targets and their families.

The next three chapters offer a series of distinct explanations of the causes of anti-integrationist violence. Chapter 3 explores what I have termed the tolerance-violence paradox: how systematic, violent expressions of racism persist in a society marked by increasing tolerance and racial diversity. Chapter 4 uses acts of anti-integrationist violence in Los Angeles, where the majority of targets are African American and the majority of perpetrators are Latino gang members, to differentiate the role that issues of geography and neighborhood dominance play in the construction of localized racial hierarchies. Chapter 5 examines anti-integrationist violence though the lens of socioeconomic status, or class. Profiling neighborhoods in which anti-integrationist violence occurred that are working-class, middle-class, and affluent, I suggest that in some cases of anti-integrationist violence, the perpetrator's class, or that of the targets, may have at least as much significance as their race.

The final chapter and the conclusion are prescriptive, suggesting how, given the existence of this sort of violence, it might be possible to improve the experiences of integrating minorities. Chapter 6 does this in a straightforward manner by looking quite broadly at the issue of legal remedies for anti-integrationist violence, from hate crime statutes to the Fair Housing Act. Special attention is paid in this chapter not only to details of the laws in a variety of jurisdictions, but also to how each type of law works "on the ground." The book concludes with an analysis of the impact of anti-integrationist violence on housing integration and a comprehensive formula for curbing its most harmful effects.

1

The Roots of Contemporary Move-In Violence

Though many Americans may imagine that racially segregated housing in the United States is a direct descendent of slavery, in actuality
the history of the integration of housing by race is more complicated.
Blacks and whites were much more likely to be housed in the same
neighborhood in the nineteenth century than they are in the twenty-
first century.

Starkly racially segregated neighborhoods are a relatively recent phenomenon. Until the twentieth century, the vast majority of blacks living in the North lived in close proximity to whites in "racially-mixed
neighborhoods, usually on blocks with many white neighbors."[1] Prior
to 1915, "Negro housing [in the North] did not differ from that of any
other race."[2] This did not mean that primarily black areas did not exist;
rather, blacks were not confined to black neighborhoods, and at that
time many blacks lived in racially mixed neighborhoods. This chapter
explores integrated living arrangements during the antebellum period
and after the Civil War. It then analyzes the onset of violence associated
with housing integration, which began to occur decades after whites
and blacks began to live in the same neighborhoods.

Mixed-Race Neighborhoods before and after the Civil War

Though the living arrangements were significantly different in the antebellum North and South, for blacks and whites in both regions of the
country there was a history of proximity in housing before the Civil War.
In the pre–Civil War South, black slaves lived on plantations with whites.
In southern cities, slaves lived in urban compounds in close proximity to

their masters. In both the North and the South, it was convenient for black workers, whether slave or free, to live near the whites for whom they worked.[3] House-by-house examination of neighborhoods in large cities in the antebellum period in the South shows mixed blocks of black and white residents.[4] For instance, in Richmond, VA, communities of free blacks were interspersed among German and Irish immigrants.[5]

In the antebellum North, in cities like Cincinnati, free people of color often lived side by side with whites, rather than being confined to an exclusively black environment. In Cincinnati it was not just the case that a few blacks lived among whites; rather, "whites lived on every street where blacks resided and . . . usually outnumbered blacks on these streets."[6] Whites dominated the Cincinnati neighborhoods where the largest numbers of free blacks lived. In one of these areas, Bucktown, "black and white residences were intermixed along every street where blacks lived. It is of significant importance that despite prejudice and discrimination in virtually every other aspect of urban life, residential patterns were not a racial issue, and blacks and whites shared the urban living space."[7]

After the Civil War, freed from the bonds of slavery, many southern blacks migrated from rural to urban areas. From 1865 until the 1890s, throughout the country blacks made their home in both all-black residential areas and much more racially mixed areas. In suburban Chicago's North Shore, Philadelphia's Main Line, and New York's lower Westchester County, entirely black areas were populated by the cooks, mechanics, and gardeners who worked for the well-off.[8] There were slums as well, but these were not necessarily exclusively black. Prior to the 1920s, the slums in which blacks lived contained what Ira Berlin described as "a mélange" of whites and blacks.[9]

These areas were not characterized by racial interaction, but the closeness of residence was still significant, given what followed: violence occurring when blacks tried to occupy the same neighborhood. Laws proscribing integrated blocks or integrated neighborhoods generally did not exist in either the North or the South in the late nineteenth and early twentieth centuries. At this time in the South, racially mixed neighborhoods may have been frowned upon but nevertheless were permitted. For instance, upper-middle-class blacks who could afford to do so were allowed to live in white neighborhoods even in the South.[10]

In the postbellum period, truly integrated neighborhoods frequently developed from necessity. Poorer whites such as widows or unskilled laborers lived among blacks because they could not afford to move out of the neighborhoods in which blacks lived.[11]

It was not just the South where blacks and whites lived in close quarters after the Civil War. In Detroit, on the Near East Side, blacks and whites lived side by side in the postbellum period. In some cases semi-skilled or unskilled immigrants lived in houses next door to blacks and in other cases lived even closer, as boarding places on the Near East Side housed people of a variety of backgrounds. The 1880 US census of Detroit reveals that even in areas with the highest number of blacks, blacks and whites lived in adjoining dwellings.[12] Similarly, in Cleveland, prior to the 1880s there was significant integration of blacks, with no section of the city being more than 5 percent black.[13] Even though most of the blacks in the city lived in just three neighborhoods, they were nevertheless integrated throughout each of these neighborhoods.[14]

Expulsion, on the Road to Segregation

Racially integrated housing may have been an outgrowth of antiracist idealism after the Civil War. James Loewen, who has documented the expulsion of African Americans from white spaces after 1890, insists that for a time immediately after the Civil War, antiracism played a significant role in American political life. Loewen maintains that the period between 1865 and 1890 was somewhat of a "springtime of race relations," during which many towns and counties throughout the northern United States demonstrated their antiracism by welcoming African Americans from the South.[15] Freedom provided empowerment and the space to occupy a new place in society. Describing this era, Loewen reminds his readers that in the period between the end of the Civil War and 1890, African Americans had "voted, served in Congress, received some spoils from the Republican Party, worked as barbers, railroad firemen, midwives, mail carriers, and landowning farmers, and played other fully human roles in American society. Their new rights made African Americans optimistic, even buoyant."[16]

Unfortunately, by the 1890s the springtime of race relations had begun to subside into a cold, harsh winter. In towns and cities across the northern and southern United States, once-blurry racial lines began to solidify. Loewen describes deepening racism sweeping the country after 1890. The first victims of this racism were Chinese Americans. Chinese Americans lived in virtually every town in the West until 1884, making their living mining gold and working as farmers, on the railroad, as domestic servants, and fishermen, among other things.[17] Between 1885 and 1920, many cities and towns in the western United States forcibly expelled Chinese Americans. In Idaho, for instance, in 1870 Chinese were one-third of the population of the territory. In the 1880s, white Idahoans began to assault and murder Chinese residents. In 1886, an anti-Chinese convention helped galvanize support for expelling Chinese residents. Over the course of the 1890s, Chinese were expelled from several Idaho towns.[18] Similar incidents occurred in cities and towns in California, Oregon, and Washington as Chinese residents were driven out and Chinatowns, where Chinese Americans had been living, were burned to the ground.

Following the Chinese exclusion, US census and historical records reveal a similar expulsion directed at African Americans beginning in 1890 and lasting until between 1930 and 1940. In 1890 just 119 counties—excluding the traditional South—had no African Americans. By 1930, this figure had nearly doubled, increasing to 235 counties, as towns around the country went "sundown": African Americans were expelled and told not to let the sun set on them in a particular town. Frequently, the process of going sundown involved violence. For instance, in July 1899 in Carterville, Illinois, white miners killed five African American strikebreakers. The whites were all acquitted and the remaining African Americans were forced to leave Carterville.[19] African Americans forced out of sundown towns went to a variety of places. For instance, some all-black towns like Mount Bayou, Mississippi, were voluntarily established during this period.

In large cities, the sharpening of racial lines, while not as stark as the blatant expulsion in sundown towns, occurred nevertheless. Analysis of census records reveals that even though blacks and whites lived in close proximity to one another in the postbellum period, in the early twentieth century this began to change as residential segregation between native whites and blacks sharply increased in cities around the country.[20] The index of dissimilarity is a tool used by social scientists to calculate the extent to which groups are distributed throughout the

hell . why?

population. Using a range from 0 to 100, the index of dissimilarity is used to assess the degree of segregation of two groups from each other in a particular location. Zero signifies complete integration, while 100 represents total segregation. In 1870 in Milwaukee, Wisconsin, data at the ward level showed a dissimilarity index between American-born whites and blacks of 56.9.[21] This means that for blacks to be evenly distributed among the white group, 56.9 percent of blacks in the city would have to move to a white ward. In 1910, the index of black-white dissimilarity had risen to 66.7.[22] Maps of distribution of blacks in the city of Chicago in 1900, 1910, and 1920 depict increasing concentration of the black population over time and consequently increasing segregation from whites as Chicago's black population increased.[23]

Using the Law to Enforce Segregation: The Rise of Segregation Ordinances

The first racial zoning ordinances in the United States were used against Chinese residents of West Coast cities in the late nineteenth century.[24] The western experience aside, it was not until the early twentieth century that such ordinances were created in other cities. More than two dozen cities around the South passed segregation zoning ordinances restricting blacks to particular neighborhoods, blocks, or streets.[25] One of the first such ordinances aimed at blacks was created in 1910 in Baltimore, Maryland. The Baltimore law was ostensibly designed for "preserving peace, preventing conflict and ill feeling between white and colored races in Baltimore city, and promoting the general welfare of the city by providing, so far as practical, for the use of separate blocks by white and black people for residences, churches and schools."[26] The Baltimore ordinance did not apply to mixed blocks where both African Americans and whites lived. Rather, it was designed to prevent integration in the future by prohibiting residential integration by street blocks where all members of a single race, black or white, lived.

The ordinance had been created in response to African American moves into white neighborhoods, particularly of the sort made by George McMechen and his family. In the summer of 1910, McMechen purchased a house in the Eutaw Place neighborhood, an all-white area in Baltimore, just ten blocks west of his former home in the Negro district. McMechen was a law graduate and practicing attorney, and as was true of many other targets of anti-integrationist violence, his new home in one of the most fashionable areas of Baltimore was an attempt to capture some of the benefits of his wealth and status. In other words, he was attempting to move "up." After the family moved in, the McMechens needed police protection from whites who were threatening violence. Concerned that other blacks intended to "plant themselves on Madison Street and Eutaw Place," ten thousand citizens of Baltimore petitioned the mayor and city council, requesting that officials "take some measures to restrain the colored people from locating in a white community and to prescribe a limit beyond which it shall be unlawful for them to go."[27]

Public officials responded, and Baltimore's first racial segregation ordinance was signed into law in December 1910. After a constitutional challenge, this ordinance was followed in quick succession by a second and then a third ordinance, both of which were also challenged and subsequently struck down. Despite the legal troubles these ordinances encountered in Baltimore, in 1912 ordinances were promulgated in Mooresville and Winston-Salem in North Carolina. The following year similar ordinances mandating segregation were passed in Asheville, North Carolina; Richmond, Norfolk, and Roanoke, Virginia; Atlanta, Georgia; Madisonville, Kentucky; and Greenville, South Carolina. Within a few years, ordinances regulating interracial housing in other cities—Louisville, Kentucky, and Birmingham, Alabama—followed.[28]

The black community did not take the passage of these ordinances lying down. Wide-scale resistance, some of which involved lawsuits, was spearheaded by local and national branches of the National Association for the Advancement of Colored People (NAACP). The NAACP had been fighting to eradicate restrictions on housing for African Americans since the early 1900s. The New York office of the NAACP worked with local black and white members of the Louisville real estate exchange to create a case that would most effectively challenge segregation ordinances. Louisville's ordinance prohibited "any colored person" from moving into and occupying a residence on any block where the greater numbers of residences are occupied by white persons. In the end, the legal strategists decided that the best challenge would involve having William Warley, president of the Louisville branch of the NAACP, enter into a contract to buy a lot on a white block from Charles

Buchanan, a white real estate agent. Warley's offer specified, among other things, that he did not have to accept a deed to the property or to pay for it "unless I have the right under the laws of the state of Kentucky and the city of Louisville to occupy said property as a residence." Warley and Buchanan were colluding, so Buchanan sued to compel specific performance of the contract. The state court ruled that Louisville's ordinance prevented Warley from performing.[29]

The Louisville case was appealed to the US Supreme Court. In making its decision, the Court evaluated a number of defenses, including the view that such ordinances promote public peace by preventing race conflicts, and that such ordinances protect property values. The Court said that while the protection of the public peace was important, "this aim cannot be accomplished by laws or ordinances which deny rights created or protected by the Federal Constitution." In other words, constitutional rights were more important than protecting racial peace. The Court also dismissed the argument about property values: "It is said that such acquisitions by colored persons depreciate property owned in the neighborhood by white persons. The property may be acquired by undesirable white neighbors or put to disagreeable though lawful uses with like results." The Supreme Court struck down Louisville's segregation ordinance, holding that it was not a legitimate exercise of the police power of the state and directly violated the Fourteenth Amendment.[30]

The decision in Buchanan v. Warley had wide-ranging consequences for the constitutionality of racially restrictive zoning ordinances around the country, if not for the integration of housing in general. In response to the Supreme Court's decision in Warley, courts also struck down ordinances in cities as diverse as Birmingham and Baltimore. This did not prevent cities from enacting other racial zoning ordinances. For instance, in 1926 Birmingham enacted an ordinance replacing the one that had been invalidated by the court. The new law was justified by protection for the "health, safety, morals, and general welfare" and did not specifically favor any one race—whites were as circumscribed from occupying property in black districts.[31] Making up 40 percent of Birmingham's population but confined by the segregation ordinance to just 16 percent of the city's land, African Americans who lived in Birmingham were not happy with the new ordinance. As is discussed later in this chapter, Birmingham's racial zoning law was eventually challenged in the early 1940s.

At the end of the 1920s, other legal breakthroughs were made in the stubborn edifice of segregation. The Supreme Court's ruling in *Harmon v. Tyler* in 1927 prohibited state and local ordinances that required written consent before minorities could move to an area.[32] White landlords and real estate agents, however, continued to refuse to show or rent accommodations in white neighborhoods to blacks.[33] Even if African Americans were allowed to live in white neighborhoods, in many cases blacks were unable to get mortgages from banks if they wanted to purchase in white neighborhoods and were frequently denied home insurance as well.

Cities and towns did not necessarily change overnight, nor did segregation proceed at the same speed in every area. While some places, like sundown towns, changed overnight, in other areas the process of segregation was much more gradual. In Brooklyn, New York, for instance, ward-level census statistics indicate that blacks were still well distributed throughout the population in 1890, with the black population not exceeding 10.2 percent in any area of the city. Though segregation increased, in 1910 blacks still lived in a variety of areas of Brooklyn, and census data show them to be less segregated from native whites than were Chicago Italians.[34] In Los Angeles, the period from the 1890s through 1920 was labeled the "Golden Era."[35] Blacks had ready access to homeownership and lived in many different areas of the city.[36] Perhaps the most remarkable city in this regard was San Francisco, where there was no readily identifiable exclusively black area.[37] The *San Francisco Chronicle* bragged in 1904 that "colored citizens" were allowed to rent in most parts of the city.[38] The Chinese were a much larger minority than African Americans and were much more segregated in San Francisco's Chinatown than African Americans. The Fillmore District was an area that had the largest number of blacks.[39] In fact, it was not until the mid- to late 1940s that blacks came to dominate a single area of San Francisco.[40]

Minority Integration during the First Migration: Squeezing into Already Cramped Quarters

Organized conflicts over African Americans living in proximity to whites began with the sharp increases in the sheer numbers of African Americans in cities. African American populations in northern cities exploded with the first Great Migration of southern blacks in the early part of the twentieth century. Fleeing violence and lack of opportunity in the South in search of jobs and a better life, roughly 1.5 million blacks left the southern United States for New York, Detroit, Chicago, Los Angeles, Philadelphia, and smaller cities in the North, Midwest, and West. Their exodus caused the numbers of blacks in the South to shrink and a corresponding increase in the black population in northern cities. In New York, for instance, between 1890 and 1910, more than sixty thousand blacks moved to New York City, tripling the number of black residents.[41] During the same time, Philadelphia's black community grew by more than two and a half times, reaching roughly two hundred thousand people, or 11 percent of the population.[42] Over the same twenty years, from 1890 through 1910, Baltimore's black population grew from fifty-four thousand to nearly eighty-five thousand, which was 15.5 percent of the population of the entire city.[43]

Some of the movement during the first Great Migration stemmed from the demand for industrial workers focused on the buildup leading to World War I. Northern employers offered blacks significant economic incentives, and in response approximately 400,000 blacks moved north between 1916 and 1919.[44] In the decade between 1910 and 1920 the black population in New York rose from 91,709 in 1910 to 152,467 in 1920.[45] Even more significant was the growth in the black population in cities in the upper Midwest. Between 1910 and 1920, Detroit's black population increased more than sevenfold, reaching 40,838.[46] Over the same time period, Chicago's black population also increased significantly, rising from roughly 44,000 to approximately 110,000 just ten years later.[47]

The end of World War I did not stop blacks from leaving the South. Many southern blacks (including veterans) had trouble finding work after World War I, as the nation's war industry collapsed. It was not just the northern United States that experienced a significant growth in the black population in the 1920s. In Los Angeles, over the 1920s the black population increased significantly, rising to nearly 39,000, which at that time in the area constituted a "visible presence."[48]

In many cities, for reasons of poverty or discrimination, blacks often lived in the worst areas of the city. In Baltimore, one of the black ghettos was the Biddle Alley neighborhood, a filthy slum that was "literally and figuratively at the bottom of what was becoming the black section of Baltimore" in 1903. Animal feces and garbage lined the streets of Biddle Alley. A 1903 report described the condition of the slum:

Privy faults and cesspools overflowed into alleys and oozed into the basement, kitchen, and living areas. Cholera and typhoid were a constant threat, and the district was the tuberculosis center for the city: According to one health department official, "there is not a house on Biddle Alley, in which there has not been at least one case of tuberculosis." Biddle Alley was the "lung block."[49]

Not every black migrant experienced the difficulties of living in slums like Biddle Alley. Living conditions faced by those moving north differed depending on where they were going. Northern cities were differently situated to deal with increases in their black population. In New York and Philadelphia, for instance, preexisting black areas or ghettos expanded in an attempt to accommodate the new migrants. In other cases, doubling or tripling of the black population placed too much pressure on the tiny number of neighborhoods that African Americans traditionally occupied.

Given the conditions of the ghettos, irrespective of the size of the black quarter, in most cities in the Northeast and Midwest black ghettos were especially challenged to provide housing for the burgeoning black professional class. Though realtors and whites selling to them charged them a premium to purchase housing in white neighborhoods, black professionals had the means to escape the overcrowded ghettos. Black professionals and others leaving the overcrowded "black belts" in large cities in the Midwest and Northeast were the first targets of violence by whites resisting housing integration.

While prior to the Great Migration a small number of black residents had been easily accommodated in white neighborhoods, when large numbers of blacks attempted to move out of the overcrowded black belts and into white neighborhoods, whites' acceptance vanished. In some cases, whites moved out of neighborhoods as blacks moved in. In others, black attempts to move into houses and apartments in white neighborhoods began to be seen as an invasion that must be resisted, if possible by organized groups. Property owners' associations in white areas began to concentrate on keeping blacks out of the neighborhood.[50] These organizations paid attention to the changing real estate market, monitoring sales and placing pressure on whites not to sell to blacks. Meetings were organized to educate fellow citizens about the perceived dangers of blacks in the neighborhood. Publications denounced blacks, and violence was directed at black residents of white neighborhoods and those whites (including white real estate brokers) who sold to them.[51] In Chicago, between July 1917 and March 1921, fifty-eight homes of black families who moved into white neighborhoods were bombed.[52]

In Philadelphia, blacks migrating to the city had few housing options outside the slums near the banks of the Delaware River or the cramped row houses in North Philadelphia. As in Chicago, when blacks in Philadelphia tried to move outside traditional black areas, they faced treatment similar to that encountered by Thomas Henry, who moved to a South Philadelphia neighborhood inhabited by Italian, Eastern European, and Irish immigrants in the summer of 1923.[53] Before the Henrys could get settled in, warnings and threats of violence were sent to the family. Henry ignored these warnings. A few days later a small mob led by Tony Pecoro came to the house and ordered Henry to leave. The mob then barged into the Henrys' home and set the furniture on fire. For trying to protect the family's belongings, Henry was "set upon and badly beaten."[54]

In a number of cities, concerns about blacks moving to white neighborhoods set off large conflicts that ignited huge portions of the city. Some of the worst rioting in Philadelphia took place in the summer of 1918, when blacks attempted to expand the boundaries of South Philadelphia's black district. The riot may have been prompted by the move by Julia Bond, a black female probation officer, to Ellsworth Street in Grays Ferry, a white working-class neighborhood. Someone in the white mob threw a brick into Bond's window on July 26, 1918.[55] Mobs threw rocks at the homes of Bond and other blacks in her neighborhood and engaged in other violence for nearly a week.

At this time white hostility was of paramount importance in determining where blacks lived; white animosity—often in the form of violence—restricted blacks' housing choices.[56] White fear of blacks was directed at any breaches of the color line. Upper-middle-class blacks were frequently the target of resistance despite having similar—and in some cases, higher—class status than those whites already living in the neighborhood. Take the case of Dr. Alexander Turner, a prominent black doctor in Detroit and the chief of surgery at the black hospital. Despite his status, Turner, who had also held appointments at two of

Second ghetto

the major white hospitals, faced opposition from his neighbors when he moved to a white neighborhood on Spokane Avenue in Detroit in 1925. Five hours after the family had moved in, white residents broke the house's windows, ripped down the phone lines, and tore tiles off the roof. A group of whites pretending to be representatives from the mayor's office knocked on the door, and after they were admitted, thirty or forty charged in and began destroying property. Turner was nearly overtaken by the mob as he rushed out of the home in fear. In the evening, he signed over the deed to his house to the neighborhood improvements society that had spearheaded the violence.[57]

Though in the 1920s the mobs were often successful at getting blacks to move away, some blacks were able to use the scant legal remedies available to resist white pressure. When Robert Waddell moved to the all-white Hills section of Brooklyn in 1921, some of his white neighbors, who had at first tried to block the sale to him, sent a threatening note saying that if he did not move out, "you and members of your black family will be killed."[58] With the intervention of the NAACP, which contacted the police commissioner, the threats ceased. Samuel Browne, who was threatened after purchasing a house in an all-white area of Staten Island in 1924, also turned to the NAACP for help. With the organization's help, Browne sued and ultimately settled out of court with ten white residents who had been indicted on conspiracy and intimidation charges.[59]

Perhaps the best-known story of black resistance to white neighborhood violence in the 1920s was the case of Ossian Sweet. Sweet, a black doctor, purchased a home on Garland Avenue, four miles east of downtown Detroit, in 1925. Soon after he and his wife and daughter moved in, mobs of hundreds of whites began to gather outside the home. Sweet, his brother Henry, and his family were accompanied by several other men who were in the home and armed for the family's protection. The mob began to throw stones at the house, shattering windows. Henry Sweet fired into the crowd, killing a white man. Ossian, Henry, and several others were charged with the man's murder. James Weldon Johnson of the NAACP brought in Clarence Darrow to defend Henry Sweet, who was eventually acquitted. At that point the charges against Ossian Sweet and the other black men were dropped. Ossian Sweet remained owner of the house on Garland Avenue until 1958, when he sold it to a black family.[60]

Violence, white flight, discrimination against African Americans moving to white neighborhoods in the wake of the Great Migration— all of these factors certainly took their toll on black-white housing integration. Before the Great Migration began, northern cities displayed much more integration than existed by the 1950s (see table 1.1). Census records from ten cities in 1910 show that many cities had low levels of residential segregation between blacks and native-born whites. With each passing decade, as the numbers of African Americans rapidly increased with the Great Migration, black-white segregation increased as well. By the 1950s, Boston, Buffalo, Cincinnati, Cleveland, St. Louis, and Syracuse had segregation indexes exceeding 80 percent.

The Federal Housing Administration and African Americans' New (Raw) Deal

In the 1930s, the Great Depression slowed the pace of African American movement from south to north. Those blacks who had already moved north remained cramped in black ghettos in many cities, since President Roosevelt's New Deal promise to create a nation of homeowners was, at least with respect to African Americans, a raw deal. For African Americans, several New Deal policies made an already difficult situation far worse. One example of this was the Federal Housing Administration (FHA), created in 1934, which guaranteed the mortgages of qualified borrowers, repaying lenders if the borrowers defaulted.

The FHA's loan program was a massive entitlement program responsible for doubling the percentage of Americans who owned their homes between 1930 and 1960.[61] The FHA's underwriting guidelines were set forth in the agency's *Underwriting Manual*. Borrowing from earlier maps, created by the Home Owners Loan Corporation (HOLC), the FHA rated the quality of neighborhood housing stock and racial composition in 140 metropolitan areas on a scale from A to D. The best neighborhoods had A and B ratings and were colored green and blue on maps. The neighborhoods where the agency judged the borrowers (and ultimately the lender's money) to be most at risk were given C or D ratings and colored yellow or red on maps. As one might expect, primacy was placed on maintaining property values. With respect to the issue of racial balance, the manual stated, "If a neighborhood is to retain stability, it is necessary

Table 1.1

Indices of Residential Segregation between Blacks and Native-Born Whites, 1910, 1920, 1930, and 1950, Selected Cities

City	1910*	1920*	1930†	1950†
Boston	64.1	65.3	77.9	80.1
Buffalo	62.6	71.5	80.5	82.5
Chicago	66.8	75.7	85.2	79.7
Cincinnati	47.3	57.2	72.8	80.6
Cleveland	60.6	70.1	85.0	86.6
Columbus	31.6	43.8	62.8	70.3
Philadelphia	46.0	47.9	63.4	74.0
Pittsburgh	44.1	43.3	61.4	68.5
St. Louis	54.3	62.1	82.1	85.4
Syracuse	64.0	65.2	86.7	85.8

Source: Stanley Liebersoll, Ethnic Patterns in American Cities (New York: Free Press of Glencoe, 1963), 122, table 38.

* Indices computed from ward data.

† Indices computed from census tract data, except community areas used for Chicago.

that properties shall continue to be occupied by the same social and racial classes."[62] The FHA counseled against "adverse influences" leading to the introduction into white neighborhoods of "unharmonious racial groups."[63] Mixed neighborhoods, which could amount to those containing just a few black residents, were awarded a D rating; homeowners who wished to buy homes in those neighborhoods were generally unable to secure FHA loans.[64] In addition to refusing loans to those who lived in neighborhoods with even a single black family, FHA officials initially required that racially restrictive covenants be written into the deeds of properties that were to receive mortgages.

These FHA regulations had a powerful effect on overall segregation patterns in the 1930s and 1940s. The effect of the appraisal guidelines was to make those who were able to purchase homes in homogeneous white neighborhoods eligible for loans. By contrast, those wishing to buy in racially mixed neighborhoods were not able to secure government-backed mortgages. The implication of the appraisal guidelines can clearly be seen in Los Angeles, one of the metropolitan areas that the HOLC rated. Los Angeles neighborhoods that had homogeneous populations and racial covenants barring property from being sold to nonwhites were given A ratings. Neighborhoods with homogeneous populations yet close to neighborhoods where minorities lived were accorded a B rating. Those neighborhoods in Los Angeles that had been assigned a C rating by the agency displayed "indications of infiltrations of Jewish families" or contained a "few Mexicans and Japs." A grade of D was awarded to neighborhoods with even a few black families. If the neighborhood had a D rating, it was redlined, and lenders were strongly cautioned against lending to those who wanted to buy properties in those areas.[65] In Los Angeles, of seventy-two "red" rated areas, all but two had racial minorities living in them.[66]

The FHA guidelines played an important role in encouraging segregation. First and foremost, blacks paid the steepest price because the FHA appraisal guidelines would not support their purchases in either white or black neighborhoods. Black and mixed neighborhoods were redlined, and FHA polices discouraged the mixing of "inharmonious races and classes."[67] This meant that blacks may have been unable to secure mortgages in white neighborhoods. In addition, whites who had an interest in purchasing in mixed neighborhoods were less likely to be able to secure mortgages because of these neighborhoods' lower ratings. The appraisal guidelines thus had the effect of steering whites into homogeneously white, rather than mixed, neighborhoods. Finally, the guidelines created an incentive for whites who had already purchased in white neighborhoods to oppose minority integration. According to the appraisal system, if blacks moved into a once homogeneously white neighborhood, the neighborhood might lose its A rating, and white homes would lose value, as the FHA would be less willing to underwrite mortgages for new homebuyers in the neighborhood, or second mortgages for existing homebuyers. It wasn't just homeowners: the guidelines also affected housing developers. When deciding where to locate a new housing development, developers paid attention to the appraisal guidelines because the guidelines were also used for FHA assessment of funding for home loans.

The FHA underwriting guidelines were not the only government housing programs during the New Deal that excluded African Americans and helped to reinforce racial segregation. The 1937 United States

:ing Act authorized the Federal Housing Administration in the
:rtment of the Interior to spend $500 million for slum clearance
and low-income housing projects.[68] By eradicating some of the sub-
standard housing where African Americans had been living and replacing it with new low-income housing, this project was designed to
help improve black living conditions. Unfortunately for those African
Americans living in the housing to be razed, the law did not guarantee
that blacks who had been displaced by housing would have access to
the new housing being built.[69] Frequently, the slums in which blacks
lived were replaced by highways and parks, and the new units were
placed in white areas, which because of violence and threats by whites
were inaccessible to blacks. In cases where some allowance was made
for blacks who needed housing, there was nowhere near one-to-one
replacement of demolished units.[70] In Chicago, for instance, between
1935 and 1945, slum clearance projects destroyed 7,000 units occupied
by blacks, replacing these with only 1,662 new units.[71]

When African Americans pushed by slum clearance began to move
to white neighborhoods in the 1930s and 1940s, their moves proved
as controversial as moves in the 1920s. For instance, in 1937, after an
African American doctor purchased property in an all-white area of
Atlanta, white homeowners forced the doctor out of the neighborhood.
In Dallas, after several blacks bought homes on Howell Street, white
residents embarked on a campaign of resistance that resulted in nearly
twenty bombings over a fifteen-month period. Many of the white residents in the neighborhood gathered in demonstrations in front of their
black neighbors' houses and also picketed the houses of whites willing
to sell to them. Black newcomers' houses were stoned and a black phy-
sician's house was burned to the ground.[72] Despite lobbying by the Dallas NAACP, city officials did little to help blacks targeted by violence,
which did not begin to abate until the onset of World War II.[73]

The Second Migration of Blacks: Integration
during the World War II Years

The jobs created by the mobilization for World War II spurred a massive second migration of African Americans from the South. Between
1941 and 1945 thousands of blacks moved to Detroit, Baltimore, Los ➤

Second migra

Angeles, Chicago, and San Francisco. Scholars estimate that approximately fifty thousand African Americans moved from the Deep South to Chicago during the war years.[74] Between 1940 and 1946, the black population in Los Angeles more than doubled.[75] The black population of the San Francisco Bay area increased even more, tripling between 1940 and 1944.[76]

Congress had prepared for the increase in pressure on existing housing stock by passing an amendment to the United States Housing Act of 1937, which authorized the Federal Housing Administration to provide either loans or subsidized housing for defense workers. During World War II, under this program and other programs, the federal government had provided housing for thousands of Americans.[77]

African American arrivals faced terrible housing pressures as they were forced to cram themselves into already crowded black ghettos. As the newcomers flooded Chicago, Baltimore, Los Angeles, and San Francisco, cities made a few attempts to satisfy the congressional mandate and build housing to accommodate them, but such efforts ran afoul of whites unhappy with providing housing to blacks. In Detroit in 1942, when city and federal officials designated the Sojourner Truth housing project for black war workers, white residents from the area erupted in protest.[78] When the first black family moved into Sojourner Truth, black supporters and their white opponents clashed; at least 40 were injured, and 220 were arrested.[79] New black settlers in Los Angeles faced similar treatment. Whites in the Allied Gardens district of Compton "threw rotten fruit at the newly purchased homes of incoming black settlers, smearing them with paint, tearing at rosebushes, cutting off electricity, and burning crosses in their front yards."[80]

Similar violence followed black attempts to escape the overcrowded black ghettos in Chicago during the 1940s. When blacks attempted to move into traditionally white areas, there was a precipitous increase in the number of violent attacks. In fact, in that respect, the late 1940s have been compared to 1917–1921, "when one racially motivated bombing or arson occurred every twenty days."[81] At the time, as in the case of whites' reaction to blacks moving in to the Allied Gardens district in Los Angeles, in Chicago hundreds, if not thousands, of whites aimed violence at individual homeowners moving in.[82] When blacks moved out of Chicago's Black Belt into the immediately surrounding white neighborhoods, their homes were attacked. Between May 1944 and July 1946, forty-six black homes were reported attacked by vandalism, arson, or bombing. Several of the incidents were serious. Twenty-nine of the incidents were firebombings, in which three people were killed.[83]   *Recont 9.*

In addition to places like Chicago that were part of the Great Migration, in response to the war production effort African Americans also moved to industrial cities like Portland, Oregon. Despite its location significantly outside the traditional South, as migrants found upon arrival, the city had plenty of race-based prejudice and discrimination to offer. The Oregon Ku Klux Klan had been quite active; some estimates put membership of the KKK in Oregon at 200,000 in the early 1920s.[84] The state of Oregon had at first refused to ratify the Fifteenth Amendment guaranteeing freed slaves the right to vote. Oregon also had some of the most antiblack laws until the late 1920s.[85] Prior to World War I, negative attitudes toward African Americans meant that employment and educational opportunities for Portland's small black population—2,000 out of 340,000 total population in 1940—were limited as well, with black men largely being restricted to jobs as red caps and porters, and black women struggling to find work as domestics and janitors.[86]

Negative attitudes toward African Americans in the state restricted available housing opportunities. The Portland Realty Board had long forbidden its members to sell property in white neighborhoods to African Americans and Asian Americans.[87] The strict legal prohibitions in place in other cities were unnecessary in Portland, since public disdain generally kept blacks out of most Portland neighborhoods. Despite this ugly history of racism, black workers nevertheless came to Portland. As a somewhat large number of blacks (fewer than 300 out of 2,500 other workers) began to arrive in Portland in 1942, Portlanders reacted with alarm and began erecting new "Whites Only" signs throughout the downtown area and especially in businesses close to the train station, where migrants could encounter them soon after arriving in the city. The "whites-only" policy applied to neighborhoods as well, with new African Americans coming to Portland for war jobs being restricted to the city's tiny black quarters. To accommodate the newcomers,

[c]ots were set up in the black Elks Lodge, in churches, and other black-owned buildings. Many people were forced to sleep on pool tables, share

the backseat of a car, or use someone else's bed during the day. Because no White families could be counted on to house African Americans, the Black community had to accommodate nearly twice its numbers.[88]

As in Detroit and Chicago, in Portland the city's attempts to build housing to accommodate black war workers coming to the city were met with resistance. In 1943 the Housing Authority of Portland (HAP) completed construction on a 40,000-resident community, Vanport City, the largest World War II federal housing project in the United States. Despite federal guidelines prohibiting discrimination in housing built with federal money, HAP allocated some units for blacks and allowed only African Americans to be eligible for these units. White residents also protested government attempts to house black war workers in Portland neighborhoods. They signed petitions demanding that officials "counteract, disrupt, and cancel the intention of those planning to house Negroes and other undesirable persons in all districts in which we have our homes."[89] Eventually, blacks were housed far from white Portlanders in neighborhoods just outside the city limits, with housing for city workers within the city limits remaining explicitly whites-only.[90]

The Postwar Period: Scarcity and Exclusion

After the war, with the return of veterans from Europe, the country plunged into a serious housing crisis. The housing crisis for blacks, including black veterans, worsened. To alleviate some of the pressure on housing, in 1944 President Roosevelt signed into law the Servicemen's Readjustment Act, or G.I. Bill, which provided tuition assistance and mortgage loan guarantees. Veterans Administration mortgages were very generous housing subsidies, as they provided a low interest rate and waived the down payment requirements. The VA also guaranteed up to 50 percent of a home loan (topping out at $2,000) for returning veterans. In 1945, the $2,000 mortgage limit was raised to $4,000 so that eligible veterans were able to receive 100 percent financing on homes that were appraised at up to $12,000.

The federal government did not have specific rules preventing blacks from receiving government funds. Unfortunately for black veterans, however, FHA appraisal guidelines did not support the disbursement of VA loans for black purchases in white neighborhoods.[91] In cases in which black veterans were able to find other financing for homes in white neighborhoods, like other African Americans, they often faced the challenges imposed by deed restrictions. Many pieces of property sold in the postwar period were covered by deed restrictions, in the form of private covenants that restricted the homes from being sold to African Americans, Jews, and other minorities.

Such was the case for Frank Louis Drye, a decorated black veteran of both world wars. In 1947, Drye purchased his dream home, a house in the Country Club Park neighborhood of Los Angeles. In Los Angeles, the postwar period was marked by severe restrictions on where African Americans could live. Black neighborhoods had begun to decay and while thousands of whites were being offered a government-assisted hand, thousands of African Americans in Los Angeles were crowded into dilapidated and rat-infested Little Tokyo, after Japanese Americans had been forcibly removed to internment camps.[92] Country Club Park was predominately white when Drye moved into the house with his wife, Atoria, and their five children. Years later, Drye's youngest son, who was thirteen at the time, recalled neighbors organizing to oust his family, along with the Stricklands and the Stewarts, the two other black families who had moved into the neighborhood.[93] Within two months of the Dryes' arrival, nine white families, led by Clarence Wright, a Presbyterian pastor who lived across the street from the Dryes, sued to enforce the deed restriction, which prohibited the property from being sold to individuals "not of the Caucasian race." Ultimately, the Dryes were able to remain in the property, but only because they were able to prevail in court.[94]

The Fight against Racial Covenants

The widespread use of racial covenants like that attached to the Dryes' property significantly restricted the housing choices of African Americans during the housing shortages of the 1940s. The pervasiveness of such covenants had led to a litigation campaign by the NAACP Legal Defense and Education Fund (LDEF) against them. There were several smaller suits against the covenants in cities around the country, many of which the organization lost.[95] Challenging restrictive covenants was a difficult battle because the covenants were private contracts among homeowners, and consequently courts were challenged to find the state action that implicated the Fourteenth Amendment's guarantee of equal protection. In the 1940s, LDEF's luck began to change. One early victory came when the organization prevailed in a 1945 case in Los Angeles involving, among others, the actress Hattie McDaniel, the first African American to win an Academy Award for her portrayal of the house slave Mammy in *Gone with the Wind*. McDaniel was one of the defendants in a suit brought by the West Adams Improvement Association, which alleged that racial covenants were attached to the properties that she and several other black film stars had purchased in the Sugar Hill neighborhood.[96] The NAACP won McDaniel's case in Los Angeles, but an even more significant development for the battle against restrictive covenants nationally came in 1948 with the organization's win in *Shelley v. Kraemer*.[97]

Shelley v. Kraemer involved a black couple, J. D. Shelley and his wife, who had purchased a home on Labadie Avenue in St. Louis in 1945 from Josephine Fitzgerald, who was white. The trial court found that the Shelleys did not know that the property contained a restrictive covenant preventing the property from being used or occupied by any persons except those of the Caucasian race.[98] Other owners of property covered by the covenant filed suit, asking that the Shelleys not be allowed to take possession of the home and that judgment be entered divesting the Shelleys of title and awarding the title to the home to the grantor or someone else of the court's choosing. The trial court decision in the Shelleys' favor was reversed by the Supreme Court of Missouri. The case was appealed to the US Supreme Court, where the Court agreed to hear it along with *Sipes v. McGhee*, a Michigan case in which white neighbors sued to enforce a racial covenant.[99]

When *Shelley v. Kraemer* was appealed to the Supreme Court, the Court evaluated whether the Fourteenth Amendment could prevent whites from selling their properties with discriminatory restrictions.[100] Previous cases had clearly established that the Fourteenth Amendment guarantee of equal protection did not apply to discriminatory private conduct. Because of this, the Court held that the restrictive covenants, standing alone, did not violate the petitioners' rights. In an imaginative and novel move, the Court did, however, find for the petitioners,

ing that court enforcement of racially restrictive covenants constitutes state action implicating the Fourteenth Amendment.[101] In other
words, white homeowners were free to attach restrictive covenants to
their property, but if a homeowner sued to enforce a violation of the
covenant, court enforcement of such covenants would be state action
and would violate the Fourteenth Amendment.

Shelley and *McGhee v. Sipes* were not the only wins in the area of
restrictive covenants. In *Hurd v. Hodge*, a Washington, DC, case that
was a companion to *Shelley* and *McGhee*, the Court invalidated the
enforcement of restrictive covenants using a slightly different approach.
Because it involved property in the District of Columbia, the Court
considered whether the Civil Rights Act of 1866 prohibited the judicial
enforcement of covenants.[102] This statute provided that all citizens of the
United States had the same right "to inherit, purchase, lease, sell, hold
and convey real and personal property, and to full and equal benefit of
all laws . . . as is enjoyed by white citizens."[103] The Court proclaimed that
the petitioners in this case had been denied such rights by virtue of the
action of the federal courts of the district. The Court used strong language to prohibit the enforcement of racial covenants in the District of
Colombia:

> That the Negro petitioners have been denied that right by virtue of the
> action of the federal government courts of the District is clear. . . . Solely
> because of their race and color they are confronted with orders of court
> divesting their titles in the property and ordering that the premises be
> vacated. . . . Under such circumstances, to suggest that the Negro peti-
> tioners have been accorded the same rights as white citizens to pur-
> chase, hold, and convey real property is to reject the plain meaning of
> language.[104]

In the end, *Shelley v. Kraemer* was somewhat of a mixed blessing. The
NAACP was able to use the case to convince the Federal Housing Administration that it should not underwrite loans to racially restrictive properties.[105] In 1949 the FHA declared that it would no longer underwrite loans to
properties covered by racial restrictions. Despite this, the Supreme Court's
decision in *Shelley* did not bring an end to the use of the covenants. Covenants were still attached to many pieces of property, and neighborhood

organizations in white neighborhoods, which had been strongly supportive of such covenants, still advocated their use.[106] After the Supreme
Court's decision in *Shelley,* in order to comply with the law, some neighborhoods changed the language of racial covenants to wording that did
not prohibit particular races but rather referred to "undesirable peoples."[107]
In other communities, neighborhood organizations harassed those property owners who breached the covenants and sold to minorities.[108]

The Postwar Housing Boom and the New Front in the War on Integration

The increased demand for housing prompted by veterans returning from World War II led to a postwar housing boom in cities and,
as discussed below, in the suburbs. Unsurprisingly, during the postwar
housing boom, housing for blacks remained in very short supply, for a
variety of reasons. First, as described above, racial covenants covered
a number of houses. Even though these were no longer enforceable by
law, the very existence of the covenants and the belief that they could be
enforceable made white sellers less likely to make their homes available
to African Americans seeking housing. Second, there was little federal
government assistance in the form of mortgages for mixed-race neighborhoods. In the city of Philadelphia and its suburbs, a postwar building boom between 1946 and 1953 created 120,000 new homes; unfortunately, just 347 of the 120,000 were available for African Americans to
purchase.[109] In Los Angeles in 1945, blacks could occupy only 3 percent
of the new private homes constructed, despite the fact that they were
over 12 percent of the people moving to the city.[110]

In the postwar period, a new front opened in the war on integration—the suburbs. Government assistance in the form of financial
backing for the VA and FHA mortgages created a segregated housing
market ripe for anti-integrationist violence. The postwar period was
one of rapid suburbanization, fueled by government rules that made
mortgage insurance more available in suburbs and in cities. Both the
FHA and VA mortgage programs provided mortgage insurance freely to
newly constructed homes, rather than existing housing stock. Encouraged by significant government investment in the interstate highway
system, schools, private development, and mortgage incentives in the

How was this explained? Defended? Still robbery?

1940s and 1950s, millions of Americans left cities and moved to the new suburbs; in 1954 *Fortune* magazine estimated that nine million Americans had moved from the city to the suburbs in the previous ten years.[111] This mass exodus had a profound effect on the city neighborhoods left behind. In Philadelphia, for instance, between 1950 and 1960, 700,000 whites moved to Philadelphia suburbs. In Chicago over that same time, more than one million whites moved to the suburbs.

Though the suburbs were symbolically and literally wide-open spaces containing spacious new houses for whites, this was not the case for African Americans. Suburban incorporation allowed suburbs to control zoning, which local officials used to keep suburbs white, according to the historian David Freund.[112] After *Buchanan v. Warley*, the process of exclusion was largely race-neutral, taking the form of bans on public housing, minimum lot size requirements, and the exclusion of apartments. If any of these measures failed and a black family managed to buy a home in a sundown suburb, writes the sociologist James Loewen, incorporation often conferred on the municipality the right to take the individual's property for the "public good."[113]

The war against housing integration in the suburbs, perhaps because in many cases it was waged after battles against integration of city neighborhoods, was focused more distinctly on measures that prevented blacks from moving in, rather than forcing them out. Take, for instance, Levittown, Pennsylvania. Levittown is located in lower Bucks County between Trenton, New Jersey, and Philadelphia. One of several massive suburban developments created by the developer William Levitt, Levittown, Pennsylvania, was completed in 1958. With sixteen thousand homes, it seemed to have room for every kind of middle-class worker, from factory workers to teachers, as long as they were white. Though *Shelley v. Kraemer* had been decided a decade earlier, racial covenants were attached to all of the homes in Levittown because for two decades the Levitt organization had publicly and officially refused to allow its houses to be sold to blacks. Levitt took this position because, as he saw it, "We can solve a housing problem, or we can try to solve a racial problem, but we cannot combine the two."[114] Though the covenants attached to Levitt's houses were unenforceable, they nevertheless had the effect of preventing the houses from being shown, and ultimately sold, to African Americans. As late as 1960, not a single one of the eighty-two thousand

"race-neutral"

wow

houses of Long Island's Levittown was owned by someone black.[115] Little progress has been made integrating Long Island's Levittown; it was still 97.37 percent white in 1990.[116] Twenty years after that, the 2010 census indicated that Levittown, New York was only 0.91% black.[117]

White suburbs close to large black populations in places like Detroit, for instance, were cognizant that they occupied a whites-only space. Because of the war industry and the deterioration of southern share-cropping, the black population of Detroit had risen to over 300,000.[118] Though such a large number of African Americans lived and worked in Detroit, they were unable to live in nearby suburbs like Dearborn, Royal Oak, Grosse Pointe, and Warren. In Royal Oak, David Freund writes, though Detroit's white suburbanites were "invested in main-taining their communities' racial homogeneity and protecting—even celebrating—the privileges that came with their whiteness," they did not openly discuss race.[119] Though race was not discussed, keeping out blacks was foremost in the residents' minds. In 1947, when the Royal Oak Land Company petitioned to have its thirteen-acre parcel rezoned to allow the construction of a 265-unit apartment complex, residents mobilized to defeat this change. Despite a housing shortage in the city, Royal Oak homeowners collected signatures, spoke out at city council meetings, and in the end were able to block the rezoning.[120]

There were noted exceptions to the suburbs' "bloodless" war against integration. One of the most famous incidents of housing-related vio-lence directed at minorities in the 1950s occurred in Cicero, Illinois. In July 1951, Harvey Clark Jr., a black bus driver, moved his family from the South Side of Chicago to suburban Cicero. The Clarks were the only black family in the twenty-unit apartment building. After the family moved in, teenagers broke into their apartment and vandalized it. For two days, a mob of between two thousand and five thousand whites attacked the Clarks' apartment building, burning and looting it. Order was restored only when 450 National Guardsmen reported to aid the 200 Cicero and Cook County sheriff's police attempting to quell the disorder.[121]

The (Few) Remaining City Residents: Standing Their Ground

In the 1950s and 1960s, many of Detroit's white residents who remained in the city were united in opposition to open housing. White Detroiters

had received assistance from the FHA, the HOLC, and the VA in the form of mortgage guarantees and loans, which meant that by the 1960s, more than 60 percent of whites were able to purchase homes.[122] These individuals were not willing to allow blacks to enter their neighborhoods. Between 1943 and 1965 approximately two hundred neighborhood organizations—"civic associations," "homeowners associations," and "improvement associations"—were created to defend their neighborhoods against black entry.[123]

In the early to mid-1950s, at the beginning of the era of widespread minority integration in Detroit, organized civil disorder was a powerful weapon. White opponents did not just use collective action, but also directed individualized threats at minority homeowners who had just moved to the neighborhood. Newcomers suffered harassment in the form of broken windows, anonymous threats, firebombings, and other types of vandalism designed to drive them out.[124] The experience of Easby Wilson, who bought a home in a white neighborhood on Detroit's Northeast Side in 1955, serves as a case in point. Wilson's new home was in the Coralville area, a white working-class neighborhood populated largely by fellow autoworkers. Only one other black family lived in the Wilsons' new neighborhood. After the Wilsons closed on their house, angry white neighbors waged a war of constant harassment. Just before they moved in, a vandal broke into the house, turned on all the faucets, and blocked the kitchen sink, flooding the basement. Black paint was splashed on the walls and floors. After the Wilsons had cleaned up the mess and left, someone broke all the front windows in the house. Over the course of the next several months, individuals threw eggs, rocks, and bricks at the Wilsons' windows, threw paint at the front of the house, and even put snakes in the basement. The attacks continued until the Wilsons moved out.[125]

The incidents directed at the Wilsons were like hundreds of others directed at blacks who crossed color lines between World War II and the 1960s. In Detroit, between the end of World War II and 1960 there were more than two hundred incidents of harassment, stoning of houses, arson, and physical attacks directed at blacks moving to white neighborhoods.[126] Thomas Sugrue suggests that these incidents may have stemmed from plant closings, a recession, unemployment, and limited housing options for the white working-class residents. "A potent mixture of fear, anger, and desperation animated Whites, who violently defended their neighborhoods. They could flee, as vast numbers of white urbanites did, or they could hold their ground and fight."[127]

The scale of anti-integrationist violence was even worse in Chicago. Between 1943 and 1946, the Chicago Council Against Racial and Religious Discrimination documented fifty-nine separate attacks on black homes, including "twenty-nine arson-bombings, twenty-two stonings, three shootings, three housebreakings, and two stink bombs."[128] One of the longest-running acts of resistance against minority integration by white neighborhoods occurred at the Trumbull Park Homes, a Chicago Housing Authority (CHA) development located in the neighborhood of South Deering. The historian Arnold Hirsch has written about the crowds of one thousand to two thousand whites who gathered in August 1953 outside the home of the Howards, a black family who had moved to the Trumbull Park Homes. At the time, South Deering was a heavily ethnic neighborhood on the city's far southeast side. A very fair-skinned African American, Betty Howard, had been presumed white when she selected, and was allowed to move into, the development. Though state law and CHA policy officially mandated nondiscrimination, Trumbull Park was one of four CHA developments that were all-white in the early 1950s.[129]

In response to this first breach of the color line, crowds threw bricks and rocks through the Howards' windows. They also threw fireworks; sometimes more than a hundred exploded in a single night. After the unrest focused on the Howards, blacks traveling though South Deering were attacked as well. The Howards moved out in May 1954, but the CHA moved other blacks in, and the white community continued to harass the newcomers. South Deering whites, Hirsch writes, congregated on street corners near the development, "'so the negroes can see them', and have no doubts that a crowd was 'waiting to catch them.'"[130]

Well into the late 1950s, on the West Side of Chicago, in countless incidents white residents behaved similarly to the neighbors of the Howards, the Clarks, and the Wilsons. Blacks moving to the West Side of Chicago in the late 1950s, and real estate brokers who sold them houses, received threats and were targeted with violence. In some cases this led to riots, like that occurring near the end of July 1957 in the Italian community of North Lawndale on Chicago's West Side. The violence started with six or seven whites attacking black picnickers, after which a mob of approximately a thousand whites gathered around a building occupied by two African American families. Members of an organized group broke windows in the house.[131] William Glover, who purchased a two-story flat in the white neighborhood of East Garfield Park in February 1957, was also targeted with violence. After the family first moved in, their furnace and boiler were destroyed. Several months later the Glovers' garage was burned down and their car was set on fire.[132]

Supporting Integration

Not all Chicago residents opposed minority move-ins. Some in the Chicago area were actively engaged in providing support for minorities attempting to move to white neighborhoods. The American Friends Service Committee (AFSC), the Chicago Committee of Racial Equality (CORE), the Catholic Interracial Council, and the Urban League were all active in promoting fair housing in Chicago in the 1950s. After the riots in Cicero, the AFSC created a fair housing program that supported African Americans moving to white neighborhoods. During an interview, one longtime AFSC member active in the fair housing movement in Chicago for several decades recalled what Chicago was like for minorities moving to white neighborhoods in the late 1940s:

> [A] typical pattern was that there was rigid segregation. It was enforced by violence. At times when a family moved into what was considered a white area, the actions of the opponents were everything from surrounding the house and throwing rocks and threatening to actually setting fires to buildings. And, the police were for the most part on the side of the rioter. It would not, with one important exception, disperse the crowds. They would stand by and maybe after a few hours go around and say, "Well, we've got to move on now." But they didn't do anything to stop the violence. There was one police captain, whose name was Commander Hackett and he was the only one that we could rely on to disperse the crowds. . . . "When you're gonna have a move, you pray for rain or [for] Hackett." Because fools won't fight in the rain and . . . Commander Hackett did his real duty. He dispersed the crowd. There was, in addition to the American Friends Service Committee, the Urban League and two of

the Jewish organizations and a Catholic Interracial Council were allied in trying to open up housing for African Americans and trying to damp down and hold the violence.[133]

In the late 1940s, this interviewee said, the AFSC worked with black families who had the means to purchase a home or an apartment in a white suburban neighborhood. Whites working with the AFSC went to the neighborhood pretending to be buyers, and when they returned told black families what the home or apartment in the white neighborhood was like. On the strength of the AFSC report, the family then purchased the home. At that point the difficult day of move-in came. The organization prepared for it by notifying the police:

> around 4 o'clock or something in the afternoon and we'd say, "We've come to tell you that this African American family is going to move into such and such address and we know that you will want to do your job in protecting them and we will be helping them while you do this." And most police, publicly, gritting their teeth, but didn't react the way that Cicero did, they tried to avoid any crowds.[134]

Neighbors had to be dealt with as well. Members of various fair housing organizations would canvass neighborhoods to advise the neighbors that an African American family was moving in and request their help. The organizations were trying to find white neighbors who would be cordial to their new neighbors. The AFSC had mixed results, with most whites acting coldly dismissive, a few thanking the organization and expressing the hope that the newcomers would be good neighbors, and in rare instances, whites in the neighborhood actually befriending the newcomers. On the move-in nights, members of the AFSC would spend the evening at the new home to provide families with some reassurance. The interviewee recounted, "I remember staying all night with families, sleeping on their couch that they'd just moved in, just to give a kind of assurance and have a telephone, particularly if a telephone hadn't been installed yet, so that the family would have some sense of help and security that it might not otherwise would have had."[135]

After move-in, the AFSC supported the families with follow-up calls to find out whether their move-ins went smoothly or whether the harassment continued. Supporting the families and preparing for their arrival made a significant difference. It helped families to persevere for a few months until the harassment died down. Eventually, in most cases after a few months, the new family was "usually pretty good to their neighbors, so their kids would eventually play with the neighborhood kids. . . . that was often the first step in getting to a normal situation."[136]

Crossing the Housing Color Line in the South in the Postwar Period

The postwar housing crisis hit African Americans in southern cities as well as northern ones. The housing shortage posed a unique challenge to the African American community in the South, which normally sought solutions that could be addressed only within the confines of the Jim Crow system.[137] In the postwar housing crisis, however, there seemed to be no solution for blacks in the South other than moving into white neighborhoods. As in the North, southern blacks crossed physical barriers and crossed into neighborhoods that had been zoned white to find housing.

Some of the most violent clashes over housing in the South in the postwar period occurred in Birmingham, Alabama, nicknamed "Bombingham." Between 1946 and 1965 there were fifty dynamite attacks directed at African Americans.[138] In 1946 Sam Matthews, a black drill operator, bought property and built a house at the very edge of an all-white neighborhood. Matthews challenged the city's racial zoning, and after US District Court Judge Clarence Mullins declared Birmingham's racial zoning law unconstitutional, a skull and crossbones were painted on Matthews's house, indicating to Matthews that it would be dangerous to move in. The next day, Matthews's vacant house was destroyed by dynamite.[139] For the next twenty years, vigilantes continued to bomb the homes of those who moved into disputed areas.

The thousands of black veterans who returned to Atlanta after World War II found that, as was the case in cities in the North, the city had destroyed residences in the traditional black neighborhoods and failed to replace them with new housing, so blacks had to seek acceptable homes in white neighborhoods.[140] In Atlanta, black expansion into white neighborhoods was first resisted by extremists—the Ku

Klux Klan and an Atlanta-based organization of brown-shirted fascists known as the Colombians. The Colombians chose to defend the largely working-class white Ashby Street neighborhood with a combination of intimidation and violence. In 1946, the Colombians posted the neighborhoods they were targeting with signs, announcing (inaccurately, for racial zoning had been outlawed) that the area was "zoned as a white community." Roving gangs of Colombians also attacked blacks whom they saw walking through these neighborhoods. Finally, as in communities in the North, Colombians bombed the houses of blacks who bought on Ashby Street.[141] The Colombians folded after one of their leaders was sentenced to prison. A new organization of the Ku Klux Klan stepped into the breach, physically attacking blacks who moved into white neighborhoods.

In 1947, the job of white neighborhood defense in Atlanta moved from extremists to a series of community organizations, including the West End Cooperative Corporation (WECC). The WECC was founded by Joe Wallace, a local businessman and Klansman. The organization's tactics were similar to those of community organizations in other cities that were mobilized against minorities moving in. When blacks were noticed moving into the neighborhood, a mob gathered around the house, and Wallace approached the buyers with an offer to repurchase.[142] When offers to repurchase or threats failed, the WECC resorted to violence. A black beautician who purchased a home on Ashby Street was first warned by Wallace not to move in, and later that night her house was firebombed.[143] Violence directed at blacks who bravely crossed the various neighborhood color lines erected by white community organizations in Atlanta continued until the early 1960s.

North of Atlanta, African Americans attempting to cross the color line in Louisville experienced similar violence, though it was not as severe as in either Atlanta or Birmingham. After World War II, as in other cities, blacks remained restricted to a small number of housing developments. There were very few suburban homes that blacks could freely purchase in the Louisville metropolitan area. It was not an issue of demand. Real estate agents simply refused to show homes to blacks wishing to buy in white neighborhoods, and whites gathered in mobs to harass whites who considered selling to blacks.[144] One study of housing in the Louisville metropolitan area suggested that blacks had access to about 1 percent of the roughly twenty thousand new homes built in the postwar period in Louisville.[145] When they were able to break through and purchase houses in white neighborhoods, white residents responded with violence.

One of the more noteworthy cases of anti-integrationist violence in the Louisville area involved a shadow purchase. Faced with difficulty finding the type of suburban ranch that he desired in Louisville, in 1954 the black World War II veteran Andrew Wade approached Anne and Carl Braden, a white couple he knew from working with them on Progressive Party candidate Henry Wallace's presidential campaign. Wade convinced the Bradens to act as shadow purchasers to help him obtain a house on Rone Court in Shively, a small town west of Louisville. Once the purchase was complete and Andrew and Charlotte Wade began occupying the house, the white developer, James Rone, realized that an African American couple owned the house. As word spread about blacks living in the neighborhood, violence began to be leveled at the family. Soon after moving in, the Wades had rocks thrown though their windows, shots fired at their house, and a cross burned nearby.[146]

The campaign to get the Wades to move out took place on multiple levels. In addition to violence leveled at the Wades' home, the home insurance company cancelled the Wades' home insurance, and consequently the mortgage company demanded payment of their home loan in full. Unidentified persons threatened the shadow purchasers, Anne and Carl Braden, and their children, sometimes calling the house, other times showing up in person. The violence was particularly frightening as both couples' children were threatened as well. At the time of the harassment, the Wades had a two-year-old and Charlotte Wade was pregnant with their second child.[147]

Andrew Wade reacted to the violence with stubborn defiance. For instance, while the cross was burning on his neighbor's property, Wade ran into the yard with a pistol. Perhaps reconsidering the ramifications of firing it, he instead shouted at the onlookers, "You're burning your own American flag."[148] Wade received offers to sell the house but was steadfast in his refusal to leave, proclaiming, "We intend to live here or die here."[149]

When he referred to dying in the house, Andrew Wade probably did not know how close he and his family might come to perishing in the house. In the middle of the night on June 27, 1954, less than two months after the Wades moved in, dynamite placed under the Wades' daughter's room exploded. No one was hurt, but there was significant property damage. Half of the house was destroyed, making the Wades' home unlivable. In 1957 the couple sold the property on Rone Court, never having returned to the neighborhood.[150]

Understanding White Neighborhood Violence in the Postwar Period

White reaction to minority integration in the postwar period was rooted in several factors. The postwar period witnessed a dramatic increase in homeownership. For many middle- and working-class whites who purchased their first homes in the postwar period, homeownership was a core aspect of their identity. These beneficiaries of HOLC, FHA, and VA housing policies internalized Roosevelt's New Deal vision of providing a home for every American. Roosevelt's rhetoric of expanding homeownership to the masses reinforced the values around homeownership and achievement that many immigrants brought to this country. Government-assisted loans smoothed the path to homeownership, and had the power to set homeowners on the path of upward social mobility.[151]

Having finally achieved the dream of homeownership in the postwar period, many whites resorted to violence to enforce the neighborhood color line. The use of violence—assaults, threats, vandalism, and firebombings of the homes of blacks who dared cross the color line—was an act of desperation. It was not especially risky behavior, however. Police were reluctant to seek out perpetrators, and even more reluctant to make arrests. Thus, whites rarely faced prosecution for crimes of anti-integrationist violence, and when they did, the charges against them were minor.[152]

At least one part of the explanation for white resistance may lie in the background of those who lived in the defended neighborhoods. Defended neighborhoods in the 1950s in Detroit included Oakwood, Dearborn, Seven-Mile, and West Fenelon. Similar neighborhoods also fighting against black integration in the 1950s in Chicago included South Deering on the city's Southwest Side, and on the West Side, West Garfield Park and Austin. In Chicago at midcentury, both West Garfield

Park and Austin were working-class neighborhoods composed of small single-family homes, apartment buildings, and two flats—homes with an apartment stacked on top of the other.[153] In Detroit, defended neighborhoods were composed of small, neat bungalows.[154] In both cities, these neighborhoods were frequently populated by a heterogeneous mix of native-born whites and working-class ethnic immigrants, or first-generation Americans who had roots in Germany, Sweden, Ireland, Italy, Poland, Russia, or other Eastern European countries. Though they (or their parents) may have come from different countries, many were Catholic, and their identities were shaped by the neighborhood's Catholic parish.[155] Defended neighborhoods in this time period were often (though not always) solidly working-class—auto workers, factory workers, teachers. In Detroit, for instance, residents of the defended neighborhoods had median incomes slightly above the city's average.[156]

Those resisting blacks' entry to their neighborhoods were multiply privileged. In addition to being homeowners, they also had the privilege of whiteness in the 1940s and 1950s, an era when being black meant suffering the indignities of Jim Crow in the South and experiencing discrimination in the North. In spite of their obvious privilege vis-à-vis blacks, those defending white neighborhoods in the postwar period may nevertheless have felt they had only a tenuous hold on any degree of elevated status. As Thomas Sugrue describes it, many of the not-yet-completely white ethnics defended their racial identity with desperation.[157] Ethnic immigrants—Slavs, Irish, Italians, and others from Europe—were newcomers to America's racial hierarchy and had to learn the contours of America's peculiar racial structure. Whiteness and the "fundamental difference from Blackness and, at other times, brownness and yellowness," did not resonate with some immigrants prior to migration to the United States.[158]

Learning the vagaries of America's racial hierarchy and where the immigrants themselves fit in it was not instantaneous, but rather a process that involved negotiating the racial organization of the neighborhoods in which they lived. Italian immigrants, for example, had to develop both affinity for the idea of whiteness and distaste for blackness in order to prevent black entry to Italian neighborhoods. Severe tensions between Italians and African Americans in Chicago neighborhoods in the mid-1940s developed as Italians came to understand

and consequently became attached to their own whiteness. Several factors were critical to the development of color consciousness among Chicago Italians, including the 1919 "Negro–white" riot, immigration restrictions, the Chicago mayoral elections in 1927 and again in 1931, and industrial unions, not to mention everyday events—chatting at the dinner table, shopping at stores, visiting dance halls, going to school. In casual discussions, friends and family of immigrants helped police the color line through their reaction to seemingly innocent "transgressions."[159]

Institutions such as the Catholic Church and settlement houses were also important teachers of the American racial structure, some of which had to do with the proper place of African Americans in white neighborhoods in Chicago. A fairly subtle message was conveyed in the diocesan policy of keeping "white" parishes "white," but some priests went further. In the 1930s, Father Luigi Giambastiani of St. Philip Benizi felt threatened by African Americans moving to his Near North Side neighborhood. Father Giambastiani was a key player in the creation of the North Side Improvement Association, whose goal was to prevent Italian Americans from selling or renting to African Americans.[160] In addition to allowing the North Side Improvement Association to hold meetings at St. Philip's, Father Giambastiani barred African Americans from attending mass, participating in the community center, and sending their children to the daycare. Giambastiani was also instrumental in the eviction of 4,700 African Americans from the neighborhood.[161]

In addition to the churches, settlement houses and social service providers were places of naturalization for Italian immigrants.[162] In other words, in addition to teaching arts and crafts, settlement houses taught immigrants how to apply for jobs and negotiate intergenerational difficulties, and generally communicated much about the process of becoming American by steeping the new immigrants in traditional American values.[163] Those settlement houses situated in predominantly Italian neighborhoods in Chicago had a policy of not allowing African Americans to benefit from the houses' activities. Social service providers adopted a similar approach, a 1930 survey revealed. According to the survey, many nursing homes, camps, homes for dependent children, convalescent care centers, nurseries, emergency shelters, hospitals, maternity homes, and the YMCA refused to admit African Americans.

immigration . . .

As a result, "Italians could encounter the color structure when entering hospital, living or visiting a relative in a nursing home, attending a summer camp or choosing a nursery school."[164]

The elaborate color structure and the system of housing segregation that it caused most definitely had a purpose—shoring up white residents who were quite vulnerable. In many cities the residents of defended neighborhoods were economically vulnerable. In the first days of white resistance to blacks moving to white neighborhoods in the 1920s, housing integration had been associated with neighborhood decline and the subsequent decline of property values. Thus, both immigrants and native-born whites assumed that if African Americans moved in, whites would move out and property values would plummet. In many cases, even the purchase of a tiny bungalow was a financial stretch for residents of working-class white neighborhoods. They occupied these particular neighborhoods because these were the only neighborhoods in which they could afford to buy homes. Frequently, one part of the reason they fought minority incursion was that they were too poor to leave if their worst fears were realized and the neighborhood declined.[165] As one white Detroiter wrote in the 1950s, "What about us, who cannot afford to move to a better location and are surrounded by colored? . . . Most of us invested our life savings in property and now we [are] in constant fear that the neighbor will sell its property to people of a different race."[166]

The process of assessing mortgageability was explicitly racialized. Take, for instance, the case of Philadelphia, where the federal Home Owners Loan Corporation (HOLC) appraisal of neighborhoods in 1937 identified older industrial and streetcar suburbs of the city as risky areas for home loans. In the assessment files that accompanied the maps, "references to hard-working Germanic stock in one area were contrasted with 'threat of Jewish encroachment.'"[167] New housing could be downgraded if it was located close to a 150-year-old black community. It wasn't just blacks and Jews who were disdained by the HOLC; neighborhoods populated by Italian, Slovak, and other Eastern European communities were also denied credit.[168]

Both the government's appraisal standards and whites' resistance to black entry were predicated on concerns about neighborhood stability. The opposite of a stable neighborhood is one that changes dramatically.

Dramatic neighborhood change—the transformation of a white working-class neighborhood into a poor black neighborhood—had occurred in many neighborhoods in the postwar period and was the nightmare of all residents of white neighborhoods. Change could be swift. In some cases, blocks in neighborhoods changed from all-white to all-black in just three or four years.[169] Many whites involved in neighborhood defense reasoned that if they allowed one black person into their neighborhood, then more would come, and with the increases in the number of black people would come crime, declining property values, and poor schools.

The horrible conditions in black ghettos—the shabby appearance of housing and the piles of garbage in crowded streets—provided all the evidence white neighborhood defenders needed that black people caused the terrible conditions that whites feared.[170] Black neighbors would destroy their peace of mind and would jeopardize the properties in which they had invested years and most of their income.[171] It was more than just money at stake. In such cases where homeowners had only a toehold on middle-class identity, their fear was that blacks, whom they knew to have lower status, moving into their neighborhood might jeopardize their own status.[172]

For middle-class whites, all-white neighborhoods conveyed respectability. In a lawsuit brought by Donald Maclean and his wife, Alma, against realty firms in Atlanta that had been selling to blacks, the Macleans argued that they and their neighbors had "established a permanent home in its present location in the belief that they could live out their lives there in peace and contentment." The Macleans accused real estate agents of trying to take away their neighborhood and give it to blacks. Allowing blacks to buy property in the area would mean that both the school and the park would be turned over "to colored persons for their exclusive use . . . thereby further . . . depriving petitioners and others of the use and enjoyment of said public park and school." The judge who ruled on the case expressed regret, indicating that a higher court compelled his decision against the Macleans.[173]

"Managing" the Inevitable

The story of housing integration in the postwar period was not always a violent one. The desperate fear that characterized many whites'

resistance to housing integration was not shared by those groups that either sought to manage racial integration or openly welcomed it. Two groups attempting to manage integration in Chicago in the 1950s and 1960s were the Good Neighbors Citizens Council in West Garfield Park and the Austin Tenants and Owners Association (ATOA). Rather than trying to stop African Americans from coming in by using legal and extralegal methods, groups in the Good Neighbors Citizens Council saw the eventual arrival of blacks in the neighborhood as inevitable and sought to prevent the neighborhood's decline in its wake. Their goal was "neighborhood stabilization," which could be achieved by preventing too many African Americans from moving in and by keeping large numbers of whites from leaving the neighborhood.[174] The ATOA, also active on the West Side of Chicago, focused on managing integration by taking on blockbusters, whose presence both preyed on vulnerable African Americans and led to white flight.[175] Some of the activities of the ATOA involved community meetings at which realtors were questioned about their practices of buying and selling and the creation of a proposed ethics code that realtors were encouraged to sign.[176]

 The residents of the Manor Park and Brightwood neighborhoods in Washington, DC, who formed Neighbors Inc. in the late 1950s, were even more supportive of integration than the Chicago organizations. One of the goals of Neighbors Inc., founded by Marvin Kaplan, a white journalist, and Warren Van Hook, a black pharmacist, was to keep their neighborhood "as a first class community of good Americans, regardless of race and religion."[177] At first solely focused on maintaining a racial balance in the Manor Park and Brightwood neighborhoods, the group began to include within its reach other nearby neighborhoods. Neighbors Inc. engaged in a variety of activities to encourage balance. One early activity of the organization involved putting pressure on the *Washington Post* and other regional newspapers to stop their practice of labeling neighborhoods "colored" in newspaper real estate ads. The organization also was careful to police middle-class standards by monitoring garbage collection, street cleaning, leaf pickup, and grass mowing in their interracial neighborhood.[178]

One of the main activities of Neighbors Inc., however, involved trying to attract middle-class blacks and whites who wanted to live in an interracial neighborhood. The ability of prospective home buyers to obtain FHA mortgages was threatened in racially mixed neighborhoods, which were highly discredited by the agency. For this reason, Margery Ware, a member of Neighbors Inc., monitored and disputed FHA judgments in which loans for houses in the neighborhood were not approved because the area was considered too risky.[179] In the mid-1960s the focus of the organization shifted as it emphasized encouraging white families to settle in the neighborhood. Though attracting whites to their changing neighborhood was a significant challenge, in the mid- to late 1960s the organization had success attracting many white families who, without the organization's efforts, might have moved to the suburbs.

The Road to the Fair Housing Act

Despite the actions of a few communities that welcomed or tried to manage integration, far too many white communities in the postwar period were not supportive of integration. By the 1960s it seemed clear that private discrimination served as a major impediment to fair housing. There were some legal remedies available to punish those who discriminated in the area of housing, punishments that stemmed from the patchwork of civil rights laws that existed at the time. State discrimination in housing was prohibited by the Fourteenth Amendment to the US Constitution, which provides that no state shall "deprive any person of life, liberty, or property, without due process of law; nor deny to any person within its jurisdiction the equal protection of the laws." Federal and state discrimination in housing was also prohibited under the Civil Rights Act of 1866, which mandates that "all citizens of the United States shall have the same right, in every state and territory, as is enjoyed by white citizens thereof, to inherit, purchase, lease, sell, hold, or convey real and personal property."[180] There was no federal statute specifically prohibiting private discrimination.

Before the passage of the Fair Housing Act, legal remedies were clearly inadequate to address even the most blatant private discrimination. Though there were a few state and local fair housing laws, the most widespread remedy was to charge perpetrators who harassed integrators with violations of the criminal law. Despite the Supreme Court's ruling in *Shelley v. Kraemer*, which held unenforceable racially restrictive covenants, private developers like William Levitt continued to use them. Similarly, neighborhood associations in white neighborhoods, which were opposed to minority integration, continued to advocate the use of racially restrictive covenants as a means of keeping African Americans out of the neighborhood. Realtors, whose code of ethics had been revised in response to the Supreme Court's decision in *Shelley v. Kraemer*, pledged not to "be instrumental in introducing into a neighborhood a character, a property or use, which will clearly be detrimental to property values in that neighborhood."[181] In interviews in the 1950s, realtors admitted that this meant that blacks should not be introduced to white neighborhoods.[182] Landlords who had property in white neighborhoods refused to rent to African Americans.

The continuing discrimination against blacks galvanized civil rights activists in the 1960s. In 1966, Dr. Martin Luther King Jr. and the Southern Christian Leadership Conference (SCLC) joined the Chicago Freedom Movement (CFM) in their struggle against racial discrimination and segregation in Chicago's housing market.[183] The American Friends Service Committee's tests of real estate offices revealed blatant racial discrimination that cut across class and neighborhood lines.[184] At the time, Chicago was deeply segregated, with blacks confined to overcrowded areas in the city's South, West, or Near North Sides. Many blacks paid higher prices than whites to live in dingy, rat-infested apartments. Those blacks who tried to escape the poor conditions in black slums by moving to white neighborhoods faced violence.

To help create support for their cause, activists staged a series of marches through white neighborhoods on Chicago's Northwest and Southwest Sides, where blacks had had trouble buying property or renting. Marchers were met in both areas with violence. Crowds threw rocks, bottles, and cherry bombs in Gage Park and Belmont-Cragin.[185] While blacks were marching through Marquette Park, white mobs burned marchers' cars.[186] Marchers were hit by objects thrown by protesters. In one famous incident, King was knocked to the ground and struck in the head by a rock thrown from an angry mob, while demonstrators shouted, "Kill him, kill him."[187]

The attention brought by CFM marches did not directly result in a fair housing bill. In 1968, however, after King was assassinated, President Johnson called for passage of the fair housing bill that had already been passed in the Senate and had been debated by the House of

Representatives. The legal scholars Leonard Rubinowitz and Kathryn Shelton suggest that Johnson and the House of Representatives selected the fair housing bill as a memorial to King because of the commitment he showed to it when he marched with the CFM.[188]

There is evidence that senators considering the bill knew about the violence faced by blacks trying to integrate. During the debate for the Senate version of the eventual act, senators paid heed to the problem of move-in violence, alluding to the failure of local officials to solve and prosecute crimes of racial violence and, in cases when they did decide to prosecute, their failure to obtain convictions. The Senate Report noted,

[A] small minority of lawbreakers has resorted to violence in an effort to bar Negroes from exercising their lawful rights. Brutal crimes have been committed not only against Negroes exercising Federal rights but also against Whites who have tried to help Negroes seeking to exercise these rights. Acts of racial terrorism have sometimes gone unpunished and have too often deterred the free exercise of constitutional and statutory rights.[189]

The reality of violent intimidation that many black homeowners experienced in the 1960s was explicitly recognized in the final legislative act. The Fair Housing Act contains a subchapter, "Prevention of Intimidation," which provides imprisonment and/or a fine for any individual who "by force or threat of force willfully injures, intimidates or interferes with, or attempts to injure, intimidate or interfere with any person because of his race, color, religion . . . and because he is or has been selling, purchasing, renting, financing, occupying, or contracting or negotiating for the sale, purchase, rental, financing or occupation of any dwelling."[190] As passed, the law had some teeth, with fines and a few fairly serious penalties. In the worst cases, when the target was killed, the penalties for violating Section 3631 allowed an individual to be sentenced to life in prison.

Conclusion

Violent reaction to racial minorities moving to white neighborhoods did not originate when minorities began to integrate in the antebellum period. In fact, prior to and even for some time after the Civil War, African Americans lived among whites largely without controversy in cities and towns in the North and South. The hardening of race relations in the 1890s led to the creation of sundown towns as African Americans were driven out of them. The Great Migration of African Americans from the South to cities in the Northeast as well as the upper Midwest placed great pressure on the traditional African American neighborhoods. As African Americans began to move out of the ghetto and into white neighborhoods, they were viewed as a threat to property values and to the condition of the neighborhoods.

The idea that African Americans were a threat to white neighborhoods was a mistaken belief that fearful residents transformed into a self-fulfilling prophecy. In many cases from the 1920s through the 1950s, those first African Americans who breached the color line and faced violent resistance from their white neighbors were professionals who had achieved significant success in order to buy into that white neighborhood. Ossian Sweet, who bought a house in a white neighborhood in Detroit in 1925, was a well-respected doctor whose class status exceeded that of his new neighbors. As such, African Americans like Sweet did not constitute a threat in the way "bad" neighbors traditionally do. Realistically, white neighbors did not have to be concerned that their new neighbors would not keep up their properties. Rather, black newcomers were seen as a threat because of what they represented—a breach of a privileged whites-only neighborhood space. With African Americans living next door, it became harder for whites to maintain the notion that their neighborhoods were exclusive spaces occupied by those at the top of the racial hierarchy.

Massive white flight from urban neighborhoods in the 1950s did not signal the end of conflict over minorities moving to white neighborhoods. The important legal reforms aimed at housing discrimination crafted during this era did not end the problem either. As the next chapter demonstrates, even after passage of the 1968 Fair Housing Act, whites in Detroit, Chicago, St. Louis, Boston, and many other cities in the Midwest, West, South, and Northeast were motivated by a mixture of fear, anger, and desperation and continued to violently resist African American moves into their neighborhoods.

2

The Contemporary Dynamics of Move-In Violence

The Fair Housing Act, passed in the wake of Martin Luther King Jr.'s assassination, attempted to address the discrimination in housing that had created the white neighborhoods in which anti-integrationist violence occurred. Though the act was an important step and eventually became a significant vehicle for the prosecution of acts of violence directed at minorities moving to white neighborhoods, by 1968, when the Fair Housing Act was passed, the geography of residential racial segregation had changed. "White flight"—a phenomenon in which whites abandoned neighborhoods after minorities moved in—had rearranged the racial distribution of urban centers. By the late 1960s many of the whites who might have resisted minority integration had fled to the suburbs.[1] Their flight, of course, did not stem solely from the presence of their new neighbors, but rather was prompted by a variety of factors ranging from the attractiveness of recently developed suburban areas to school desegregation. Changes in many neighborhoods' racial balance were both profound and swift. In some cases, for instance, neighborhoods like West Garfield Park in Chicago underwent significant racial shifts seemingly overnight, as African Americans or Latinos came to predominate in neighborhoods once fiercely guarded by whites. In West Garfield Park, in only five years, from 1960 to 1965, the African American population rose from 16 percent to between 65 and 85 percent of residents.[2]

Despite seismic shifts in the racial balance of areas like Garfield Park, a small number of white neighborhoods in large cities in the Northeast and Midwest—New York, Chicago, Boston, and the Washington, DC, metropolitan area—were occupied by whites determined to resist racial turnover. For instance, several crosses were burned in Prince George's County, Maryland, in 1977, terrifying new black residents.[3] Though the police attributed these particular cross burnings to juveniles playing pranks, some of the perpetrators who burned crosses in the 1970s did so for ideological reasons. One of the highest-profile incidents of anti-integrationist violence in the 1970s occurred when the home of the Butler family, who lived in College Park, Maryland, was repeatedly vandalized after the Butlers became the first blacks to move into their neighborhood in January 1977. Five years later, in 1982, a federal court ordered a Ku Klux Klan member to pay the family $23,000 in civil damages.[4]

In the years following the passage of the Fair Housing Act, high-profile, violent acts continued to be directed at minorities attempting to integrate. Many perpetrators were not, however, affiliated with white supremacist organizations. Rather, they were just unwilling to share their neighborhoods with minorities and could not afford to or did not want to flee. The first part of this chapter focuses on the time period immediately after the passage of the 1968 Fair Housing Act and explores the actions and preferences of working-class white ethnics living in neighborhoods like Bensonhurst and Canarsie, in Brooklyn, New York; South Boston; Yonkers, New York; and Cicero, Illinois, who, instead of fleeing or accepting their neighbors, chose to stand and fight.[5]

Those Who Chose to Stand and Fight, 1970–1990

The individuals who lived in working-class neighborhoods that strongly rejected minorities may have viewed their neighborhood as a "last stand" for a variety of reasons. In the 1980s in Chicago and New York, many of the all-white ethnic enclaves resisting minority integration were among the few remaining affordable (white) neighborhoods. Many of these neighborhoods were dominated by blue-collar workers and city employees. In the case of police officers and firefighters, their jobs required them to live within the city limits. Such neighborhoods were one of the few remaining all-white places that they could live. In other cases, residents who ended up in neighborhoods like Canarsie had moved once, and developed resentment over having previously fled minorities; they were thus exceedingly dismayed at the prospect of having to again face minority movers in their new neighborhood.

Resistance in Canarsie, Brooklyn

Working-class urbanites, especially those abiding in areas identified as ethnic enclaves, remained fiercely attached to their neighborhoods and aggressively patrolled their boundaries, resisting minority incursion. One of the most vivid examples of resistance to housing integration in the 1970s occurred in Canarsie, a neighborhood in Brooklyn. In the 1970s, middle-class blacks began moving to Canarsie, which previously had been settled predominately by Jews and Italians. Canarsie was viewed as territory many of the nonblack residents were determined to protect by preventing black in-migration to the neighborhood. Some of the whites occupying Canarsie in the 1970s were longtime residents; a substantial number had relocated to the area from other parts of Brooklyn, like Crown Heights, East New York, Brownsville, Bedford-Stuyvesant, Bushwick, and Williamsburg, that had been integrated by blacks and Hispanics.[6] Part of the desire to fight minority entry may have stemmed from the vulnerability of the residents. Even though residences in Canarsie were comparatively less expensive, white working-class buyers were often still terribly financially vulnerable. Some of the new buyers in Canarsie, who had fled neighborhoods like East Flatbush in the 1970s, felt their relatively modest incomes squeezed by high mortgage payments and property taxes.[7]

Many of the new residents in Canarsie feared that minorities moving in would jeopardize their home values, the quality of the neighborhood schools, and their children's safety.[8] In their old neighborhoods, shifting racial composition had been accompanied by changes in the neighborhood's overall socioeconomic class as minorities moved into the neighborhood's housing projects. The residents complained that the new residents were not just poor but also dirty. There were changes in culture, too. One Jewish attorney living in Canarsie, who had moved away from his old neighborhood in East New York, described changes after the arrival of Puerto Ricans. The Puerto Ricans, he complained in an interview, were "sitting outside all summer, playing dominoes, strumming guitars, drinking beer." He went on to reflect,

> The Jews were shocked by it. And then there was a robbery of a delicatessen at Dumont and Alabama Street. My family began to feel unsettled

by the men hanging around during the day, and the crime and drugs.
. . . East New York used to be quiet on the high holidays, but suddenly
there was noise and gangs and bodegas. We no longer felt comfortable
sleeping outside on mattresses on the fire escape on hot summer nights.[9]

In the late 1960s, Canarsie may have seemed like a safe place to relocate
to because the central core of Canarsie remained "lily-white" long after
minorities had moved into the surrounding neighborhoods. By the early
1970s, however, a few middle-class blacks began to move into Canarsie.
At that point, protecting Canarsie became of paramount importance to
its white residents. Block associations were formed to encourage homeowners to sell only to whites. Attempts were made to recruit whites to
the neighborhood to fill any vacancies and prevent African Americans
from moving in. Some Canarsians' behavior fell outside the law, as a
select group of residents resorted to violence to protect their neighborhood. Several houses of minorities who had moved to the neighborhood
and also those of whites who had sold to minorities were firebombed.[10]
After a Puerto Rican family moved to a block near Rockaway Parkway,
where many working-class Italians lived, their new neighbors attributed
a rash of storefront burglaries that occurred nearby to the newcomers.[11]
A band of Italian boys ousted the Puerto Ricans. One of the individuals
responsible for ejecting the Puerto Rican family boasted to the sociologist
Jonathan Rieder, "They were the filthiest family you'd ever seen, right out
of Brownsville. We got them out of Canarsie. We ran right into the house
and kicked the shit out of everyone."[12]

Canarsie was not alone. National investigations of attacks on minorities in the mid-1980s identified violence directed at minority families
moving to white neighborhoods as the most common form of violent
racism in the country.[13] A report by the Southern Poverty Law Center
(SPLC) focused on the period between 1985 and 1986 and investigated
incidents in Philadelphia, Chicago, Cleveland, and places throughout
the South. The incidents documented in the SPLC report were cross
burnings, arson, firebombings, verbal harassment, vandalism, and
threatening calls and letters, all focused on driving minorities out of
all-white or predominantly white neighborhoods. The authors of the
report seemed to recognize that readers might assume that move-in
violence occurs primarily in the South, and were careful to note that

this was a mistaken assumption. Highlighting the widespread occurrence of the incidents in question, the SPLC report noted that violence directed at minorities moving to white neighborhoods was in fact as acute, if not *more* acute, in the North, the Midwest, and the West as in the South. Spotlighting the new and unexpected locale for these incidents, the SPLC report noted, "Since 1985 the majority of the 45 arson and cross burning attempts against move-ins have taken place in the metropolitan areas of northern Midwest."[14] The report did not offer an explanation for this unexpected result.

The Decline of Mobs and the Rise of Individual Action

One characteristic that distinguishes the 1970s and 1980s from the earlier periods of resistance to minority integration is that in the vast majority of cases, the 1970s heralded the decline of mob violence directed at minorities moving to white neighborhoods. There was also a decline in mass protests associated with individual minorities who moved to white neighborhoods. For instance, in the 1940s and 1950s, as chapter 1 describes, if a black family moved to a house or apartment in a white neighborhood, mobs of white people might gather in front of the house in protest. By the 1970s, there were fewer reports of situations in which neighbors organized collectively to run minority families out of white neighborhoods.

Organized, neighborhood-wide campaigns of terror to force out newcomers were replaced in the 1970s with small groups of terrorists working to keep their neighborhoods white, or a barrage of small acts of violence committed by individuals acting alone. For instance, between 1983 and 1986, black families living in Maplewood and South Orange, New Jersey, experienced more than a hundred incidents of racial harassment ranging from car tires being slashed to lawns burned with the imprint of a cross.[15] Around the same time as the New Jersey incidents, in Chicago, on the border with Cicero, Illinois, Spencer Goffer and Patricia Franklin and their eight-year-old son moved into an apartment in an all-white neighborhood. A few days after their arrival, someone threw a tire iron through their living room window. The following evening a group of assailants spent hours screaming slurs and epithets as they threw bottles and bricks at the family's windows.

The family escaped injury by leaving through a back alley, but never returned to the house.[16] A few years later, in Toledo, Ohio, four men were arrested for having fired shotgun blasts at the homes of two black families living in a white neighborhood. The shotgun blasts occurred a few days after a cross burning on the lawn of a black family that had moved into a white and Hispanic neighborhood in Toledo.[17] Similar incidents were directed at black families moving to white neighborhoods in the early to mid-1980s in the Atlanta metropolitan area and in Cleveland, Boston, and Philadelphia.[18]

Collective action opposing integration was rarer in the 1970s and 1980s than it had been in the time before the passage of the Fair Housing Act. Potential explanations for the decrease in collective action included the availability of a legal remedy to address such violence and the lack of social support for open displays of racial hatred. Despite the general decrease in open displays of hostility, there were a few notable cases involving black families moving to all-white neighborhoods in Boston, New York, and Philadelphia where residents did organize to prevent blacks from moving in. One of the most publicized incidents of anti-integrationist violence during the 1970s occurred in the Boston area in 1976, when Otis and Alva Debnam, the first blacks to purchase a home in their Irish neighborhood, were confronted by white neighbors who mounted a campaign of racial intimidation, violence, and vandalism against them.[19] In Philadelphia there was a history of white resistance to African Americans, particularly in working-class neighborhoods. In the early 1960s, for example, a black couple who purchased a home in Folcroft, a working-class suburb, had been driven from their home with burning crosses, intimidation, vandalism, and epithets. In November 1985 Carol Fox, who was white, moved with her black husband, Gerald Fox, into a home in a white neighborhood in Southwest Philadelphia. The week the Foxes and their two children moved to the neighborhood, several hundred whites, many shouting, "Move, move, move!" demonstrated outside the Foxes' home.[20] Carol Fox told a reporter that as the family tried to move in, they were pelted with slurs. A few days before the protests at the Foxes' house, only a few blocks away in the Woodlawn neighborhood, roughly four hundred white protesters, many screaming, "We want them out!" gathered outside the home of a young black couple who had moved to the neighborhood.[21] Soon after the couple moved in, a soft drink bottle was thrown through the window. On December 12, 1985, the house was burned to the ground, destroying most of the possessions of the couple who had moved there.[22]

There were significant racial conflicts over housing in various parts of Philadelphia throughout the 1980s. Woodlawn, which had originally been built in the early twentieth century as a "streetcar suburb," was transformed in the 1940s and 1950s into a neighborhood for successful second-generation Polish, Italian, and Irish immigrants. Living in an all-white neighborhood close to a black neighborhood that had once been white may have made Woodlawn residents feel much more vulnerable to the racial balance in their neighborhood changing significantly. Many of the homeowners in the neighborhood were elderly, and because of fears of racial transition, demand for their houses was too low to produce a selling price high enough to enable them to move to other white areas. As the political scientist Carolyn Adams noted, "Unable to move, the residents of Woodlawn chose to resist the encroachment of blacks."[23]

Racial Tension in White Neighborhoods in New York City

Much of the 1980s and 1990s were characterized by extremely well publicized racial tension in several working-class white neighborhoods in New York City. Race relations in these predominantly white areas were exacerbated by three high-profile racialized attacks on blacks who were just passing through. The first incident, in 1982, involved the black New York City transit worker Willie Turks, who along with several coworkers had stopped in the Gravesend section of Brooklyn to get something to eat on their way home from work. When they tried to drive away, their car stalled and Turks was pulled out of the car and fatally beaten. His coworkers were beaten by the mob as well. A few years after Turks's murder, in December 1986, Michael Griffin and three friends had car trouble in Howard Beach, Queens. A mob of white men spotted the three black men, rushed over, began screaming racial slurs, and then started to beat them. Trying to escape, Griffin ran in front of a car and was killed. The last high-profile incident was the attack on Yusuf Hawkins, which occurred on August 23, 1989. Hawkins, a black sixteen-year-old, was accompanied by two friends who went to Bensonhurst, a working-class white neighborhood in Brooklyn, looking for a used car.

The group was attacked by a mob of between ten and thirty white men, and in the melee Hawkins was shot to death.

Even though these three attacks do not fit the traditional pattern of anti-integrationist violence, there is some connection to housing-related hate crime. First, each of these crimes occurred in neighborhoods that were predominantly white. These violent mob attacks also involved numerous perpetrators. That the crimes had so many perpetrators (far outnumbering the targets) suggests a sense of community racism, or defending one's turf against minorities. Defense of the neighborhood is a common explanation for neighborhood-based hate crime. Finally, there is the message that such crimes send. Attacks on black men who just happened by chance to be in the neighborhood send a distinct message that blacks do not belong in the neighborhood even as passersby. In addition, these crimes and the protests that followed were extremely well publicized, and therefore helped communicate to minorities throughout the metropolitan area that these neighborhoods would not welcome them as residents.

One attempt to understand the context of the racial violence directed at the black men who were attacked in Howard Beach, Bensonhurst, and Gravesend involved a study of eighty-eight white neighborhood youths from the Bensonhurst, Sheepshead Bay, Canarsie, and Gravesend neighborhoods in Brooklyn in the early 1990s. The young men were hardly model citizens, having been placed in a youth program that works with at-risk teenagers. Nevertheless, they were strongly representative of the types of young men engaged in the behavior that led to the killings of Griffin, Hawkins, and Turks. In their interviews, the youth described feeling under siege from minorities. The election of a black mayor, David Dinkins, was viewed as leading to blacks taking over the city, which diminished the young men's ability to control the face of their neighborhood.

> VINNIE: You know, Italians used to run the city. We didn't have any problems 'cause we had political juice [power]. Now the blacks have taken over, and we don't get nothin' from the politicians.
> GINO: Dinkins, he's all for the blacks, 100 percent. Not like Ed Koch who used to care about people in white neighborhoods.
> SAL: When Dinkins was elected I wanted to move out of the city.[24]

Like other whites living in working-class white neighborhoods, the Brooklyn youth viewed the neighborhood as their turf, and considered it their collective obligation to defend their territory against blacks. They also suggested that these views were shared among others in their neighborhood. As one of the youth said, "If a white guy walks my block, nobody will say anything to him. But if the black guy walked onto my block everybody puts their head out the window to make sure he leaves the block."[25]

The attitudes that those Brooklyn youth displayed—that blacks were not welcome in white neighborhoods—maps quite well onto an analysis of the big picture of hate crime and migration to white neighborhoods in New York City in the late 1980s and 1990s. In New York many of the hate crimes in this period occurred in parts of the city where the urban landscape was changing demographically. One study analyzing the location of hate crimes reported to the hate crimes unit within the New York City Police Department between 1987 and 1995 revealed that rates of racially motivated crime against Asian Americans, Latinos, and blacks rose when minorities moved into white strongholds.[26] The researchers hypothesized that racially motivated crime stemmed from white residents' battles to control areas they considered to be their territory.[27]

The precise relationship between desiring neighborhoods in which there are few people of color and committing crimes against them when they move in is unclear. The literature on move-in violence and segregation does, however, suggest that some whites who are fiercely protective of their neighborhood spaces will engage in acts of violence to discourage minority incursions. This may be more likely to happen in cases in which the neighborhood is close-knit or has a particular ethnic identity that residents feel fiercely driven to protect.

The 1990s: Move-In Violence Becomes "Hate Crime"

The 1986 Southern Poverty Law Center report on move-in violence noted the absence of nationwide systematic record keeping in the area of what they termed "hate violence activity." The 1990s began with the advent of a new way of thinking about racial violence in the creation of the category "hate" or "bias" crime. These crimes are crimes motivated by bias on the basis of race, religion, ethnicity, sexual orientation, and a number of other categories prohibited by law. In 1990, Congress passed the Hate Crime Statistics Act (HCSA), which requires the Justice Department to conduct annual nationwide surveys of law enforcement agencies to obtain data on "crimes that manifest evidence of prejudice based on race, religion, disability, sexual orientation, or ethnicity, including where appropriate the crimes of murder, non-negligent manslaughter, forcible rape, aggravated assault, simple assault, intimidation, arson and destruction, damage or vandalism of property."[28]

While the HCSA did not itself provide any type of additional legal remedy for bias-motivated crimes, the legislation was designed to help by encouraging local law enforcement to pay more attention to these types of crimes. The FBI created a series of publications, including *Hate Crime Data Collection Guidelines* and *Training Guide for Hate Crime Data Collection*, which could be used by law enforcement officers for training and for the development of procedures to aid in identifying hate crimes. The HCSA also required the US attorney general to publish a yearly summary of the data collected from different law enforcement agencies around the country. This report, *Hate Crime Statistics*, has appeared each year since 1993 and provides data regarding incidents, offenses, victims, and offenders in crimes motivated in whole or in part by bias against the victims' perceived race/ethnicity, religion, sexual orientation, or disability.

When combined with census figures, *Hate Crime Statistics* can allow some evaluation of the level of anti-integrationist violence. Analyses of hate crime numbers and census data from 2000 reveal links between increases in hate crimes and the migration of minorities to white neighborhoods. One study compared census data to the FBI's nationwide hate crime statistics for 1998, 1999, and 2000.[29] The segregation levels in US cities with more than 95,000 residents were measured using a dissimilarity index score, which in this case described how many blacks would have to change residence in order for the city to be perfectly integrated. This analysis found that cities with higher rates of antiblack hate crime also had higher levels of black-white dissimilarity. In other words, more antiblack hate crimes occurred in cities that were more segregated.[30]

Despite its comprehensiveness—there is no other nationwide measure of hate crime—*Hate Crime Statistics* is not the most *reliable* source of data. This is true for a variety of reasons, the most important of which is the source of the data. The data that make up the annual *Hate Crime Statistics* are submitted by different law enforcement agencies around the county. The police agencies submitting these reports vary widely in their training, data collection methods, reporting practices, and investigative procedures regarding hate crime. Thus, in some jurisdictions there may be no reports or inaccurate reports at best. For instance, in 2008, even though 13,690 agencies participated in data collection, 11,545 agencies (some 84 percent of all agencies reporting) reported that *not one* bias-motivated incident occurred in their jurisdiction in 2008.[31] Agencies reporting no bias-motivated incidents were unlikely to have dedicated personnel charged with identifying and investigating bias-motivated crime.

A far more accurate yet less comprehensive way of measuring the relationship between housing segregation and the number of hate crimes occurring in a city is to use individual hate crime reports and compare them to segregation levels in a particular city. Examination of data on hate crimes in New York City in the 1990s and Boston in the mid-1980s, discussed in more detail in chapter 5, suggests that race-based hate crimes were strongly linked to the migration of minorities to white neighborhoods. For instance, Jack Levin and Jack McDevitt analyzed all the hate crimes identified by the Boston police over a three-year period in the 1980s, and "moving into a neighborhood" was the third most likely cause of hate crime.[32]

The passage of the HCSA in 1990 brought significant national attention to bias-motivated violence. As a result, many jurisdictions passed special statutes criminalizing bias crime. The precise content of these statutes is described in more detail in chapter 6. Regardless of the statutory arrangement, bias crime provided a new and sorely needed legal remedy for anti-integrationist violence. The majority of bias crimes are "low-level" crimes—vandalism and assault—from a criminal law perspective. Low-level crimes are frequently not even investigated by the police.[33] Because of this, the new category of bias crime brought much-needed attention to incidents that might not have been investigated by the police, let alone prosecuted. In fact, to deal with the rigors of investigation of this new type of crime, police departments around the country established specialized units. The prosecution of such crimes, discussed in more detail in chapter 6, is also a challenge, requiring special resources and skills.

The increased attention created by hate crime legislation and prosecutors' offices did not put an end to bias-motivated violence occurring as a result of minorities moving to white neighborhoods. One analysis of hate crime data collected by the police and census data from 1990 and 2000 in California revealed a correlation between increases in hate crimes and the migration of minorities to white neighborhoods.[34] In addition to this research, news accounts drawn from newspapers around the country suggest that minorities living in or moving to white neighborhoods continue to be attacked. In 2007 alone, from the East Coast (New York and Philadelphia) to the West (California), in the South and Midwest, minority families experienced cross burnings, graffiti, arson, and verbal harassment committed by their neighbors upon their move to white neighborhoods. The violence of the 1940s and 1950s is eerily similar to incidents occurring since 2000. For instance, in one of several incidents that took place in Philadelphia,[35] Sean Jenkins, a black construction worker, and his girlfriend made plans to rent a house in a quiet, predominately white neighborhood in December 2007. Immediately prior to their taking occupancy, white vandals broke first-floor windows in the house and wrote on a wall, "All n[igger]s should be hung."[36] Later, when Jenkins's girlfriend went to clean the house, a young white man yelled at her, "all n[igger]s taking over the neighborhood!"[37] After these events, the couple changed their mind about the house.

In some cities, like Chicago, crimes directed at minorities who moved to white neighborhoods were part of a continuous battle over housing integration. The struggles over housing integration that Chicago experienced in the 1950s, as described in chapter 1, continued as minorities moved to white neighborhoods in the city and also in the suburbs. In 1998 the *Chicago Reporter* compared hate crime statistics with population change in 265 suburbs in the metropolitan area between 1990 and 1997. The results suggested that hate crimes were more likely to strike in areas undergoing demographic change. Suburbs with a white population of between 70 percent and 90 percent that experienced a significant change in their minority population accounted for more than half of all suburban hate crimes in the metropolitan area.[38]

Newspaper accounts from the 1990s show Chicago to be littered with incidents of anti-integrationist violence. Incidents involving attacks on African Americans who had moved to white neighborhoods in and around the Chicago area occurred in Elwood Park (1992, 1998), Berwyn (1992), Portage Park (1998), Glenwood (1994), Ashburn (1996), and Mount Greenwood (1996, 1999). Most of the victims were black, but Hispanics were also targeted. One such incident involved hate graffiti placed on the property of three Hispanic families who had moved to Portage Park in 1998. Though some neighbors were not happy with the graffiti, others viewed their new neighbors as criminals, and felt the treatment was appropriate. One neighbor told a reporter, "They deserve it. This was a nice neighborhood until *they* [the Hispanic families] moved in. People want them out of here."[39]

A similar lack of sympathy for targets and support for perpetrators of move-in violence were offered by neighbors of the Campbells, new black residents of Berwyn, another Chicago suburb. When Clifton Campbell, a Jamaican immigrant, his wife, and three children moved to Berwyn in March 1992, the suburb was 98 percent white. The day after the Campbells moved in, someone threw a brick through a window in the family's house. The following day someone set fire to the Campbells' porch. Though one neighbor quoted seemed dismayed by the crime and felt that the family should not move, several others seemed more supportive of the perpetrator. One neighbor, who declined to be identified, told a reporter, "I feel bad their house got burned . . . but real estate people should have told him that this is an all-white neighborhood, and they should've expected it. I want them to leave. I don't want my property value to go down."[40] The Campbells subsequently put their house up for sale.

Another incident in suburban Chicago involved Andre Bailey and Sharon Henderson, a black couple who moved to Blue Island, Illinois, in the summer of 1996. They moved from south suburban Harvey, and like that of many minorities moving to white neighborhoods, the Bailey-Hendersons' relocation was a move up the social ladder, prompted by their wish to live in a better neighborhood. Soon after the Bailey-Hendersons moved in, someone set fire to a pile of leaves in their front yard and the tires on their car were slashed.[41] The family's dog Bingo was shot with a pellet gun. Then, on June 12, 1996, their neighbor Thomas Budlove burned a six-foot cross on their lawn. Charged with a hate crime, Budlove eventually pled guilty and was sentenced to two hundred hours of community service. Bailey said that after the crime,

Table 2.1
News Accounts of Anti-Integrationist Violence, 1990–2010

Type of Incident	Number of Incidents
Arson/firebombing	44
Cross burning	96
Harassment & verbal threats	102
Homicide	3
Physical attack	28
Racially motivated shooting	20
Vandalism	162
Total	455*

*The number of incidents here differs from the number in Figure 2.1. Figure 2.1 captures the number of families who were targeted. In several cases, families experienced several incidents. Table 2.1 captures and categorizes the total number of incidents that the news stories reported.

the children were worried about leaving the house. "I'd give them a look, telling them it's okay to go outside." Nearly three years after the crime, the Bailey-Hendersons testified that they lived in fear of another racially motivated attack.[42]

A National Look at Bias-Motivated Violence, 1990–2010

My own analysis of newspaper stories published on move-in violence between 1990 and 2010 reveals that these incidents in Chicago were just a few of the hundreds of attacks targeted at minorities moving to majority-white areas across the country in that period (see table 2.1). The events were not restricted to any particular geographic area of the country and occurred in cities in every region of the country.

The Tip of the Iceberg

Figure 2.1 shows 432 crosses placed in the approximate geographic location where each incident occurred. Each of the crosses in figure 2.1 represents a minority family who experienced race-based

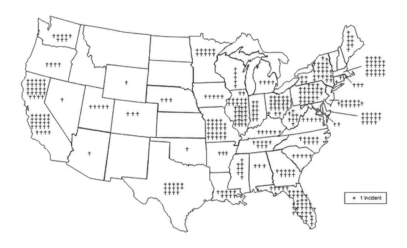

Figure 2.1. Incidents of Anti-Integrationist Violence, 1990-2010.

harassment while living in, or upon planning a move to, a white neighborhood. These 432 incidents, however, are just the tip of the iceberg. Though these types of incidents are frequently not reported, the majority of the incidents depicted here have been reported to law enforcement because media attention often spurs law enforcement attention. Also, I argue that these incidents are underrepresented because the individual symbols depicted in figure 2.1 represent only one incident. In many of these cases (as is typical of hate crimes generally), a particular family may experience several incidents before realizing that the incidents are bias-motivated or before they find reporting the crime to police to be justified. Incidents directed at families' homes often consist of vandalism or other property damage. For all of these reasons, many incidents directed at minorities who have moved into white neighborhoods never get reported to police and never end up as media accounts. Those targeted by this type of crime may be loath to admit that they are being targeted because of their race. Reluctance to admit the reality of race-based treatment is true for hate crimes in general, but may be even more likely in cases of anti-integrationist violence, where individuals are targeted at their homes. In addition, many of the incidents identified are vandalisms, and targets may feel more comfortable attributing the incidents to other sources. A final reason that this catalog represents only a small percentage of the cases that have occurred in the past several years is that often individuals who experience crimes directed at them because they have moved to a white neighborhood are terrified, and end up leaving the neighborhood without reporting incidents to the police.[43]

Frequently, the incidents directed at the integrating family occur within days, weeks, or a few months of their move to a predominately or all-white neighborhood.[44] Occasionally, the home targeted is one that a black or other minority family is contemplating purchasing, has just purchased, or has under construction.[45] For instance, in September 2004 in Gary, Indiana, a newly constructed Habitat for Humanity home for a black family in a white neighborhood was marked with racial slurs and Ku Klux Klan insignia and then burned.[46] In a few cases, the targeted family or individual had lived in the neighborhood for many years, but the action is unambiguously aimed at getting them to move, and as such can have disruptive potential. One woman who lived in Portland for nine years had a cross burned on her lawn. According to police, it was the eighth racial incident at the home in two months. Though she'd lived in Portland for nine years, the harassment and the cross burning made her reconsider the decision to make Portland her home. When asked about the cross, she admitted being terrorized: "All of a sudden I'm wondering if it's worth staying."[47]

That there is any "waiting period" between a family's move-in date and the crimes being committed marks a distinct difference between contemporary acts of anti-integrationist violence and those committed in the 1950s and earlier. As chapter 1 describes, in the earliest years of black integration of white neighborhoods, white residents of the neighborhood were primed for black families' arrival and violently erupted within days, if not hours, of the families' taking up residence in their new homes. Violence occurring so quickly was in part a symptom of the mob violence attendant to the earlier period. One significant characteristic of anti-integrationist violence in the 1990s is that incidents are almost always the result of individual action—one perpetrator—and rarely if ever involve large groups of perpetrators.

The Geography of Violence: North and South, Rural and Urban, Working-Class and Upscale

Figure 2.1 depicts 432 incidents of violence directed at racial and ethnic minorities moving to all-white or predominately white neighborhoods. The violence is not limited to one area of the country; rather, there is broad diffusion of incidents throughout the United States.[48] This does not mean that incidents in this catalog are not clustered in particular regions of the country. Over the twenty-year period between 1990 and 2010, in twenty-seven states fewer than ten incidents were identified. Instead, the vast majority of incidents seem to be concentrated in just eight states, with the largest number of incidents occurring in California (48), followed by Florida (40).[49] The region of the country with the greatest concentration of incidents is the southern United States, followed closely by the midwestern United States. Perpetrators in just four states—Ohio, Missouri, Illinois, and Pennsylvania—were responsible for 23 percent of the total number of incidents countrywide (see figure 2.2).

Incidents of anti-integrationist violence occurred not just in cities and suburbs, but also in rural areas during this period. These accounts also suggest that incidents occur in working-class white neighborhoods as well as affluent neighborhoods and upscale developments.[50] One example of such an incident occurring in an upscale area involved the targeting of George and Samirah Aziz-Hodge, the only African American family in their Fort Lauderdale neighborhood. The Hodges awakened the morning of July 14, 2004, to the image of a cross burned on the lawn of their Country Club Estates home.[51] Other incidents targeting individuals living in upscale neighborhoods are discussed in chapter 5.

Incidents reported run the gamut of criminal offenses, including arson and firebombing, cross burning, harassment and verbal threats, murder, racial epithets, racist graffiti, and vandalism. Some of these, like murder and arson, are serious crimes, while others, like "racial epithets," fall into the category of behavior that most likely can be criminalized only if it fits the legal definition of harassment. Figure 2.3 shows the number of different types of incidents.[52]

The perpetrators' intent in these crimes is often quite clearly expressed—they wish to drive the family from the neighborhood. In

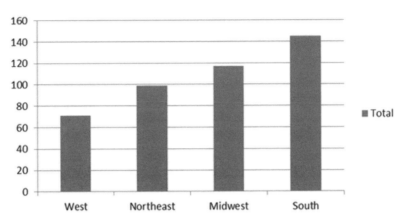

Figure 2.2. Incidents of Anti-Integrationist Violence, 1990-2010, by Region.

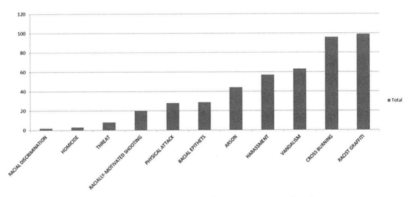

Figure 2.3. Incidents of Anti-Integrationist Violence, 1990-2010, by Type.

many cases, it is the language that is used that makes the perpetrators' views so crystal clear. "Go home" and "Get out" are common phrases scrawled on bricks that are thrown through windows or written next to racial epithets on the targets' garages, front doors, fences, and other pieces of property.[53] Scrawled on the sides of the targets' homes, the epithets are there not just for the targets to see, but for their neighbors as well. When someone writes, "Go back to Africa where you came from"[54] and other vulgarities on the side of the home of a black person or another racial or ethnic minority who has moved into a white neighborhood, it serves, at least in part, as a public shaming. Often (though not always) the incidents occur soon after the individual moves to the white neighborhood. Families may find it particularly difficult and sometimes mystifying when they suffer harassment as they are moving into the neighborhood. For instance, vandals spray-painted racial slurs on the exterior of Sang Huynh's new home in Happy Valley, Oregon, and left a book of matches next to a clear plastic bottle filled with what the police thought was gasoline. The note said, "Last warning. We will burn your house down if we have to." Phong Tran, Sang Huynh's wife, lamented, "It's just terrible because we just moved here, and it's my dream area. . . . How were we supposed to know this would happen?"[55] Perpetrators' vivid use of racist graffiti packs a double punch: it exposes both the newcomers' difference and their vulnerability. The use of slurs, painted on the newcomers' property, does this in the cruelest way, because it forces the target to first see it, and then clean it up.

In some cases, the perpetrators' intent is spoken directly to the targets. In another case, the day after a black woman in Orlando whose house had been repeatedly vandalized found a burning cross on her lawn, a teenager told her that those responsible for the cross burning did not want more black people in the neighborhood.[56] In a 1995 case from the Chicago metropolitan area, a nineteen-year-old white man approached a sixty-three-year-old black woman as she pulled weeds in her yard, yelled slurs at her, and "threatened to blow up her house" if the woman and her disabled husband did not move from the predominately white suburb.[57]

Those targeted by this type of violence are well aware that the perpetrator's intention is to force them out. Many end up leaving the neighborhood. To pack up and leave the neighborhood has important implications because, as indicated earlier, many minority families have chosen to move to white neighborhoods because the new house in which they were victimized was their dream home.[58] For others, the house in which they eventually find themselves harassed seemed simply like a safe place to raise their family.

Rather than leaving, some individuals targeted by anti-integrationist violence take the opposite approach—they dig in their heels and refuse to leave. The Bradshaws, a black family who had moved to the Southwest

Side of Chicago in 2007, found "Niggers Beware" scrawled on their garage door and were angry and surprised. The family described feeling violated but not intimidated: "It was a threatening message. 'Beware' means something. But it doesn't mean that we're going to leave. This is our home and we will leave on our own accord."[59]

Anti-Integrationist Violence and the Power of the Hate Crime Label

The most serious incidents in this catalog—murder, arson, firebombing, and cross burning—are similar in intensity to the incidents described in chapter 1, for example, the experience of the Clarks, a black family who moved to an apartment in Cicero, Illinois, an all-white suburb of Chicago, in 1951. The Clarks endured a number of acts of violence, and the apartment was eventually firebombed. Though some minority families moving to white neighborhoods were targeted with firebombing, the context of the violence and the reaction of their neighbors were different. In the case of the Clarks, their neighbors were united in their opposition to the family. In the 1950s and 1960s, resistance to minority newcomers was organized, even if loosely. In the Clarks' case, a mob of whites estimated at between two thousand and five thousand gathered to burn and loot the apartment building where the family lived.

Contemporary incidents of anti-integrationist violence tend not to involve mob violence or organized neighborhood opposition to the family's presence. Though there are exceptions to this, often when a minority neighbor is targeted by racial violence, neighbors express shock that such an incident could have occurred in their community. One of the important impacts of the label "hate crime" is that this identifier provides a context for acts of anti-integrationist violence. The hate crime label allows incidents to make it past the threshold of being considered "ordinary" run-of-the-mill vandalism. Many acts of anti-integrationist violence involve racial slurs in some way—slurs scrawled on houses or cars as an act of vandalism, slurs written on crosses before they are burned, harassment involving racial slurs—so the race-based nature of the crime is clear.

Race-based crimes are now labeled hate crimes by the authorities. Thus the perpetrator and everyone associated with the perpetrator are labeled "racist." Because of the taint in mainstream society associated with the label "racist," even in cases where the perpetrator's intention may seem unambiguous, perpetrators deny that their actions have such implications. In the wake of such incidents, neighbors of the individual targeted may reject any implication that the neighborhood is racist. For instance, when a house that was being sold to a black family was burned down in a predominately white neighborhood in West Roxbury, Massachusetts, neighbors were concerned that they were being portrayed as racists in news accounts. "We are not racists," Elaine Ziff, a resident of the community, said.[60]

In addition to rejecting the label of "racist" for the community in which an incident occurs, neighbors frequently offer support to the family targeted by racist violence, in sharp contrast to the 1950s and 1960s, when neighbors frequently supported those attacking the integrating family. Support may be expressed in a variety of tangible and also intangible ways. Tangible offers of support come from neighbors and businesses alike in the form of offers to repaint slurs scrawled on property.[61] A neighbor awakened Brenda Snow, a black woman living in St. Petersburg, Florida, at 6:30 a.m. in July 2004 to show her the Nazi and Ku Klux Klan symbols that had been painted on her house and car. The story of the arrest was broadcast on the local news, and neighbors, local businesses, and even strangers pitched in to help with the cleanup.[62] In some cases the family's home has been so damaged that they are in need of housing, and their city government or local hotels may provide temporary accommodations for the family while their home is being cleaned or repaired. Intangible expressions of support may come in the form of the verbal affirmation that the target is a part of the community. Related to this are unity marches showcasing the community's standing with the individual targeted by the violence.[63] One of the strongest expressions of support, however, is condemnation of the perpetrator and his actions.[64] One vivid example of this involved the response to a black woman's house being set on fire in the Tremont neighborhood in Cleveland, Ohio, in 2007. The crime was one of several aimed at blacks in the neighborhood over a two-month period. Speaking about the perpetrator, Ward 13 Councilman Joe Cimperman exclaimed bitterly, "This jackass, whoever did this, is not [part of] West 12th Street. . . . We're going to find the jerk that did this and run him out of town on a rail."[65]

The Effect of Anti-Integrationist Violence on Targets

Though the context of contemporary acts of anti-integrationist violence is very different from the past in that such crimes are frequently the acts of individuals, and neighbors often provide important assistance, such crimes can still cause terrible damage. The psychological research has demonstrated that targets of bias-motivated crimes suffer substantial harm.[66] In at least one case, the monetary damage from anti-integrationist violence was in the millions of dollars. On December 6, 2004, a fire estimated to be one of the costliest residential fires in the history of the state of Maryland caused up to $10 million in damage to the Hunters Brooke development in Indian Head, Maryland. The arson, which destroyed ten houses and damaged sixteen others, was later determined to have been set because a number of residents of the planned development were African American.[67] The residents of the Hunters Brooke development were comparatively lucky, because the houses were under construction and not occupied. Minorities who are targeted with fire-bombings of houses they are occupying do not just have their homes severely damaged but may also lose many, if not all, of their possessions.

Even if a house is not destroyed, property damage in these types of cases can be extensive because the perpetrator's intention is to drive the family out or prevent them from moving in. Such was the case for Ruby Fleeks, a black woman preparing to move her family into a house in Wichita Falls, Texas, a city 125 miles north of Dallas. The day before Fleeks moved in, two white men, one of whom lived across the street from the home that Fleeks was set to occupy, set fire to the house, causing $15,000 in damage. The fire prevented the family, who had already moved most of their belongings into the house, from occupying the dwelling.[68]

Even if a family decides initially to tough it out after damage, they may be eventually "crimed out" of the neighborhood. The Walkers, a black family living in Volusia, Florida, experienced $50,000 in property damage when vandals broke in to their home in August 2002, vandalizing and defacing the walls with racial slurs and swastikas. Two years before the break-in, the family had discovered in their yard a Barbie doll painted black hanging from a rope. Later, someone placed a coil of nails around their dog's neck. Nineteen months after the break-in, in 2004, vandals set fire to the Walkers' car, leaving the message "never forget" spray-painted on their driveway. After the car fire, as is so often the case with targeted families, the Walkers elected to move.[69]

Even more significant than the property damage that such attacks cause is the emotional scars that families incur in the wake of such violence. Perhaps because of the bitterness and cruelty of these attacks, families often sustain serious trauma as a result of acts of anti-integrationist violence. One study analyzed survey data obtained from bias and non-bias assault victims from the city of Boston. The authors' results revealed that those targeted by bias-motivated crime were more likely to feel the effects of victimization more intensely and for a longer period of time.[70] Bias crime victims experience nervousness, depression, and difficulty concentrating, and tend to focus on their attack at a higher rate than do non-bias victims.[71] The Boston study also found that bias crime victims may feel as if they don't want to live any longer, more than do non-bias victims.[72] Given all of these psychological effects, it is not surprising that the authors of the study found that, on the whole, victims of bias crime experience a greater degree of difficulty coping with victimization.[73]

Seemingly small incidents, from a property damage perspective, may have a significant emotional impact. For instance, *Johnson v. Smith* involved a civil rights action filed by the black plaintiffs against two whites who, on August 15, 1990, burned a cross in the Johnsons' yard and threw a brick through the window of their house, which had been occupied by white persons before the Johnsons moved in. As a result of the incident, two of the Johnsons, Steve and Tracy, moved out of the neighborhood. They indicated that their move was prompted by the fact that they were planning on starting a family and didn't want to raise their children in a racially hostile environment. In the wake of the cross burning, a third member of the family, Tina Johnson, became increasingly fearful and distressed, having to take medication to calm her nerves.[74]

In some cases the sheer cruelty of anti-integrationist violence is what destabilizes targets. Perhaps because in so many cases the attacks are designed to get the targets to leave their homes, perpetrators' behavior takes on special intensity. Take the case of the Williamses, an African American family who moved to Fox Lake, Illinois, in August 2001.

On the night of August 30, 2002, several former members of a white supremacist organization accosted Tywon Williams, Juwon Williams, Deona Williams, and a friend while they were walking home from a football game. The men fled in terror but the assailants, who had knives, caught the lone woman, Deona Williams, and trapped her against a parked car. After taking off his shirt to reveal a tattoo of a swastika, one of the assailants, Shaun Derifield, held a knife to Deona's throat. As Deona pleaded with Derifield not to kill her, Derifield threatened, "Remember our faces, nigger! This is our town and you better get out of it before we kill you! We're going to kill you and your whole f——ing family if you don't get out of town."[75] Derifield and the other assailants were identified and eventually named in a suit brought by the Williamses alleging, among other things, intentional infliction of extreme emotional distress. A federal court specifically ruled on the issue of whether the defendants had intentionally caused extreme emotional distress by trapping Deona Williams against a parked car with a knife held to her throat while they threatened her, behavior that the defendants admitted. In the opinion, ruling on the Williamses' motion for summary judgment, the court recognized the cruelty of the defendants' actions and their impact:

> Defendants admit that they approached plaintiffs while carrying knives, intentionally threatened plaintiffs with physical harm, and trapped Deona Williams against a car with a knife to her throat. *It is clear that defendant's conduct is beyond all possible bounds of decency.* In addition, no reasonable trier of fact could find other than that Defendants' conduct was intentional, and that Defendants knew that there was a high probability that their actions would cause severe emotional distress. . . . Thus, no reasonable trier of fact could find other than that Plaintiffs in fact suffered severe emotional distress.[76]

In addition to the cruelty that often characterizes the incidents of anti-integrationist violence, targets of anti-integrationist violence are often one of a small number of (if not the only) minorities living in a white neighborhood. Courts have recognized that this may isolate them, which can increase their feelings of vulnerability and consequently lead to more trauma in the wake of attacks. Such was the case for Linda and

Isaiah Ruffin, a black couple who moved with their family to the small, rural all-white community of Horton, Alabama, in 1991. The Ruffins were some of the first blacks to live in that area. In response to the Ruffins moving into the community, the Alabama Empire Knights of the Ku Klux Klan burned a cross in the Ruffins' yard fifteen feet from the family's front door. The cross burning tore this family apart. All members of the family had to undergo some sort of treatment for the mental anguish that the event caused. After a second cross burning a year later, Isaiah Ruffin remained, and Linda Ruffin took the couple's children and moved back to Ohio.[77]

Severe emotional trauma may also be caused by a family's vulnerability to further attack. After the first attack, the family may realize that there is nothing they can actually do to protect themselves or their children from the next attack. Parents report that children have trouble sleeping after the attack. On Long Island, New York, the house of a Mexican immigrant family, the Garcias, was firebombed over the Fourth of July weekend in 2004. The family lost everything in the fire, which gutted the home. The firebombing condemned the family, in the words of the mother, to "a life of emotional scars." The couple's six-year-old cried whenever the family drove by their gutted house. The mother told reporters that the family had become so despondent that they were considering returning to Mexico despite slim job opportunities there.[78]

The threatening nature of anti-integrationist violence often causes parents to worry about the physical and emotional dangers to which they are subjecting their children. In these cases children are often especially traumatized. For instance, in addition to their children being taunted with racial insults, one black family in a rural area of West Virginia discovered a black cross on their property, from which dangled two dead black ducks.[79] Children can be literally caught in the crossfire of violence, like the eight-year-old son of Mattie Harrell, who had moved her family to an all-white neighborhood in Vineland, New Jersey, in 1994.[80] Not long after the Harrells moved in, at 2:04 a.m. three days before Christmas, a white man, Charles Apprendi, fired several rounds from a .22-caliber shotgun at the Harrells' house.[81] The shotgun blast tore into the wall near where Harrell's eight-year-old son would have been sleeping.[82] The man later told police that he had fired at the house because he didn't want blacks living in the neighborhood.[83] The crime, Harrell later recounted, "tore the whole family up. We will never be the same."[84] Harrell said that she and her husband divorced, in part as a result of the stress the hate crime caused. Though her son escaped injury, for several years afterward he had trouble sleeping.[85] In the case of the Smalls, a black family living in an isolated all-white rural area in northwest Florida who had a cross burned on their lawn, their two teenage children decided to join the military several months after the cross burning, at least in part "to escape the racial bigotry that the cross burning represented."[86]

The Loss of Money, Property, and Opportunity

If the family's home is destroyed or badly damaged, they may not have a place to live. Even if the home is not wholly destroyed, minorities might choose not to stay. In the wake of acts of anti-integrationist violence, minorities may, as one court said, "get the hint" and leave the neighborhood.[87] If the incidents have occurred pre-purchase, minorities may decide not to finalize the purchase of a piece of property.[88] The consequences of not completing a purchase in a white neighborhood may extend beyond the mere loss of money to the individual family. In many cases the move to a white neighborhood by a minority family is an attempt to escape crime and pursue greater opportunity. If the act of anti-integrationist violence creates a disincentive to live in white neighborhoods, then the family has lost out on a host of potentially wealth-maximizing advantages.

Families may want to leave, but it may be harder for some to go than others, especially if the crimes against them are well publicized. As a result of well-meaning television coverage designed to help the Garcias, landlords recognized the family and, as a result, were afraid to rent to them for fear their property might be damaged or destroyed in subsequent attacks. In a similar case, also on Long Island in 1992, the Macks, a black couple, and their two children faced similar difficulty finding housing after the home that Mr. Mack had rented for his wife and children was vandalized and set on fire. After the incident, the landlord tried to break the lease, and Mr. Mack indicated that publicity about the incident would make it difficult to find another house in Suffolk County.[89]

In the vast majority of cases, anti-integrationist violence comes to the target, as perpetrators deface the homes and property on which the targets live. Violence then is directed at the target at home, a location that is in many ways inescapable, and also emotionally laden. Perpetrators are not only attacking targets where they are most vulnerable, but also where many who have been threatened go for sanctuary. Thus, the violence is largely inescapable. The shock of the incident is compounded by the difficulty that parents have explaining the violence to their children. Dave Turner, an African American living in Glendale, California, discovered racial slurs painted on walls throughout his house, which was under construction. Vandals also took a hatchet to the bathroom walls, bursting pipes and flooding the house. When Turner discovered the violence he said, "I never experienced anything like this, and now I have to convey this to my children."[90] Another father, a thirty-five-year-old African American chef who found the letters "KKK" and the shapes of three crosses burned into the lawn of his Metairie, Louisiana, home in 2008, commented that the hardest part was explaining the meaning of crosses and the Ku Klux Klan to his nine-year-old son. The father had to explain to the child why someone might not like the boy because of his skin color—a painful conversation that he'd never imagined having to have.[91]

The Meaning of Symbols of Racialized Violence: The Burning Cross and Other Signs

Perpetrators of anti-integrationist violence use a variety of signs— burning crosses, spoken slurs and epithets, and race-based vandalism—to convey that African Americans are not wanted in a particular neighborhood. These signs are threatening because their meaning often invokes a legacy of violence.

The burning cross, one of the most vivid symbols used by contemporary perpetrators of anti-integrationist violence, harkens back to the burning crosses that were part of many outdoor Klan rallies during the KKK's heyday. The rallies were often held on high places where the enormous "burlap-wrapped and kerosene-soaked wooden cross" could be seen from a distance.[92] The Klan used burning crosses to terrorize blacks, labor organizers, and anyone who transgressed social boundaries.[93] In the 1940s, the burning cross was used solely for intimidation; crosses were burned in the early 1960s to terrorize blacks involved in civil rights activism. In January 1964, for example, more than 150 crosses were burned near black homes and churches in Louisiana.[94]

Today when African Americans are targeted by anti-integrationist violence, they feel the legacy of the burning cross as an instrument of racialized violence. As the black woman mentioned earlier in this chapter who had a cross burned on her lawn in Portland in 1992 said of cross burning, "[I]t means the same to me as it did to my parents and grandparents and great grandparents. It means you're not wanted, that your life is in danger."[95] Seeing a charred cross that had been burnt on her lawn in 2000 had a similar effect on LaWanda Holmes, a twenty-year-old black woman in Atlanta. Holmes burst into tears when she saw the burnt remains of the wooden cross. "I was thinking it was the KKK. I was terrified. I thought of all kinds of stuff: churches being burned, bottles being thrown through windows, houses being set on fire." After the cross was burned, Holmes stayed with her mother, afraid to return to the mostly white neighborhood where she lived.[96] One member of a black family who had a cross burned in their yard remarked eloquently,

> From our point of view this is not only a hate crime but an act of domestic terrorism. The image of a burnt cross in front of our home conjures feelings of distrust, confusion, and quite honestly fear. Fear for our young children and concern about our safety. We are law abiding, productive members of this community and cannot imagine what reason anyone would have for doing such a horrible thing.[97]

Even when the burning cross is not itself used, its violent legacy may be invoked by the use of markers that will trigger fears of the Ku Klux Klan. Perpetrators who have no affiliation with the Ku Klux Klan frequently scrawl the letters "KKK" on African Americans' garage doors, walls, and fences.[98] Many of the perpetrators in vandalism cases are juveniles, and it seems that even young people know that "KKK" can cause terror. One black family, the Overstreets, began to be harassed soon after they moved into their Riverside, California, home in the mid-1990s. Their home and cars were defaced with "KKK" and the phrase "will [*sic*] hang you if we see you." The family also had their windows smeared with feces. Mr. Overstreet said that the incidents were so frightening that he would not let his children outside alone. Police attributed some of the incidents to "youngsters" because the vandals used crayons and the writing was small.[99]

Racialized violence may lead its targets to recall the violence of Ku Klux Klan even if "KKK" is not written and a cross is not burned. A black man, Gregg Macintosh, moved to a majority-white neighborhood in southwest St. Louis in 1986. Eggs were frequently thrown at his house, slurs were yelled at him, and, in 1993, his house was painted with racial epithets and then set on fire. He described his reaction to seeing the charred, smoldering ruins: "The first thing that came to my mind when I saw the house was the movie *Mississippi Burning*, and it kind of reminded me how vulnerable I am."[100]

Though targets of anti-integrationist violence may be frightened, some bravely resist, and refuse to leave. Such was the case for Irene Bailey, who is African American. Bailey discovered one morning in 2008 that overnight vandals had scratched racist graffiti into the paint of the family's two cars and slashed the tires on one of the cars, causing $4,000 in damage to the vehicles. Bailey told her three youngest children, "We are not going to let anybody chase us out of our house, and we are not moving, so don't be afraid."[101]

Does a City's History of Violence Increase the Likelihood of Resistance?

In some locations, violence associated with housing integration in the 1990s could be somewhat expected, given the location's past history of housing-related violence. Such was the case with the struggle surrounding the integration of public housing in Vidor, Texas. Located in East Texas, Vidor had a strong history of housing segregation. In the 1920s, the Ku Klux Klan forced blacks out of town. Vidor then became a "sundown" town. In the early 1990s, Joyce Dennis, a Vidor native, recalled a hand-printed sign next to the exit off the highway into town that warned, "Nigger, don't let the sun set on you in Vidor."[102]

Vidor's legacy of racial violence may have affected some blacks' desire to live in Vidor, but government policies also deliberately excluded African Americans. In 1980 the civil rights lawyers Mike Daniel and Betsy Julian brought a class action suit on behalf of hundreds of black applicants for and residents of public housing. In their suit they alleged that the US Department of Housing and Urban Development (HUD) had discriminated against them in the allocation of public housing, not just in Orange County, the county where Vidor is located, but also in thirty-five other Texas counties. The court ruled in the plaintiffs' favor in 1985, with Judge William Wayne Justice ruling that HUD had intentionally created, promoted, and funded racially segregated housing in East Texas in violation of the United States Constitution and federal civil rights laws.[103] In 1992, US District Court Judge Justice ordered the thirty-six East Texas counties to integrate seventy all-white housing complexes or face stiff penalties and fines.[104]

In response to housing officials' announcement of plans to integrate Vidor, Ku Klux Klan members began a "Keep Vidor White" campaign, holding rallies, passing out literature, and parading through the public housing complex dressed in Klan regalia to dissuade blacks from moving in.[105] Grand Dragon Mike Lowe, head of one of the two Klan organizations opposed to the integration of Vidor public housing, insisted that his organization was not composed of violent white supremacists but rather "separatists" who were opposed to integration because blacks caused crime. "Anywhere we have had integration, we have crime," said the Vidor KKK leader.[106] Lowe suggested that after blacks moved to the development, residents should not harass them, but rather "isolate them and maybe they'll get the hint."[107]

In early 1993, two black men were the first to move into the seventy-four-unit public housing complex in Vidor.[108] Two women and their families followed, but after being harassed by strangers and threatened by neighbors and the Klan, both families moved out within two weeks of their arrival. One of the women reported that a neighbor who was a self-described Klan supporter passed a message to her through the apartment manager indicating that if the newcomers' children ventured into the neighbor's yard, they'd be beaten with a baseball bat.[109] The end of this particular integration story and the cautionary tale stemming from HUD's attempt to integrate public housing in Vidor in the early 1990s is set forth in the conclusion of this book.

Resistance to Integration in Places without a History of Racial Violence

Given the ugly history of race relations in Vidor, Texas, one might have expected resistance to housing integration in the 1990s. Dubuque, Iowa, a city of fifty-seven thousand with few minorities, had a very different history, but a surprisingly similar experience once plans were made to integrate the town. The city's plan stemmed from a desire to increase the area's ethnic diversity, in the wake of arson at the home of a black official of the local NAACP chapter in October 1989. The official's garage had been set on fire and police found in the remains a small wooden cross with a racial slur and the words "KKK lives."[110]

After the cross burning, the mayor and other leaders closely examined the city's demographics and saw that of Dubuque's 57,546 residents, just 331, roughly 1.5 percent of Dubuque's population, were black. This was the smallest percentage of any Iowa city.[111] As the mayor said, "This town was just too white, and we felt we should do something about it."[112] City officials established a Constructive Integration Task Force, which created a nine-page plan, "We Want to Change," that established a goal of bringing a hundred minority families to the city over a five-year period. It also provided financial incentives to encourage local businesses to reach out to minority job applicants and offer them jobs in Dubuque. The plan also suggested ways to protect new hires who were minorities.[113]

Soon after city officials began to publicize the integration plan, a number of crosses were burned in residential areas outside apartment buildings. There were also a series of racially motivated incidents of vandalism over a period of five months in 1991. Two individuals accused of the cross burnings admitted to an affiliation with the white supremacist organization National Association for the Advancement of White People, an extremist organization started by the failed Louisiana gubernatorial candidate David Duke.[114] Most of the cross burnings were not aimed specifically at individuals who were in the process of integrating, but at least one was. Early one morning, a cross was burned and a brick was thrown through the apartment window of Alice Scott, a black woman who had recently moved her three children to Dubuque to escape escalating violence in Milwaukee.[115]

Racial violence around housing integration occurring in Boston, Massachusetts, was not quite as much of a surprise as it was in Dubuque, given the racialized battles over school busing in the 1970s. As in Vidor, in Boston the racial integration of public housing in the 1990s, which had been intentionally segregated until a lawsuit forced its integration, was controversial. An official in the Boston Housing Authority had kept public housing in the traditionally Irish neighborhoods of South Boston and Charlestown white, and housed blacks in developments located in predominantly black neighborhoods. South Boston and Charlestown's opposition to the integration of the housing developments is discussed in more detail in chapter 5. The violence associated with housing integration was not, however, limited to South Boston and Charlestown. In other areas of the city, minority integration of predominantly white neighborhoods did not always proceed smoothly. For instance, in September 1996, a black family who had intended to purchase a house in a white neighborhood in West Roxbury was firebombed, which caused $100,000 in damage to the home. Like a number of other black families that face such violence prepurchase, the family backed out of the purchase.[116] In another area of the city, the North End, a black family who moved into an apartment in Boston in 1992 found the words "No Niggers" spray-painted on the front of the brownstone they moved into that week.[117] Six months earlier, according to a neighbor, within a week of another black family's arrival, "No niggers" was painted on their building.[118] Other neighbors may have shared the views of the perpetrator, as several neighbors who were interviewed by the *Boston Globe* indicated that they did not want blacks living in the neighborhood. As one resident told the *Globe* reporter, "We don't want any blacks here because we are afraid. We don't want them in our neighborhood. In Roxbury, in Dorchester they're isolated. Away from us. But not here."[119]

Conclusion

Forty years after the passage of the Fair Housing Act and twenty years after the passage of the Hate Crime Statistics Act, acts of anti-integrationist violence are still part of the national landscape. In many areas of the country, violence has been targeted at racial and ethnic minorities who plan to move to, or are living in, white neighborhoods. There are significant changes in the form this violence takes in the contemporary period, with few incidents occurring as the result of organized collective action. Instead of organized groups of neighbors opposed to minorities taking up residence in "their" neighborhoods, minorities who cross the color line more often face a series of incidents often committed by a single perpetrator or a small group of perpetrators aimed at forcing them to leave the neighborhood. Such incidents—ranging from cross burning and firebombing to graffiti on cars and homes—may occur over a period of time. They may cause severe damage to property. Often, irrespective of the monetary damage the family suffers, these attacks also cause significant emotional damage. Frequently, families targeted by racial harassment in white neighborhoods move out, unwilling to subject themselves to the possibility that they may be attacked in the future. If the families remain, they may be fearful that the attacks will escalate.

The experiences of the racial and ethnic minorities described in this chapter are, of course, not descriptive of all of the experiences of minorities integrating white neighborhood between 1970 and 2010. In some communities in the United States, whites and racial and ethnic minorities live together peacefully, with minority newcomers welcomed. What makes some instances of housing integration acceptable and others not? This is explored in the next chapter.

3

Anti-Integrationist Violence and the Tolerance-Violence Paradox

The popular stereotype of American racial violence is captured by the movie *Mississippi Burning*. This 1988 Oscar-winning movie starred Willem Dafoe and Gene Hackman in a fictionalized account of the FBI investigation into the real-life murders of three civil rights workers killed in Mississippi in 1964. The picture that *Mississippi Burning* presents of racial violence is fairly distinct. If the movie can be said to create an archetype, racial incidents (1) are serious, violent crimes—murders; (2) occur in the Deep South; and (3) involve the Klan or some other extremist group. Highly publicized dramatic incidents of racial violence, like the dragging death of James Byrd, a violent crime perpetrated by the white supremacists Bill King and Russell Brewer in Jasper, Texas, in 1998, seem to underscore the idea that contemporary racial violence also fits this picture.

Unfortunately, if we are only looking for incidents of racial violence that fit the *Mississippi Burning* archetype, we will miss contemporary acts of hate crime, and the subset of hate crime on which I focus, anti-integrationist violence. This chapter's goal is to move beyond the myth of the extremist perpetrator that is so central to the *Mississippi Burning* archetype. I do this by explicitly analyzing the roots of the majority of contemporary acts of racial violence (including anti-integrationist violence). In divining the roots of acts of anti-integrationist violence, I will carefully examine perpetrators' justifications for their behavior, as laid out in court testimony and news reports.

Who Commits Racialized Violence?

It is not surprising that Americans believe that most hate crimes are committed by members of organized hate groups. The imagery of the burning cross used by the Ku Klux Klan remains a vivid symbol of an organized hate group responsible for countless acts of racist violence committed all over the country for more than 150 years. Ku Klux Klan marches and ritual cross burnings also are well publicized, fueling the assumption that racial violence is committed primarily by members of extremist groups. Hate groups—white supremacist organizations like the White Aryan Resistance, the National Alliance, and the World Church of the Creator, to name a few—are also alive and well, and the activities in which their members engage are often publicized.

While it may have at one time been true that hate groups were responsible for most of the hate crimes committed in this country, in the last two decades that attribution is inaccurate. Statistics gathered by the Center for Democratic Renewal and the Southern Poverty Law Center show that the militant white racist movements have only about 25,000 "hard-core" members, roughly another 150,000 "sympathizers" who purchase literature or attend rallies, and possibly another 450,000 supporters who read their literature.[1] Analyses of hate crimes reveal that the majority are not committed by members of organized hate groups.[2] For instance, the map of acts of anti-integrationist violence since 1990 presented in chapter 2 depicts 432 incidents directed at minorities who have moved to white neighborhoods. Only four cases with identified perpetrators involved individuals affiliated with extremist groups. These findings are consistent with other research on hate crimes, which suggests that most perpetrators are "regular" people who do not have any contact with organized hate groups. As Jack Levin and Jack McDevitt write, "hate crimes are more often committed under ordinary circumstances by otherwise unremarkable types—neighbors, a coworker at the next desk, or groups of youngsters looking for 'bragging rights' with their friends."[3]

To begin to understand why perpetrators commit acts of anti-integrationist violence, we must place such incidents in proper perspective along with other hate crimes. Levin and McDevitt created a typology of hate crimes, a classification system for identifying particular types of hate crimes based on the offender's motivation. Ku Klux Klan members and individuals involved in other hate groups commit the rarest kind of hate crimes, "mission" hate crimes prompted by the desire to "rid the world of evil by disposing of members of a despised group."[4] Acts of anti-integrationist violence directed at minorities who have moved to white neighborhoods are not mission crimes but rather are considered defensive hate crimes. In defensive hate crimes, offenders are motivated by the desire to protect their neighborhood by those they consider intruders. As the perpetrators of defensive hate crimes see it, "their community, means of livelihood, or way of life has been threatened by the mere presence of members of some other group. Hatemongers therefore feel justified, even obligated, to go on the 'defensive.' Characteristically, they feel few, if any, pangs of guilt in savagely attacking an outsider."[5]

Perpetrators of defensive hate crimes are reacting to threats and thereby target particular individuals or groups whom they consider to be a threat. Those targeted for harassment or violence may represent an economic threat—when the perpetrators fear that their homes are declining in value—or the perpetrators may just be reacting to a symbolic loss of "turf" or "privilege" when, to quote Levin and McDevitt, "they come into our neighborhood, and begin to 'take over.'"[6] There is not a sense of individuality in such crimes—any member of the target's background will be viewed as posing a threat and therefore is vulnerable to attack. Perpetrators intend for their attacks to send a message, for instance, the message that blacks are not welcome on the perpetrator's block.[7] If the message is not understood by the target, then there is escalation. "A black family moving into an all-white neighborhood is first warned; if they don't heed the warning, then their windows are broken; and if they still refuse to move out, their house may be firebombed or worse."[8]

The Tolerance-Violence Paradox: The Surprise of Racial Violence in the Era of Obama

Many contemporary targets of racial violence in the post–civil rights era are caught off-guard by the incidents. Frequently, multiple incidents may have to occur before the family even realizes that someone has a problem with their presence. Vanessa Glover, a black woman who lived in a home in an ethnically diverse neighborhood in Cleveland, Ohio, found "KKK" and "No Niggers—Move Out" scrawled in the alley next to her home. Though she was aware of the graffiti, she didn't think much of it at the time. Two days after she noticed the graffiti, an arsonist set fire to her garage. Her house, a few feet from the garage, escaped damage only because a newspaper delivery man alerted Glover to the early-morning fire. The next victim was not so lucky. Early the next morning, July 31, 2007, another black woman in Glover's neighborhood, Rogina Weakley, was awakened by a crackling sound emanating from her front porch. Weakley investigated and found a gasoline-soaked T-shirt on fire, which quickly ignited the entire home. Weakley and her family survived, but the house was destroyed. Glover found the events emotionally taxing: "Because I had to stop working to be here for my children, because I'm not going to let my children just be out here and there's someone like that out there," said Glover. "There's no telling what they could do. . . . I really want to stay in this neighborhood, but I'm frightened."[9]

Once the targets and neighbors realize what has happened, they are often stunned and shocked. When asked to comment on a cross burning, racist graffiti, or other incidents, more often than not they respond by saying that in this day and age they cannot believe that someone would commit such an act. For instance, in reacting to the crimes directed at Weakley and Glover, the executive director of Cleveland's NAACP, Stanley Miller, commented, "Something like this is not supposed to happen in 2007. . . . Those are things that we had to deal with back in the '50s and '60s and we should not have to deal with it today and the NAACP refuses to let that happen on our watch."[10] The surprise publicly expressed by those interviewed in the wake of acts of anti-integrationist violence is in clear contrast with attitudes expressed in the 1950s and earlier, when angry, often stone-throwing, mobs gathered in front of homes of blacks who had moved to white neighborhoods.

The shock at such a violent hatred may stem in part from popular assumptions about who we, as Americans, are. America is increasingly racially and ethnically diverse, and the last fifty years have seen steady changes in racial attitudes that demonstrate increasing tolerance. This changing picture of who Americans are is discussed below.

Increasing American Diversity

With each US census there is evidence of increasing American diversity. Though the non-Hispanic white population is still both numerically and proportionally the largest major race and ethnic group in the United States, other groups are growing far more quickly. Between 2000 and 2010, Hispanic immigration led to a 43 percent increase in the Hispanic population. This increase of roughly fifteen million Hispanics accounted for nearly half of the increase in the total US population since 2000. As table 3.1 shows, just over 72 percent of the people listed their race as white alone. Contrast this with figures from 1980, just thirty years earlier, when 80 percent of individuals indicated that they were white.

Though the country is more racially diverse than it has ever been, the census reveals that we still live in very separate spaces, as segregation, particularly black-white segregation, has changed very little over the last twenty years. Though analysis of census data after 1980 initially showed the nation to be making moderate progress in integrating, the pace of change has slowed over the last twenty years. Between 1980 and 1990 there was a five-point drop in the country's average level of black-white segregation, as measured by the dissimilarity index.[11] There was a slower rate of change in the 1990s (only a four-point drop) and in the first decade of the twenty-first century (just a 5.2-point drop) in the average black-white dissimilarity index.[12] Traditionally, black-white segregation tends to be lowest in areas where the black community is smaller (less than 5 percent of the total population), but since 2000 black-white segregation has increased in these areas. In metropolitan areas with 20 percent or more blacks, black-white segregation is high; on average the dissimilarity index declined just 3.4 points since 2000.[13]

Based on national averages, the experience of African Americans with respect to the type of neighborhood in which they live is dramatically different from the experience of whites. Analyzing the experiences of whites, Hispanics, Asian Americans and blacks, sociologists have identified an "average" or "typical" neighborhood based on the average of experiences for all the members of each group.[14] Using data collected from 331 metropolitan areas across the United States between 2005 and 2009, they concluded that the average white person lives in

Table 3.1
Racial Identification, US Census, 1990–2010

| | 1990 | | 2000 | | 2010 | |
Race	Number	% of Total Population	Number	% of Total Population	Number	% of Total Population
Asian	7,273,662	2.9	10,242,998	3.6	14,674,252	4.8
Black	29,986,060	12.1	34,658,190	12.3	38,929,319	12.6
Hispanic	22,354,059	9.0	35,305,818	12.5	50,477,594	16.3
White	199,686,070	80.3	211,460,626	75.1	223,553,265	72.4

Sources: Data for 1990 taken from "Historical Census Statistics on Population, Totals by Race 1790 to 1990, and by Hispanic Origin, 1970 to 1990, for the United States, Regions, Divisions and States," http://www.census.gov/population/www/documentation/twps0056/twps0056.pdf. Data for 2000–2010 taken from "Overview of Race and Hispanic Origin: 2010," 2010 Census Briefs, http://www.census.gov/prod/cen2010/briefs/c2010br-02.pdf.

Note: Percentage totals may exceed 100 because the census counts "Hispanic" as an ethnicity, and "black," "white," and "Asian" as "race" categories. This means that some Asians, whites, and blacks may also be listed in the "Hispanic" category.

a neighborhood that is more than 77 percent white, 7 percent black, 10 percent Hispanic, and 4 percent Asian American.[15] By contrast, the average black person lives in a neighborhood that is 48 percent black, 34 percent white, 14 percent Hispanic, and 3 percent Asian American. On average, both Asian Americans and Hispanics live in the most diverse neighborhoods. The "typical" Asian American lives in a neighborhood that is 21 percent Asian American, 49 percent white, 8 percent black, and 18 percent Hispanic, while the typical Hispanic lives in a neighborhood that is 46 percent Hispanic, 36 percent white, 10 percent black, and 6 percent Asian American.[16]

[handwritten margin note: Must vary by state!]

Increasing Tolerance

In 2011 there is widespread belief that in the post–civil rights era, blacks and whites actually do "get along." The popular assumption concerning positive race relations is borne out by survey research. For instance,

Gallup surveys administered between 2002 and 2008 reveal that blacks and non-Hispanic whites feel a sense of optimism regarding race relations between the two groups (see figure 3.1). When asked to rate relations between the various racial and ethnic groups, approximately 70 percent of whites agreed that relations between the two groups were either "very good" or "somewhat good." There is a racial divide on this, with blacks being somewhat more pessimistic in their views of race relations, but the majority, some 61 percent of all blacks surveyed, see relations between the two groups as either very good or somewhat good.

In some ways, violence directed at minorities who move to white neighborhoods is an anachronism that recalls a bygone and far less tolerant era. Violent and unambiguous expressions of racism seem to reflect the long-dead past not just because of many Americans' perceptions that relations between blacks and whites are good, but also because of national conversations—prompted by the election of Barack Obama—regarding Americans' increasing racial tolerance. In the immediate post-election period, news articles about Barack Obama's presidency frequently assumed that the fact that a black candidate had been elected president of the United States for the first time was a definitive sign of racial progress.[17] Surveys administered by Gallup just after the election in 2008 suggest that the vast majority of Americans, some 70 percent, perceived Obama's election as having the ability to improve race relations.[18] Three years later, in 2011, respondents expressed a bit more skepticism regarding the progress Americans had actually made, with 48 percent of blacks and 31 percent of whites surveyed indicating that race relations had improved during Obama's tenure.[19]

The assessment that America has transcended race may be premature. In fact, there is a range of opinion among pundits and scholars regarding the depth of the racial change that President Obama's election represented. While some scholars and commentators heralded the election as evidence of a "post-racial" society, others thought it represented not quite as fundamental a break with the past.[20] Some scholars are concerned about the impact that normative pressure to appear nonracist may have on individuals' self-reports of their racial attitudes.[21] These scholars used the Implicit Association Test (IAT), a computer-based test that attempts to measure implicit or nonconscious racial attitudes. The IAT does this by calculating respondents' associations between negative or positive values and individuals of different races.[22] Comparing measures of racial bias

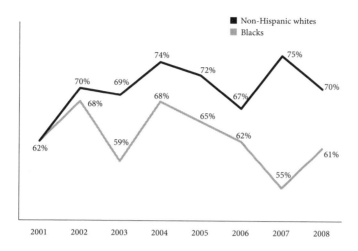

Figure 3.1. Race Relations between Blacks and Whites

Source: Gallup, "Race Relations," accessed August 1, 2012, http://www.gallup.com/poll/1687/race-relations.aspx#2.

Note: The survey question was "Would you say relations between (whites and blacks) are very good, somewhat good, somewhat bad, or very bad?" Percentages here combine responses of "very good" and "somewhat good" by blacks and non-Hispanic whites, respectively.

using the IAT taken before Obama's announcement of his candidacy for presidency and four months after Obama's inauguration, scholars found that implicit and explicit racial attitudes showed little evidence of change during his candidacy and early presidency.[23] Others thought that while the Obama victory was significant, it did not have the far-reaching potential to transform American racial and ethnic prejudice.[24] Some scholars even questioned the breadth of change that the election itself represented, noting, for example, backlash against the Obama presidency and the potential resurgence of racism that the Obama presidency could cause.[25]

The political scientist Vincent Hutchings examined the black-white divide during Obama's candidacy and then after his election and found significant divisions by race. National exit polls revealed significant correlation between Americans' (or voters') race and the candidate they supported in the presidential election. Exit polls showed that 95 percent of blacks and approximately two-thirds of Latinos and Asian Americans voted for Barack Obama. Whites, however, are a very different story: the majority, some 55 percent, voted for Senator John McCain, with only 43 percent supporting Obama.[26] While 43 percent of the white vote exceeds the percentage gained by Jesse Jackson in his 1998 presidential primary (11 percent), it nevertheless still represents a black-white racial divide that exceeds fifty percentage points. With respect to the nation as a whole, Hutchings examined survey results detailing racial policy preferences in questionnaires administered in 1988 and 2008 and found little change in the significant racial divides on blacks' and whites' views of fair job treatment, aid to blacks, and racial preferences.[27] Hutchings does not find much of an "Obama Effect": "There is little evidence to conclude that white liberals, defined as respondents identifying as either extremely liberal, liberal or slightly liberal, are more likely to support racially egalitarian policies in 2008 compared to 1998."[28]

What's Our Racial Temperature?

Even if twenty-first-century America is not yet "post-racial," the racial temperature—American attitudes on issues of race as measured by survey research—may suggest that acts of racial violence like cross burnings are inconsistent with the current state of race relations. To evaluate whether racial violence is unexpected given the current state of American race relations involves examining American racial attitudes over time. Contemporary racial attitudes in the United States are often evaluated through surveys administered to whites and blacks beginning in the 1940s. Taking the racial temperature, as it were, social scientists evaluate respondents' answers to questions addressing principles of equal treatment, social distance, beliefs about inequality, and affirmative action, which provide some context for Americans' current perspective on race relations.

Racial attitudes were analyzed for the first time in 1942, when pollsters began to ask regular questions about racial issues.[29] Looking at various issues over time with respect to race, social scientists have identified significant changes in the normative definition of appropriate relations between blacks and whites.[30] Discrimination against and segregation of African Americans were accepted by the majority of whites as recently as World War II.[31] By the mid-1990s the norm with respect to white racial attitudes was that African Americans deserve the same treatment and respect accorded to whites and that racial integration in public spaces of life was a desired goal.[32]

Table 3.2

White Respondents' Opinions on Black-White Intermarriage

Year	Approve (%)	Disapprove (%)	No Opinion (%)
1958	4	94	3
1968	17	75	7
1978	33	58	9
1997	61	30	9
2007	75	19	5

Source: Gallup, "Race Relations," accessed October 22, 2010,
http://www.gallup.com/poll/1687/Race-Relations.aspx#3.

Note: Hispanics were included in the category of whites. The survey question was "Do you approve or disapprove of marriage between blacks and whites?"

In addition to attitudes on equal treatment and the regulation of public space, one frequently discussed bellwether of change in tolerance is Americans' views on interracial marriage. Though there is still a significant racial divide in opinion in this area, there have been substantial changes over the last fifty years in the rate of white approval for interracial marriage. In 1958, just 4 percent of whites polled by the Gallup organization approved of black-white intermarriage. By 2007, nearly 75 percent of whites indicated they approved (see table 3.2).

Though equal treatment and interracial marriage are largely accepted, a substantial number of blacks, whites, and Hispanics surveyed seem to accept that race relations between blacks and whites and the continuing level of discrimination against blacks are difficult and perhaps intractable problems. In 2009, 40 percent of all Americans surveyed indicated that relations between blacks and whites will always be a problem. There was significant division in this assessment along racial lines: 38 percent of whites and Hispanics but 55 percent of blacks believed that relations between blacks and whites would always be a problem (see table 3.3). With respect to the issue of the level of discrimination against African Americans, surveys in 2008 and 2009 revealed that 51 percent of those surveyed, and 49 percent of whites, viewed race discrimination against African Americans as widespread (see table 3.4).

Table 3.3
Opinions on the Future of Black-White Relations

Year	Always a Problem (%)	Eventually Worked Out (%)	No Opinion (%)
	All Respondents		
1963	42	55	3
1999	52	44	4
2009	40	56	4
	White (Including Hispanic) Respondents		
1963	44	53	3
1999	51	45	4
2009	38	59	4
	Black Respondents		
1963	26	70	4
1999	59	36	5
2009	55	42	3

Source: Gallup, "Race Relations," accessed November 5, 2012,
http://www.gallup.com/poll/1687/Race-Relations.aspx#1.

Note: The survey question was "Do you think that relations between blacks and whites will always be a problem for the United States, or that a solution will eventually be worked out?"

Table 3.4
Opinions on Prevalence of Antiblack Racism

Year	Racism Is Widespread (%)	Racism Is Not Widespread (%)	No Opinion (%)
	Total Respondents		
2008	56	42	3
2009	51	46	3
	Non-Hispanic White Respondents		
2008	51	46	3
2009	49	48	3
	Black Respondents		
2008	78	20	2
2009	72	26	2

Source: Gallup, "Race Relations," accessed November 5, 2012,
http://www.gallup.com/poll/1687/Race-Relations.aspx#1.

Racial Tolerance and Housing

When one looks at the increase in racial tolerance over time in the public opinion data cited above, violent expressions of hatred toward racial and ethnic minorities who have moved to white neighborhoods seem inexplicable. After all, one might say that polling data show two clear markers that contemporary American society has moved beyond issues of race: significant increases in tolerance over time coupled with an awareness of any vestiges of racism by a substantial number of white Americans. Nevertheless, as chapter 2 details, there is significant evidence throughout the 1990s and continuing until the present day that minorities who move to white neighborhoods experience violence on a nearly daily basis. One might attempt to explain this violence as an indication of Americans' negative views on neighborhood racial integration and open housing. Nevertheless, as is detailed below, public opinion polls probing Americans' attitudes toward open housing administered between the 1970s and the 1990s reflect broad support for housing integration.

In fact, questions on housing cohere with the general trend of increasing racial tolerance. Since the early 1970s, Americans have shown increasing support for the concept of open or nondiscriminatory housing. For instance, one survey question on housing asked respondents whether they would support a law that allowed the owner of a property to decide whether there would be open access, or whether the law should prohibit owners from discriminating on the basis of race. This question was first asked as part of the General Social Survey (GSS) in 1973. In 1973, 63.8 percent of respondents felt that the owner should have the discretion to decide whether or not to discriminate. Only 34.7 percent of respondents felt that nondiscrimination should be the policy. By 2006, the majority's inclination toward discrimination had reversed, with more than two-thirds (some 69 percent) of respondents answering that discrimination should not be allowed and just under one-third (27 percent) answering that discrimination was acceptable (see table 3.5).

Similar results occurred when Americans were asked whether whites had a right, which African Americans should respect, to keep their neighborhoods entirely white. As shown in table 3.6, in 1972 roughly 39 percent of Americans agreed with the statement "White people have a right to keep (Negroes/Blacks/African-Americans) out of their neigh-borhoods if they want to, and (Negroes/Blacks/African-Americans) should respect that right." The number of individuals who agreed that whites had a right to prevent blacks from moving in had fallen signifi-cantly by 1996, when just over 11 percent of respondents agreed with the statement that whites have a right to keep blacks out of their neighbor-hoods. By 1996 more than 70 percent of those polled strongly disagreed with the statement.

In addition to survey research showing that many Americans have positive attitudes regarding housing, since the passage of the Fair Housing Act in 1968 a number of neighborhoods have developed that have integration as an important objective. In her book *The Failures of Integration,* Sheryll Cashin profiles people who live in stable, racially integrated communities in several areas of the country. She profiles neighbors and communities in places as diverse as Portland, Oregon; Washington, DC; Shaker Heights, Cleveland Heights, and Cleveland, Ohio; Rogers Park, Edgewater, Uptown, and Chicago Lawn in Chicago, Illinois; San Antonio, Texas; Fruitvale, in Oakland, California; Houston Heights in Houston, Texas; Southfield, Michigan; Oak Park, Illinois; South Orange, New Jersey; and West Mt. Airy in Philadelphia, Penn-sylvania.[33] These communities do not reflect the national trend of fairly stark racial neighborhood segregation. They are distinctive in two ways: first, their racial and ethnic distribution mirrors the racial and ethnic average of the city overall. Second, these communities are recognized as diverse by the individuals who live and work there.[34]

Personalizing Housing Choices: Where Would *You* Live?

Though the existence of truly integrated neighborhoods is one indica-tion of Americans' deepening appreciation of residential racial inte-gration, the paucity of such integrated neighborhoods suggests that the problem of race and housing choice is much more complicated.[35] Despite support for open housing and lack of support for housing dis-crimination, as stated earlier in this chapter, census data suggest that in 2010 the vast majority of whites in America still live in predominately white neighborhoods. Seeking to explain the disparity between Ameri-cans' attitudes and their practices, scholars have attempted to probe

Table 3.5
Opinions on Whether Owners Should Be Allowed to Discriminate in Housing

Year	Owner Should Decide (%)	Owner Can't Discriminate (%)	Neither
1973	63.8	34.7	1.6
1980	55.3	43.2	1.5
1990	39.3	59.1	1.6
2004	33.2	66.8	0.0
2006	26.6	69.0	4.5

Source: General Social Survey, "Dataset: General Social Surveys, 1972–2006 [Cumulative File]: Race," accessed November 5, 2012, http://www.norc.org/GSS+Website/Browse+GSS+Variables/Collections/.

Note: The survey question was "Suppose there is a community-wide vote on the general housing issue (open housing law). There are two possible laws to vote on. Which law would you vote for?"

Table 3.6
Opinions on Whites' Right to Keep Neighborhoods All-White

Year	Agree Strongly (%)	Agree Slightly (%)	Disagree Slightly (%)	Disagree Strongly (%)
1972	21.5	17.4	25.0	36.1
1980	15.4	15.0	28.2	41.4
1990	8.0	13.2	24.0	54.7
1996	5.1	6.0	18.7	70.2

Source: General Social Survey, "Dataset: General Social Surveys, 1972–2006 [Cumulative File]: Race," accessed October 22, 2010, http://www.norc.org/GSS+Website/Browse+GSS+Variables/Collections/.

Note: Respondents were asked to express their degree of agreement or disagreement with the following statement: "White people have a right to keep (Negroes/Blacks/African-Americans) out of their neighborhoods if they want to, and (Negroes/Blacks/African-Americans) should respect that right."

both the root of an individual's selection of a particular neighborhood and also the strength of an individual's desire or preference for neighborhoods with a particular demographic distribution. In doing this, scholars were attempting to evaluate whether neighborhood selection seemed to originate from ethnocentrism (the desire to live with members of their own group), from racial prejudice, or from some combination.[36] One of the most comprehensive evaluations of Americans' attitudes about race, housing, and neighborhood came about as part of the Multi-City Study of Urban Inequality (MCSUI).[37] The MCSUI's household survey involved face-to-face interviews conducted between 1992 and 1994 with 8,916 non-Hispanic white, African American, Hispanic, and Asian American adults living in metropolitan Detroit, Boston, Los Angeles, and Atlanta. In each city, the number and race of the respondents selected was consistent with that city's local ethnic and racial mix.[38]

To capture the respondents' taste for housing integration, interviewers presented them with a variety of neighborhood scenarios, each of which portrayed fifteen icons in the shape of a house. The houses were shaded in various ways to denote occupants of color or left blank to signify white occupants (see figure 3.2). White respondents were first asked to picture themselves living in a neighborhood depicted in card 1, a neighborhood that was all white. The respondent's hypothetical house was designated and, over the course of the interview, was located in different places in different diagrams presented to the respondent. After the first question, in which they were to imagine living in an all-white neighborhood, white respondents were shown cards with greater degrees of integration—houses designated as occupied by minorities—and were asked to describe whether they felt "very comfortable," "comfortable," "somewhat comfortable," or "very uncomfortable" with varying degrees of integration.[39]

Theoretical support for integration is distinctly different from the neighborhoods that whites choose in actuality. As indicated earlier in the chapter, analysis of data collected as part of the 2010 US census reveals that the typical white person in the United States lives in a neighborhood that is more than 77 percent white. In spite of this, a majority of whites surveyed by the MCSUI still expressed a degree of comfort living in neighborhoods that are racially integrated. A fair

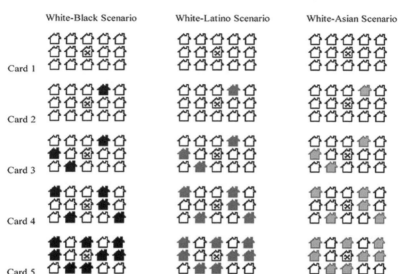

Figure 3.2. Source: Multi-City Study of Urban Inequality, Camille Zubrinsky Charles, "Processes of Racial Residential Segregation," in Urban Inequality: Evidence from Four Cities, ed. Alice O'Connor, Chris Tilly, and Lawrence D. Bobo (New York: Russell Sage, 2001), 234.

majority, at least 60 percent, of white respondents indicated that they were comfortable in neighborhoods that were depicted as having one-third of the houses occupied by black residents.[40] Despite this, whites were not equally comfortable with neighbors who are black, Hispanic, and Asian American. Racial groups occupying other housing influenced white respondents' comfort level. White respondents were significantly less comfortable (roughly 20 percent) in neighborhoods in which blacks were the dominant residents than in those in which Asian Americans and Hispanics dominated.[41]

The questions detailed above, in which a majority of whites expressed broad support for open housing, focused on the issue of housing integration in a very abstract manner. Respondents were questioned about their support for particular principles, such as "open housing" or "non-discrimination." In a similar manner, researchers operationalized support for housing by focusing on the actions of others—landlords not being allowed to discriminate. Not personalizing integration may have allowed respondents to distance themselves from the prospect of living in an integrated neighborhood and may have artificially increased support for integrated housing.

More recent research on attitudes toward housing, particularly questions asked by the MCSUI, personalize the question of housing choice, requiring that the respondent move from abstract notions of support for open housing to concrete notions of the type of neighborhood in which the individual would choose to live. In doing so, the data concerning neighborhood choice offers much greater insight into how and whether whites are more inclined toward making racialized choices with respect to housing. Data from white respondents on the neighborhood racial mix that they would tolerate thus offers the first glimpse of the attitudes that might help explain some whites' negative attitudes toward black or other minority neighbors that in some cases lead to violence.

Through responses in the surveys of general attitudes toward open housing noted above, a majority of white respondents expressed support for housing integration. But when the question of integration is finally personalized, a different picture—one much more consistent with resistance to minority integration—emerges. In addition to the issue of comfort described above, the MCSUI also probed the willingness of whites to move into neighborhoods with more than one or two nonwhite families. White respondents in Boston and Los Angeles who had previously indicated they were comfortable with minority neighbors of particular backgrounds (either Hispanic, black, or Asian American) were shown cards depicting neighborhoods with different levels of integration and were asked whether they'd consider moving into a "nice" house that they could afford in one of the neighborhoods on the shown cards (see figure 3.2).[42]

Despite their professed support for integration expressed in responses to questions regarding neighborhoods in which they felt comfortable, the vast majority of white respondents were reluctant to choose majority/minority neighborhoods, particularly if most of the residents were African American. Fewer than 30 percent of white respondents would choose a house in a majority-black neighborhood.[43] Even if the percentage of blacks was lower, whites still remained reluctant to move into a neighborhood that had more than a token number of blacks. Though 60 percent of whites had expressed comfort with a neighborhood where one-third of the residents were black, only 45 percent expressed a desire to select a house in this type of neighborhood.[44] Whites considered Asian Americans and Hispanics to be much more acceptable neighbors, with slightly more than 50 percent of whites indicating that they might choose a neighborhood where Asian Americans are in the majority and just over 40 percent saying that they would choose a neighborhood where Hispanics are in the majority.[45]

By examining racial attitudes and preferences for housing in Los Angeles, the Los Angeles Survey of Urban Inequality in 1992 and 1994 surveyed non-Hispanic whites, blacks, Hispanics, and Asian Americans of Chinese, Korean, and Japanese descent. The results suggest that for individuals from a variety of racial backgrounds, racial prejudice plays an important role in housing segregation. Analysis of the responses from individuals in each of these groups indicates that prejudice was the most significant factor in the creation of neighborhoods by race.[46] Evaluating the propensity to hold negative racial stereotypes, researchers asked white respondents whether they viewed members of the following groups—whites, blacks, native-born or foreign-born Asian Americans, or Latinos—as unintelligent, preferring welfare, speaking poor English, or being involved with drugs and gangs. The same question was also asked of blacks, Latinos, and Asian Americans. The researchers found that for whites, negative racial stereotyping and the perception of racial group competition were the two factors most associated with the desire to integrate. Unsurprisingly, whites who had the most negative stereotypes of racial and ethnic minorities were the group most likely to prefer neighbors who are also white, rather than neighbors who are members of racial and ethnic "out groups."[47]

One might hope that positive contact with racial and ethnic minorities would tend to increase the desire of whites to live in integrated neighborhoods. Unfortunately for advocates of social integration, the data suggest otherwise. Researchers found that for whites, racial attitudes may eclipse even positive personal experiences. Even when researchers controlled for white respondents' class attitudes or ethnocentrism, racial attitudes were more important: "That racial stereotyping was always more strongly associated with whites' preferences than perceived social distance suggests that whites discount their actual experience with out-group members—which presumably informed their social distance attitudes—in favor of global beliefs about a group's tendency to have 'undesirable' characteristics."[48] In other words, the best way to predict what types of housing choices someone who is white might make is to look at their racial attitudes. This is not just true of whites. Racial attitudes were important to the neighborhood choice of minority groups as well, though such attitudes were not as significant a factor as they were for whites.[49]

Negative racial attitudes do more than just affect the choices that individuals make with respect to the neighborhoods in which they wish to live. Extreme racial attitudes may affect the likelihood that one will stay in the neighborhood after African Americans move there. When asked by MCSUI researchers, 38 percent of non-Hispanic whites indicated that they would evaluate whether they should stay when presented with pictures of neighborhoods that ranged from one black family to eight black families (out of fifteen families total). The percentage of respondents who indicated that they would move out grew as the number of blacks increased.[50]

Maria Krysan's research using MCSUI data probed the responses of whites who said they would move out if blacks moved in. One group of respondents—the 'early leavers'—said they would leave if a single black family moved to their white neighborhood. Approximately 6 percent of the white respondents indicated a desire to move out if just one black family moved in because of opposition to integration in general and/or living next to African Americans in particular. This group also includes those who clearly express anger toward or mistrust of African Americans.[51] Individuals who expressed the view that living next to an African American was distasteful or who expressed their lack of trust or dislike of African Americans in very explicit terms provide the first clue that some whites might still be so opposed to living next door to a minority that they would try to force them to leave the neighborhood.

Explaining the Tolerance-Violence Paradox:
The Perpetrator's Perspective

The extremely negative views of the early leavers in Krysan's work are similar to those of the individuals who do not necessarily choose to leave when minorities, particularly African Americans, move to their neighborhoods. Instead of moving, such individuals choose to stand and fight, committing acts of anti-integrationist violence against racial and ethnic minorities who have moved into white neighborhoods. Though such behavior often has the intended effect and minorities move from the neighborhood, such perpetrators who actually commit hate crimes in their neighborhoods may face prosecution for engaging in violent behavior.

Because individuals have been prosecuted for acts of anti-integrationist violence, federal and state cases provide some insight into what perpetrators may have intended by their actions. The most common type of incident prosecuted in these cases are cross burnings, but individuals also were convicted of threats, gunshots, arson, vandalism, firebombings, and beatings, all aimed at driving the targeted individual out of the neighborhood.[52] As the work of Levin and McDevitt predicts, most of the incidents involve those unaffiliated with any sort of hate or extremist group. The vast majority of individuals targeted by the violence are African Americans who have moved to white neighborhoods, though several cases involve individuals of other races, including interracial couples.[53]

The perpetrator's intention to drive the newcomer out of the neighborhood is crystal clear in many of these cases.[54] The experience of the Waheeds, a black family who moved to a white neighborhood in Chicago in July 1986, was typical of those targeted. The day after the family moved in, the house was firebombed. The next day two members of the family, David and Aleem Waheed, were approached by one of their white neighbors, Larry Kalafut, and another man. Kalafut told them that the arsonist had "not done a good job." Later Kalafut screamed racist epithets at the Waheeds' house. Evidently, Larry Kalafut did not think that the Waheeds belonged in his neighborhood. His view in this regard became clear when David Waheed and Stephen Johnson encountered Kalafut a few weeks after the first firebomb and Kalafut shouted at them, "You niggers don't belong in this neighborhood. Go back to the other side of Western." Kalafut and several others followed Waheed and Johnson, pelting them with empty bottles and shouting, "Ku Klux Klan." At the end of August, the Waheeds' house was set on fire a second time. Kalafut was charged with arson and eventually pled guilty.[55]

Like other cases of anti-integrationist violence, the incidents directed at the Waheeds occurred soon after they moved in.[56] If the family stays in the neighborhood, they must endure several acts of violence. Often the behavior will start with small acts such as vandalism, then, if the target does not leave the neighborhood, will escalate into a much larger incident like a cross burning or firebombing. In the vast majority of cases there is evidence that the perpetrator is not happy with the integration of his or her neighborhood and his or her actions are aimed at scaring the new family so that they will leave the neighborhood.[57]

The intention to force a black family out of the neighborhood was clear in *United States v. J.H.H.* The incidents in this case took place in June 1990 and involved an eighteen-year-old, Arthur Miller III, a fourteen-year-old, JHH, and two other teenagers living in St. Paul, Minnesota. The teenagers had discussed how they were "really disgusted" that the Joneses, an African American family, had moved in across the street from Miller. In response, the teenagers decided to try to "do something about it." In the ensuing discussion, JHH suggested slashing the tires of the Joneses' car. Miller replied that that had already been done and "it didn't do no good. . . . they're still here." The group decided to "go burn some neighbors." In the early morning of June 20, 1990, the teenagers burned three crosses in the vicinity of the Joneses' house—one inside the Joneses' yard, one across the street from the Joneses' house, and one nearby, in the vicinity of an apartment building where several minorities lived. Several of the teenagers were prosecuted, and at trial Arthur Miller testified that the crosses had been burned to send a message to the Jones family to move out.[58]

Though the majority of the cases in which individuals are federally prosecuted for acts of anti-integrationist violence target African Americans, a few of the cases target whites, and also members of other racial and ethnic minority groups. When members of other ethnic minority groups are attacked, it appears the perpetrators have a similar motive to rid the neighborhood of individuals of that particular background. In a majority of these cases, the defendants' desire to preserve their whites-only space was crystal clear. For instance, *United States v. Nichols*, in Bessemer City, North Carolina, involved an attack on a group of Hispanics who had moved to a white neighborhood. As in the Waheed case, the attack was prompted by the fact that minorities—in this case blacks and Hispanics—had begun to move into the formerly all-white neighborhood of Michael Nichols and Shane Greene, two white men. Nichols and Greene had complained about the neighborhood's changing demographics, indicating that they had a problem with "niggers" and "spics" living in Bessemer City. Witnesses also saw Nichols and Greene spewing racial epithets at African Americans and Hispanics who lived in the neighborhood. On July 30, 1999, Nichols and Greene approached Julio Sanchez while he and a friend were sitting on Sanchez's front porch. One of the men assaulted the friend and tried to hit Sanchez. Nichols and Greene left and then returned with an iron pipe, which they used to break all the windows in the front of the house in addition to the windows of vehicles parked outside the house.[59]

One undercurrent running through these cases is that the offenders do not want minorities in their neighborhoods because they feel that the very presence of minorities, particularly African Americans, ruins the neighborhood. Perpetrators have expressed the fear that the presence of minorities will lead to the ruin of the offender's white neighborhood in a variety of ways. In some cases, whites who commit crimes against African American neighbors attribute problems they've seen in the neighborhood to the nearest member of a minority group. In these incidents, African Americans and, in some cases, other minorities constitute an undifferentiated mass, and a crime directed at one may be viewed by the perpetrators as helping to solve the problem. The perpetrator Nichols, described above, displayed this thinking when, as a witness testified, he was vandalizing the Latino target's home and car while screaming, "Go back to Mexico, you done got all our jobs." Sanchez, Nichols's target, had invaded Nichols's white neighborhood, and his very presence symbolized white unemployment.[60]

The use of attacks against one member of an ethnic group to send a message to the entire group (as if all members of an ethnic group are somehow in communication with one another) is a frequent theme in neighborhood attacks. In *United States v. Nicholson*, the Milwaukee-based Lee family, who were Hmong, bore the brunt of ire against their ethnic group.[61] On July 28, 1998, several teenagers, who it was later revealed did not know their victims, burned down the Lees' eight-family-member home and plotted to kill or intimidate other Asian Americans because of an earlier fight between white and Asian

American youth.[62] Andrew Franz, one of the arsonists, testified that the men "selected Hmong as targets because they wanted to 'send a message' to Asian American men in the community to leave them alone."[63]

Some incidents may be global, as in the case of the message communicated to the Hmong community by burning down the Lees' home; others are more local, prompted both by a hatred of a particular ethnic group in the neighborhood and a wish to retaliate against an individual member of the group. *United States v. Magleby* provides an example. One evening the perpetrator, Michael Brad Magleby, discussed with several friends his dislike for African Americans living in his Salt Lake City neighborhood. Magleby was particularly disparaging of the Tongans, alleged gang members, with whom one witness indicated that Magleby had gotten in a fight. Magleby and his friends decided to burn a cross on the Tongans' lawn. After the cross was constructed and taken to the Tongans' house, Magleby was too scared to burn the cross there. Instead, on the advice of a co-conspirator, Magleby burned the cross on the lawn of the Henrys, whom he did not know but had been told were black.[64]

In a similar turn of events described in *United States v. Gresser*, a cross burning on the lawn of a black neighbor of Timothy Singer and Todd Gresser in Massillon, Ohio, was prompted by an earlier altercation involving entirely different African Americans.[65] In the earlier incident, after Singer and Gresser screamed at two black youths, "Will you damn niggers turn that mother——music down!," the four men subsequently argued and one of the black men hit Singer with a piece of concrete. Though Singer knew, and later identified, where the man who had hit him lived, he did not retaliate against him. Instead, a short time later, Singer told his black neighbors, Donna and Jennings Mason, who were sitting on their front porch, "that he had a gun and a half-stick of dynamite in his pocket and was going to 'blow up all those mother——niggers.'" Early the next morning, August 13, 1989, a large wooden cross was burned accompanied by an explosion in a vacant lot across the street from Singer's home. In addition, racial epithets, "KKK," "nigger die," and "KKK, ——you, nigger," were painted on the back of several houses in the neighborhood.[66]

The "Damage" of Integration

Perpetrators of anti-integrationist violence frequently imagine that their neighborhood's property values will be damaged if a single minority family moves in. Several of the cases prosecuting individuals for anti-integrationist violence demonstrate this false assumption that if African Americans move to the neighborhood their own property will instantly be worth less. For example, in *United States v. Myers*, a black couple eventually targeted for violence had just purchased a home in a white neighborhood in Hobart, Indiana. The parents of Kelly Myers, the defendant in the case, lived across the street from the newcomers and wanted to sell their home. According to the decision in *Myers,* they were concerned that the home's value would be lessened by the presence of blacks living in the neighborhood. To scare the couple into leaving the neighborhood, Kelly Myers and her boyfriend set fire to the couple's car.[67]

The argument that a black family's presence is damaging to property values may be graphically expressed by perpetrators as part of the crime. For instance, in *United States v. Mahan*, early one morning in September 1997, an African American family discovered approximately a hundred copies of a racist flyer on their front lawn in Murray, Kentucky. The authors of the flyer made it abundantly clear that the black family, as "niggers," did not belong in their white neighborhood. Members of the community had worked hard to protect their investment, and the black family's presence in the community, the writers of the flyer argued, was going to cost members of the community when they tried to resell their homes. The flyer read,

> We don't know if you have realized this or not, but you and your family are niggers. We, as members of the white society, do not condone the idea of having niggers living in our community. We are not happy to see our property values plummet to an all-time low. We have worked hard to bring up our property value with strict community restrictions. Since the real estate appraisers have learned that niggers live in our communities, we have lost thousands of dollars on the resale value of our homes. Whoever gave you the idea that it is all right to live on [this street] is sadly mistaken. . . . Move back to the nigger section in town, to another state or community, or to Africa where you really belong.[68]

After exhorting the family to leave the neighborhood, the authors of the flyer went on to communicate in great detail the harm that would come to the family if they did not leave the neighborhood. As a further threat, the authors even warned that the police could not protect the family from the coming violence. They should move back to where they belonged or else. The flyer went on to caution,

> You have exactly 30 days to vacate the premises. Contact the police if you think this will make you rest easier at night, but not even the police can protect you from our wrath. We will see to it that you and your family are permanently removed from your eyesore of a home, the easy way or the hard way. We prefer the hard way. The choice is yours; just remember that you have 30 days and not a moment longer. We will be watching your every move, day and night. . . . Go home!![69]

In the vast majority of the situations where perpetrators allege that their property values have been affected, it is minorities themselves who are targeted. In some cases, however, it is those who facilitate or are accused of facilitating minority purchases in white neighborhoods that are targeted. In *United States v. Vartanian*, for example, the defendant was convicted for having threatened a real estate agent after she facilitated the purchase of a house by an African American family in a formerly all-white neighborhood in Harper Woods, Michigan. Standing outside the home, the defendant, who owned the property across the street from the seller, ran across the road and began ranting at the agents assembled there. Vartanian insisted that he would not have invested $10,000 in a swimming pool in his yard had he known that African Americans would move in across the street.[70] In another example of a perpetrator who committed acts of anti-integrationist violence to protect the neighborhood from minority incursion, Frank Scire firebombed a real estate agency that was under court order to show local homes to blacks in Canarsie, a Brooklyn neighborhood with many white residents strongly opposed to minority integration. Scire had convinced someone to help him by arguing, "It's good for the neighborhood, all the niggers are moving in."[71]

In some of the cases in which perpetrators act in response to the assumed threat against the neighborhood's property values, the intimidation begins quite quickly—soon after the minority moves in.[72] Sometimes it starts before a purchase is even completed. For instance, in *United States v. Tuffarelli*, Joseph Tuffarelli was charged with violating the Fair Housing Act for his role in intimidating someone who inquired about the neighborhood. One day while standing on his lawn, Tuffarelli, who is white, was approached by Mr. White, a black man, who asked about the neighborhood. In response, Tuffarelli began to shout racially derogatory remarks at Mr. White "in an effort to dissuade him from considering a move to the neighborhood." During the five-minute tirade by Tuffarelli, he pounded on the door of his neighbor's home, screaming that if she sold the house to the Whites, he would burn it down. It was later revealed that the Whites had not indicated any intention to purchase the seller's home prior to the incident.[73]

A similar case, *State v. Talley*, was prosecuted under Washington State's cross burning statute. Dave Talley was prosecuted for burning a four-foot-tall cross on his own lawn in the presence of Philip and René Smith and several others. The Smiths, a mixed-race couple, were accompanied by their three-year-old son, their friend Jeanne Tyler, and their realtor Stacy Lutzenger on a visit to the house they intended to purchase in King County. Having recently signed an earnest money agreement, they were at the house to measure the rooms for carpets and obtain window measurements for draperies. Talley saw the couple and told bystanders that having "niggers next door" would ruin his property values. Talley constructed a four-foot tall cross, erected it in his own yard, and ignited it. To attract the Smiths' attention, Talley began to "hoot and holler." When asked by René Smith whether there was a problem, he indicated that he did not talk with her "kind" and ordered her off his driveway. Disturbed and frightened by Talley's actions, the Smiths declined their option to purchase.[74]

The Value of Whites-Only Neighborhoods

There may be many reasons that whites who have committed acts of anti-integrationist violence associate housing integration with declining property values. It may be that they fear a domino effect, in which one black person moves in, others follow, and consequently whites will end up fleeing the neighborhood. As whites flee, they imagine the neighborhood

Not only explaining the mechanism (in it?)

will be transformed into a black ghetto, as has happened to many neighborhoods in central cities with the rise of white-dominated suburbs, as described in the previous chapter. There is empirical evidence to support the fact that many whites associate integration with neighborhood decline—falling property values and increasing crime. Because of this, a majority (53 percent) of whites surveyed in Detroit in 1992 would move away from integrating areas.[75] The Multi-City Study of Urban Inequality found that whites in different cities have a different taste for integration. Whites in the Detroit metropolitan area, for instance, were much more likely to leave if a single black family moved into the neighborhood than were whites living in Atlanta, Boston, or Los Angeles.[76]

If whites fear that minorities' presence will lead to some sort of change in their neighborhood, the color of the neighborhood may have significant value to whites. Associating a value, even a dollar amount, on the whiteness of a particular neighborhood makes intuitive sense, especially given the range of pure economic incentives many whites benefit from when they live in white neighborhoods. Many middle-class white suburban property owners build wealth as their property values rise, while people of color, many of whom are consigned to poorer neighborhoods in cities, experience a loss of wealth.[77] Moreover, many white suburbs have amenities that predominantly black neighborhoods, even middle-class black suburbs, lack—a system of parks and libraries, good schools, and low crime rates.[78]

Given whites' preferences and the advantages of white neighborhoods, it is less surprising that some whites harbor the desire to protect their privilege by committing acts of anti-integrationist violence. The strength of the resistance to minority incursion is expressed most clearly in cases of attacks on whites who have involvement with blacks or other people of color. Though the vast majority of the racially motivated cases prosecuted under Section 3631 of the Fair Housing Act involve situations in which Asian Americans, African Americans, Latinos, or other minorities are targeted, some of the cases involve whites who have been targeted for race-based hate crimes. When whites are targeted in this context, the perpetrators tend to be motivated by anger at the victim's interaction or association with racial and ethnic minorities. The association that most often triggers a violent racial attack against someone who is white is familial involvement with a person of color, for instance, as part of an interracial couple.[79] Lesser associations such as friendship may also prompt racial attacks.[80] In one rather unusual case, a defendant was convicted under Section 3631 for sending letters threatening the white head of an adoption agency who was trying to place African American and Asian children with white adoptive families.[81] In a similar case, a white woman who had moved to a white neighborhood with her biracial children was threatened.[82] As in other cases, few perpetrators in the case where whites are attacked express some sort of ideological commitment to racial purity. Rather, it may be the case that the perpetrators attached such a high value to preserving the whiteness of their environment that even the nonwhite partner, child, or friend of a white person constitutes a threat.

The Effect of Anti-Integrationist Violence on Housing Integration

Engaging in anti-integrationist violence is the opposite of rolling out the welcome mat for newcomers: it signals outright hostility, at least on the part of the perpetrator. Though it may be impossible to assess the precise impact of individual incidents of anti-integrationist violence on overall housing integration, there is evidence on a variety of levels that such incidents affect the choice of minorities to live in predominantly white neighborhoods. Moreover, in order for such incidents to have an impact, minorities have to know about them. Survey research from Los Angeles, Detroit, Boston, and Atlanta suggests that minorities develop clear ideas about the neighborhoods in which they are not welcome, and such ideas affect housing search behavior.[83] In this research, investigators measure hostility toward an individual's own group by asking individuals whether they believe that area residents would be upset by a new neighbor of their background. For instance, in Michigan, at least 60 percent of African American respondents indicated that residents of Warren, Troy, and/ or Dearborn would be upset by a new black neighbor.[84] The effect of the perception of hostility in various neighborhoods in each of the cities was also found to be true for Hispanics, African Americans, and Asian Americans. Perceptions regarding the hostility of different ethnic groups map on to residential segregation from whites. African Americans, the most segregated group, are also the minority group most likely to see particular areas as upset by a new black neighbor.[85]

The impact of individual instances of anti-integrationist violence on minority housing choices can be assessed in a variety of ways. Court cases and news stories make clear that in many cases of anti-integrationist violence, targets choose to leave the neighborhood rather than remain. It is also the case that particular white neighborhoods in which well-publicized hate crimes occur develop reputations that affect minorities' desires to remain in the neighborhood or to move there. In Chicago, the beating of thirteen-year-old Lenard Clark serves as an example of this effect.

On March 21, 1997, Lenard Clark and a friend, Clevan Nicholson, rode their bikes into Armor Square Park district, thereby crossing an invisible racial barrier into Bridgeport, a working-class, predominately white neighborhood populated by, at various points in Chicago's history, European immigrants from Ireland, Germany, Lithuania, Poland, Italy, and Ukraine. Bridgeport, reportedly home to five of Chicago's mayors, was a long-segregated neighborhood that had witnessed open housing marches in the 1960s. When Clark was spotted in Bridgeport, he was knocked off his bike and beaten into a coma by three white men for "being in their neighborhood." The men later bragged to their friends about keeping Bridgeport white.[86] Two of the men, Victor Jasas and Michael Kwidzinski, received probation and community service for the vicious beating, while the third, Frank Caruso Jr., was acquitted of attempted murder but convicted of aggravated battery and hate crime charges and sentenced to eight years in prison.

Though Clark's attack was certainly not the first racial attack on someone passing through the neighborhood that occurred in Bridgeport in the 1980s or 1990s, it may have been the best publicized.[87] Clark's beating led to multiple protest marches with celebrities like the Reverend Jesse Jackson, and fundraising breakfasts for his family attended by luminaries like the mayor of Chicago. Given this publicity, for more than a decade, the beating of Lenard Clark continued to serve as a symbol to African Americans of the fact that they were not welcome in Bridgeport. Though there were other attempts to ameliorate tension (e.g., the Chicago Commission on Human Rights summit with representatives of several organizations from the Bridgeport area aimed at creating a plan to fight racism), members of the African American community in Chicago did not believe that racial attitudes in Bridgeport had changed since the days of the Clark attack. While Asian American and Latino immigration to Bridgeport increased dramatically, the African American population, which was 36 percent in the city as a whole, remained below 1 percent in Bridgeport.[88] Even years after the incident, African Americans repeatedly indicated that they did not want to venture into Bridgeport.[89] When several African Americans were interviewed about housing in Chicago, none of them would entertain the idea of living in Bridgeport. One upper-middle-class young African American woman, when asked whether there was any place in Chicago she refused to live, responded,

> Definitely. Bridgeport, . . . definitely very hostile in Bridgeport and those surrounding areas. My husband and I had to get his asthma medicine one time over there. People were very rude and very hostile. We had to take a bus from Bronzeville to that area. Now, I'm not sure that that's Bridgeport but it's west of 90/94. . . . They were very rude, very hostile. . . . my husband, being from Chicago, he said we need to hurry up and get out of here. Because, you know, there've been incidents in the past. Sometimes I try to get him to go see the White Sox games, [but] he doesn't want to go because he's heard about a black man getting beaten up in front of White Sox Park.[90]

Another young upper-middle-class African American woman who had lived in Chicago for only a few years, when asked whether she would choose to live in Bridgeport, said, "No. I mean, I grew up with white people, but . . . from just the news reports and some of the things that have happened there; activities, and racial tension, . . . I don't need any of that. I'm too old for that, you know."[91] Whites who lived in Bridgeport also reported friends of color, particularly African American friends, being worried about coming to visit them. It is unclear whether Bridgeport's reputation as a place where African Americans should not live was deserved. Three individuals who work with victims of hate crime in various capacities indicated in interviews that Bridgeport was one of the neighborhoods in the city where a high number of hate crimes occurred, despite the paucity of official data confirming this.[92] Anecdotal accounts suggest that Asian Americans have replaced blacks as the largest group of hate crime victims in the neighborhood.[93]

Bridgeport residents deny that the neighborhood is racist.[94] Several Latinos and one black person who lived in Bridgeport all reported in interviews that they had not been harassed in Bridgeport.[95] Whether or not the neighborhood still deserves its reputation for being a hotbed of racial tension, however, the paucity of African Americans living in Bridgeport suggests that the beating of Lenard Clark may still serve as an active deterrent to African Americans moving into this working-class neighborhood on the South Side. *Bad arg*t

Conclusion

Sta loy :

When it comes to race, American attitudes bear some relation to a fun house mirror in which the reflection does not accurately depict the reality. The election of Barack Obama serves as a great metaphor for the tolerance-violence paradox—the continued presence of housing-related violence in an era of increasing racial tolerance. Barack Obama's electoral victory over John McCain symbolized unprecedented support among white voters, a group that had previously shown reluctance to support a black candidate. Subsequent analysis of Obama's victory reveals that viewing it as a triumph for race relations masks a significant gap between black and white electoral support.

Violent crimes directed at minorities moving to white neighborhoods seem paradoxical in light of survey data that show increasing racial tolerance on issues such as interracial marriage and even in the area of housing itself. To explain what seems to be a paradox, this chapter has looked more closely at both perpetrators' motivations and other, more personal attitudes about housing. Survey research on whites' housing choices reveals that while theoretically in support of housing integration, many white Americans reject integrated neighborhoods. Perpetrators of anti-integrationist violence, of course, are the most extreme example of this, choosing to fight to keep their neighborhoods all-white. The justification that these perpetrators offer—the protection of property values—is similar to that of white residents who do not commit crimes but nonetheless reject housing integration. In other words, the way to explain the paradox is that, while many whites may be more tolerant of interracial interaction, for many this still does not extend to sharing neighborhoods with minorities, particularly African Americans.

So they say they are tolerant..

4

Racism or Power?

Explaining Perpetrator Motivation in Interethnic Cases

When Channise Davy first laid eyes on the cream-colored, three-bed-room bungalow on a peaceful street in Duarte, a small town in Los Angeles County, California, she thought she had found the perfect place to call home. The charming little house was accented by red and yellow roses in the front yard, with a nectarine tree, a red swing set, and a small gazebo in the backyard. In April 2009, the thirty-one-year-old black beauty salon owner moved her four children from North Holly-wood into the lovely house in Duarte. Davy did not think much about the fact that her family would be the first blacks to move to their block.

Unfortunately, as Davy later learned, others in the neighborhood found her race to be significant. About a month after Davy had moved in, she entered the front door of the house to find the hardwood floors, mirrors, and televisions defaced with the word "nigger." The vandals also destroyed furniture and ransacked dresser drawers. No room in the house was left untouched. The scope of the violence impressed law enforcement. "As far as hate crimes go," Sergeant Tony Haynes of the Los Angeles County Sheriff's Department later said, "it's probably one of the worst ones I've seen in my career."[1] Davy turned down city offi-cials' offers to send volunteers to clean up. She and her family moved out immediately after the crime, with no intent to return.

Though Sergeant Haynes had not seen worse hate crimes, at first glance this incident seems identical to other contemporary acts of anti-integrationist violence in that it fits the following pattern: a black per-son moves to a neighborhood and soon after experiences vandalism accompanied by racial slurs and epithets. A closer look at Davy's case reveals that the harassment directed at her was slightly different from the instances of anti-integrationist violence described in the preceding chapters. Davy had not moved to a neighborhood that was predominantly white. Instead, Davy's neighbors were mostly Latino. Authorities believed that the incidents directed at Davy, and countless similar attacks directed at African Americans moving to Latino neighborhoods in Los Angeles from the early 1990s until 2008 or 2009, were committed by Latinos.

Explaining Perpetrator Motivation

Because they are slightly atypical, the incidents directed at Davy raise the issue of perpetrator motivation. In other words, why did the perpetrator vandalize the victim's home or burn a cross on the victim's lawn? While it might be assumed that the perpetrators of these crimes are card-carrying racists, divining perpetrator motivation is rarely straightforward even in more typical cases. As the previous chapter highlights, research on hate crimes aimed at minorities who have moved to white neighborhoods demonstrates that the perpetrators are rarely ideological extremists or members of organized hate groups.[2] The question then becomes what prompts these incidents. This chapter and the next explore three different explanations for perpetrators' behavior—racial prejudice, social class, and power. In discussing each of these explanations, I deconstruct the role of race-based understandings of anti-integrationist violence by using attacks on African Americans in Los Angeles as a case study.

Interethnic Hate Crimes

Interethnic acts of anti-integrationist violence raise some challenges for our understanding of anti-integrationist violence. First, interethnic hate crimes involving minority victims and racial and ethnic minority perpetrators are not what we expect when we hear the term anti-integrationist violence. When the perpetrators of these crimes are also people of color from similarly disadvantaged backgrounds, our understanding of the racialized reasons that perpetrators engage in such violence is challenged. One of the biggest challenges has to do with the role of race in understanding what is motivating those committing these acts of violence. If members of minority groups are committing crimes against other minorities, are the perpetrators motivated by ideological racism? Are such crimes struggles for turf?

Blacks and Latinos in America, and in Los Angeles

The acts of move-in violence I describe in this chapter involve crimes committed by Latinos against African Americans in Los Angeles. "Latinos," and nothing more specific, is how the perpetrators are described in court cases, human rights organizations' materials, and press accounts. This is slightly problematic because the term "Latino" is a catchall phrase that encompasses people of Cuban, Puerto Rican, Dominican, Mexican, and South and Central American descent. This generic lumping under the term "Latino" of individuals from different countries with different national histories does not do justice to the complex relationship that Latinos from different regions have with African Americans. For instance, as the political analyst Earl Ofari Hutchinson notes, due to the history of political oppression that drove Central Americans to the United States, blacks, Salvadorans, and other Central Americans as a group have a relationship characterized by cooperation rather than friction.[3] This applies as well to Salvadoran gang members, who are not known to be involved in turf wars with black gangs. Context matters as well. Blacks in Chicago and New York have lived in close proximity with Puerto Ricans and have cooperated since the 1960s on electoral and housing issues and school reform.[4]

In addition to the countries of origin of Latino immigrants, in any given geographic space, Latinos may have a variety of other issues that influence their perspectives on race relations. In Los Angeles, the very diverse Latino community includes individuals of Mexican and Central and South American descent; it includes seventh-generation Californians and people who have only just arrived, either legally or illegally.[5] These differences among "Latinos" are added to economic, political, educational, and religious backgrounds, all of which may influence their perspective on—and consequently their interactions with—African Americans.

Despite the diversity of the Latino community in Los Angeles, there is evidence of several moments of cooperation between Latinos of many different backgrounds and African Americans. In exploring cross-racial political activism in Los Angeles, the historian Daniel Widener offers several examples of cooperation between Latinos and African Americans, from strong fraternal links between the Black Panther Party and the Chicano activist group the Brown Berets in the 1960s to multiracial labor organizing in the 1990s.[6] With respect to civil rights, African Americans and several other ethnic groups help sustain the Mexican American Community Service Organization, described by the historian Shana Bernstein as the first civil rights organization serving the Mexican-origin population of Los Angeles.[7] Latinos and African Americans as well as other ethnic groups were also part of a multiethnic, multigenerational response to a variety of political issues, including Proposition 187, NAFTA, and the police attack in 2007 at an immigrants' rights rally.[8] This history of interracial cooperation between Latinos and African Americans in Los Angeles makes the violence directed at African Americans in places like Duarte and Hawaiian Gardens in the 1990s even more notable.

The Battle against Blacks in Los Angeles

The violence directed at Davy and her family was one of several attacks on African Americans in predominantly Latino areas from the early 1990s through 2008–2009. One study of hate crimes in Los Angeles County between 1994 and 1997 using statistics gathered from several different Los Angeles County police departments found that African Americans had been disproportionately targeted.[9] For instance, in 1997 African Americans accounted for only 10 percent of the county population, but they were 56 percent of all race-based hate crime victims.[10] The authors also found that there had been a disproportionate increase in the number of African American victims of racially motivated crimes. Over that time period, the most significant increase in perpetrators by race was among Latinos. Field interviews and police reports revealed crimes clustered in, among other areas, Hawaiian Gardens and Harbor Gateway.

Similarly, data collected by the Los Angeles County Human Relations Commission show that over the 1990s, blacks were the victims of an average of 50 percent of the crimes reported (see table 4.1). In the

early 1990s, members of Latino gangs began to target African Americans living in predominantly Latino neighborhoods.[11] The commission
separated out the number of antiblack hate crimes committed by Latinos in 1998 and 1999. In 1998, 76 (34 percent) of the 219 antiblack hate
crimes reported to the commission were committed by Latinos.

After 1999, the number of cases in which blacks were attacked by
Latinos showed blacks to be a large percentage of hate crime targets,
despite making up less than 10 percent of the population. The commission noted that in 2006, African Americans were targeted for attack in
59 percent of the reported racial hate crime cases. Fifty-two percent of
the known suspects in these attacks were Latino. By 2007 Latino gangs
had become, according to the commission, the region's leading perpetrators of violent hate crimes, with the largest number of racial crimes
involving black victims.[12]

The Origins of Antiblack Hate Crimes in Los Angeles County

In the early 1990s, when attacks on African Americans living in the Los
Angeles area first started to occur, many were typical acts of move-in
violence reminiscent of behavior directed at African Americans moving
to white ethnic neighborhoods like Canarsie or Yonkers in New York.
Though it was similar in form, what distinguished the harassment of
African Americans in Los Angeles is that instead of being concentrated
in a single geographic area like a neighborhood, incidents were spread
out over communities blanketing Los Angeles County. For instance,
one of the first incidents that authorities focused on in the early 1990s
involved hate crimes directed at African Americans in Azusa, which
was at the time a working-class city of about fourteen thousand located
in the foothills of the San Gabriel Mountains. In 1991, the Los Angeles County Human Relations Commission reported that Latinos committed nine hate crimes in Azusa against African Americans.[13] Most of
these crimes involved Latino youths and included racial harassment—
slurs and epithets—and assaults, several of which were violent.

The violence continued in 1992. For nine months, Latino youth,
whom the FBI believed to be members of gangs, subjected Lori Martin
and her family to a campaign of terror—first vandalizing their property, then throwing rocks and bottles at the family car and harassing

Table 4.1

Hate Crimes in Los Angeles County, CA, 1997–2000

	1997		1998		1999		2000	
Type of crime	N	%	N	%	N	%	N	%
Antiblack								
All Perpetrators	273	55.8	219	50.2	232	50.7	279	49.6
Latino Perpetrators	—		76		67		—	
Anti-Latino	76	15.5	90	20.6	85	18.6	132	23.5
Anti-Asian	32	6.5	33	7.6	34	7.4	30	5.3
Antiwhite	89	18.2	72	16.5	81	17.7	93	16.6

Source: Los Angeles County Human Relations Commission.

Martin's children with slurs and threats. Deborah Judge, a black neighbor of Martin who moved in six months later, was also harassed. Complaints to the police fell on deaf ears. When one of the youths fired eight shots at their homes, Judge and Martin both moved out that same night with only their clothes and minor possessions.[14] When Martin returned several weeks later to retrieve her furniture, the door to her home was open and more graffiti was scrawled on the outside walls. The walls in the interior were smeared with mustard and lipstick.[15]

As the violence directed at African Americans in communities in Los Angeles County continued, random attacks began to occur more frequently. A few months after the incidents directed at Judge and Martin, in March 1993, Los Angeles County sheriff's deputies began investigating several incidents targeted at black families living in Hawaiian Gardens, in Los Angeles County. According to the 1990 census, two-thirds of the residents were of Hispanic origin and only 5 percent were African American. Beginning in the 1990s African Americans were beginning to move to Hawaiian Gardens.[16]

Between 1996 and 1997, thirty-four incidents were reported to the Hawaiian Gardens Police Department.[17] All but one of these incidents targeted African Americans and all of the suspected perpetrators were Latino. The most serious of the incidents in Hawaiian Gardens involved the firebombing of an African American family's house. During the

firebombing one of the five suspects allegedly yelled, "Nigger."[18] In several cases, African Americans living or passing through predominately
Latino neighborhoods were shot and killed by Latino gang members.
Though Latino gang members were responsible for the attacks, many
of the attacks against African Americans were directed at those who
were not involved in the drug trade at all. Though innocent people are
sometimes killed in gang crossfire, police also rejected that particular
scenario; law enforcement officials indicated that there was not really
an African American gang presence in Hawaiian Gardens.[19] Nor did
the attacks stem from Latino gangs fighting with black gangs over drug
territory.

The attacks on African Americans seemed clearly to be motivated by
gang members' desire to force African Americans out of their neighborhoods. Most of the incidents were believed to have been committed by the Losquitos gang. One member of the gang said, "Three [mur-
ders] ain't that much. . . . believe me, there should be a lot more dead
ones. They know if they come into our neighborhood they better get
the f——k out."[20] One of his friends added, "niggers come here thinking
they're gonna take over, but there ain't no blacks here and there never
will be."[21] Understanding the gang's message, many African Americans
left the neighborhood. As one victim forced to move said, "they don't
want any blacks in their neighborhood. We've moved real close to the
barrio, and they don't want us there."[22]

"They Don't Want Us Here": Targeting of African Americans in Highland Park

Attacks in Azusa occurred at the same time that African Americans
moving to Highland Park began to be targeted by Latino street gangs.
One of these gangs was Avenues 43, named for one of the avenues that
crosses Figueroa Street in Los Angeles. Police identified the Avenues as
being responsible for several attacks against African Americans between
1995 and 2005 in Highland Park. Located in the hills and ravines northeast of downtown Los Angeles, Highland Park was a neighborhood
that Latinos had dominated for many years. Asian Americans, African Americans, and non-Latino whites made up roughly 30 percent of
the population in 2006.[23] According to experts, the Avenues' territory

included all of Highland Park and parts of Cypress Park, Glassell Park, and Eagle Rock.[24] One of the gang's objectives became to drive African Americans out of the Highland Park neighborhood. These intentions were communicated by threats and racial epithets scrawled on walls in the neighborhood and also by personal attacks aimed at African Americans, including women and children who had no gang affiliations.

According to prosecutors, who later charged five members of the Avenues gang with hate crime violations, many of the gang's attacks were entirely random. Between 1995 and 2005, some of the incidents included the shooting of a fifteen-year-old African American boy while he was riding a bike, the pistol-whipping of a black jogger, and the beating with a metal club of a black man standing at a pay phone. One of the most telling cases involved gang members drawing outlines of human bodies in chalk on a black family's driveway. In the event the family missed the gang's gruesome message, the chalk outlines were accompanied by a racial slur. In another incident that clearly demonstrated the gang members' views that African Americans didn't belong in the neighborhood, gang members knocked a black woman off her bike and assaulted her. The gang members later brandished a box cutter at the woman's husband, threatening, "You niggers have been here long enough."[25]

The most tragic cases of racial intimidation of African Americans in Los Angeles involved those black residents and passersby who were killed in the Highland Park neighborhood. Kenneth Wilson was an early victim of the Avenues gang. One evening in April 1999, several Avenues gang members came upon Wilson, who was black, parking his Cadillac. One of the gang members, Martinez, asked if anyone wanted to kill a black man. In response, three other gang members jumped out of the car and opened fire on Wilson's car, killing him instantly.[26] Another of the gang's victims was twenty-eight-year-old Christopher Browser. On December 11, 2000, Browser was shot three times in the head at close range by Avenues members while he was waiting for the bus.[27]

Police identified the killers in both the Browser and Wilson murders. In addition to murder, the gang members who shot Browser and Wilson were charged with violating the civil rights of African Americans in the Highland Park neighborhood. Los Angeles Police Officer Elias Villaseñor, a gang expert who testified at the trial of Portofirio Avila, a member of the Avenues gang and one of the defendants charged with Browser's and Wilson's murders, noted that one of the motives for Browser's murder was that the Avenues targets African Americans, like Browser, who are in their territory.[28] The court noted that the Avenues gang did not want blacks around their area and had regularly beaten Browser. Testimony from those affiliated with the gang showed that gang members had planned to burn down Browser's house, but when they saw him standing at the bus stop, they shot him in the head instead.[29] Wilson's and Browser's murders, combined with evidence from other crimes directed at African Americans in the Highland Park neighborhood, eventually led to the conviction of four members of the Avenues gang for hate crimes violations.

Eradicating the Black "Threat" in Harbor Gateway

Other areas in Los Angeles County were also plagued by Latino gang members' attacks designed to rid the areas of the African American population. For more than a decade, beginning in the early to mid-1990s, African American residents of the Harbor Gateway neighborhood in Los Angeles were terrorized by Latino members of the 204th Street gang. Harassment of and attacks on African Americans in the Harbor Gateway neighborhood included slurs and epithets written on walls in the neighborhood, assaults, and even murders.

Over a ten-year period, authorities attributed to the 204th Street gang several murders of African American residents of Harbor Gateway who had no ties to street gangs. For instance, in 1997 an eleven-year-old African American with no gang ties, Marquis Wilbert, was shot and killed by a 204th Street gang member who rode by on a bicycle. Two years later, in April 1999, Mario Martinez approached two African American men who were not affiliated with a gang and opened fire with a .357-caliber handgun, fatally wounding Michael Richardson. At Martinez's trial, one police officer testified that 204th Street gang members were engaged in "a pattern of escalating acts of violence against their African American neighbors designed to force them to move."[30] In 2003, thirty-nine-year-old Eric Butler was shot to death while he was leaving the Del Amo market. Gang members considered the market—the neighborhood's only business—to be part of their territory.

One of the best-known cases of violence directed at African Americans in Harbor Gateway occurred in December 2006, when fourteen-year old Cheryl Green was shot and killed as she stood talking with friends.[31] Cheryl Green's killers were caught and charged with murder and hate crime violations. Overall, according to the Los Angeles police department statistics, from 1994 to 2005 in Harbor Gateway there were nearly five times as many homicides, assaults, and other violent crimes perpetrated by Latinos against black victims as by blacks against Latinos.[32] Some of these crimes may not have been motivated by bias or a deep desire to drive the African Americans out, but because of the campaign of attacks committed by the 204th Street gang, black residents of Harbor Gateway may have nevertheless felt that, in instances when the perpetrators were Latino and the victims were black, the crimes were bias-motivated.

The effects of the attacks by the 204th Street gang were long-lasting. Even after Cheryl Green's murderers were caught and prosecuted, residents of Harbor Gateway told reporters that they still lived in fear of the gang.[33] Gang members had carefully cultivated that fear by shooting at black residents, yelling racist insults, and defacing walls with racist graffiti.[34] Black residents of the neighborhood were careful to avoid Latinos in general, and many blacks became afraid to venture north of 206th Street, the gang-created boundary for African Americans.[35] Gang members patrolled the streets, circling the neighborhood on bicycles. In some cases gang members drove through the neighborhood shooting, and blacks ran for cover. Fearful of encountering members of the gang, black children often played inside. In order to keep them safe, though they could ill afford the time, black mothers drove their children to school. Crackdowns by the police abated the violence, but it returned when funds necessary for police patrols dried up.

Even when residents were not injured or killed, these crimes had a significant impact on those targeted. In several cases, black residents of Latino neighborhoods had moved to the neighborhood to avoid crime and gang-related behavior in their previous neighborhoods. Their new addresses and the surroundings in Azusa, Torrance, Duarte, and Canoga Park suggested that they would be safe from gang-related violence and death. Being targeted because of their race was a surprise and a shock. The attacks terrified many of the families, who fled the area quickly if they could afford it. After the attacks on her rental house in

Duarte, Channise Davy moved into a hotel. After the subsidy that had allowed her to live in the hotel expired, she said she didn't know what to do but reiterated that she was not returning to the neighborhood.

Like other incidents of anti-integrationist violence, the attacks may have been so terrifying at least in part because of the paucity of African Americans living in the neighborhoods where the attacks occurred. Those targeted, like other hate crime victims, may have felt that they were outnumbered in the area. Take incidents that occurred in Azusa in the early 1990s, and later in 2001. By November 1991, nine hate crimes committed by Latinos against blacks had been reported to the Los Angeles Human Relations Commission.[36] The previous year had seen only two reports of hate crimes of any perpetrator-victim configuration.[37] In 2001, Azusa had a population of roughly forty-eight thousand people, about 60 percent of whom were Latino and only 4 percent of whom identified as African Americans. In 2000, there were thirteen hate crimes, including three firebombings of African Americans' homes. The following year, in 2001, three homemade bombs were thrown into the homes of African American families with children.[38] Given the long history of attacks against African Americans, police investigated the three bombings in 2001 as hate crimes.

The Links between Race-Based Harassment in Los Angeles and Anti-Integrationist Violence Elsewhere

There are important similarities between the violence directed at African Americans in the Los Angeles metropolitan area and incidents of move-in violence occurring in other cities around the country. As chapter 3 describes, hate crime experts classify neighborhood-based hate crimes that fit the pattern of anti-integrationist violence as defensive bias attacks. Defensive bias attacks are committed to protect the offender's neighborhood from intruders. The purpose of these attacks is to force those targeted by the attack to leave. As distinguished from those who commit hate crimes for ideological reasons, offenders may have only a moderate commitment to racial bias or racism.

Racism-based attacks directed at African Americans by Latinos may seem counterintuitive because of the issue of linked fate. There are several reasons to believe that Latinos might perceive linkages in fate between their own group and African Americans. For instance, with respect to figures describing median income, housing, and educational achievement, Latinos have status that is similar to, if not worse than, that of African Americans.[39] In addition, Latinos report experiencing discrimination at rates most similar to that of African Americans.[40] In Los Angeles, Latinos are nearly as segregated as blacks. In order to achieve our random spatial distribution of the population, 68 percent of blacks would need to relocate. For Latinos, this figure is 63 percent.[41]

There is also the issue of being seen unfavorably by other groups, especially whites. Again, there is a similarity between the perception of Latinos and that of African Americans. Survey research has shown as well that whites' views of blacks and Hispanics are both unfavorable. The 1990 General Social Survey, for instance, found that more than 50 percent of whites rated blacks and Hispanics as less intelligent than whites.[42] A similar percentage of white Americans surveyed rated blacks and Hispanics as prone to violence, too.[43] More than two-thirds of whites rated blacks and Hispanics as actually preferring to live off welfare.[44]

Notwithstanding these commonalities between blacks and Latinos, studies of the racial attitudes of Latinos in Los Angeles County and elsewhere reveal that Latinos living in the United States have many negative attitudes toward African Americans. Research on Latino attitudes suggests that Latinos have a preference for maintaining social distance from—i.e., they have little desire to interact with—African Americans.[45] Evidence that Latinos wish to maintain social distance includes Latino preferences for neighborhoods with few African Americans.[46]

Some Latino immigrants may have brought negative stereotypes from their countries of origin. Hutchinson argues that racism toward African Americans among Mexican immigrants stems at least in part from cultural programming in Mexico, where television networks have broadcast American sitcoms and gangster shows that portray African Americans as clowns, buffoons, and crooks.[47] Also quite popular in Mexico was *Memim Pingin,* a cartoon that starred a character possessing "grossly distorted monkeylike features, a bald head and big ears. His mother was a fat bandanna-wearing mammy."[48] Contemporary ads in Mexico sometimes portray individuals in blackface with distorted features—caricatures that in the United States would be considered racist.[49] Of course Mexico is not the only place Latino gang members might have picked up stereotypes about African Americans. For native-born and immigrant Latinos, some of these negative racial attitudes may have been acquired here in the United States as they assimilated and adopted mainstream white culture's negative views toward African Americans.

There is evidence that Latino attacks on African Americans unaffiliated with gangs were motivated by a combination of stereotypes and racist ideology. In 2011 the Justice Department indicted fifty-one members of Azusa 13 for terrorizing blacks. As one former member of the gang who grew up in the neighborhood testified, "We're brainwashed to think that if we let a black family in, then their [gang] cousins are going to come from Compton."[50] There was also some evidence of racist ideology in the gang's targeting of blacks, which is different from other defensive attacks, where offenders generally display little commitment to racist ideology. In Los Angeles, law enforcement officers found neo-Nazi material in the possession of some Latino gang members accused of attacking African Americans in Harbor Gateway.[51] Law enforcement reports also indicated that some Latino gangs have been linked to white supremacist groups known for attacking blacks in prison.

The randomness of the attacks against African Americans in Los Angeles and the rhetoric employed during many of them suggest that, as in incidents of move-in violence in other areas of the country, these have many of the characteristics of defensive attacks. As such, those attacked were not targeted because their behavior violated the neighborhood's social norms but rather because their very presence in the area was offensive. The attacks seem to have been motivated in part by suspicion that African Americans would bring harm to the neighborhood. The idea that African Americans moving in cause harm to the neighborhood, however, is speculative rather than empirical. Like other incidents of anti-integrationist violence in white neighborhoods around the country, it is not as if those who were targeted had behaved in a manner that invited attack. In many cases, the attack began soon after the individual had moved to the neighborhood, so the perpetrator had not had time to assess the new arrival's conduct. In addition, it was rare that the perpetrator of the violence had any direct contact with the individual targeted prior to the attack(s).

Most cases of African Americans targeted by anti-integrationist violence seem almost fungible. Rather than having "provoked"—even

unintentionally—the attacks, almost any African American moving into that particular space is just as likely to be attacked. As in struggles in Yonkers, Canarsie, and other areas that similarly rejected an African American presence, African Americans moving to particular Latino neighborhoods in Los Angeles were moving in on another ethnic group's territory. This has important consequences for African Americans' freedom, personal safety, and housing rights. When just being black is a violation of territorial boundaries, there is nothing African Americans can do to avoid being targeted besides move to another area. Because it is impossible for individuals to change their race, if they remain in the area they are always vulnerable to attack.

Demographic Changes as a Trigger

There is significant research to suggest that defensive hate crimes are associated with demographic shifts.[52] The black presence in Los Angeles was small until the early 1940s. Attracted by the mobilization for World War II, the city's black population increased from 63,744 in 1940 to 233,082 in 1946.[53] This increase in the black population sparked anxiety and conflict among many whites, though not necessarily people of other racial groups, because African Americans, Latinos, and Asian Americans had a history of interacting relatively peacefully and even occasionally forming political coalitions.[54] Peaceful interaction among African Americans, Asian Americans, and Latinos continued with their involvement in the war industry. The black population in Los Angeles continued to grow, but even black and Latino gangs existed in relative peace before the 1990s.

By the early 1990s, however, significant demographic changes were afoot. The 1990 census revealed a sudden influx of low-income refugees and immigrants into some of the city's most economically depressed neighborhoods. There was a significant (62 percent) increase in the number of Latinos in the Los Angeles area since 1980. By 1990, the expanding Latino population had begun to overtake black majorities in traditionally black areas like Watts and several other areas of South Central Los Angeles, and had even begun to challenge black majorities in other areas of the San Fernando Valley. By contrast, the black population in the county as a whole had decreased (see table 4.2).

Table 4.2
Racial Demographic Trends in Los Angeles County, CA, 1980–2000

	1980		1990		2000	
Race		%		%		%
Black	943,968	12.6	992,974	11.2	930,957	9.7
Latino	2,066,103	27.6	3,351,242	37.8	4,242,213	44.6
Asian	434,850	5.8	954,485	10.8	1,137,500	10.3
White	5,073,617	67.9	5,035,103	56.8	4,637,062	29.6

Sources: US Census Bureau, "General Population Statistics: California," Table 15, Persons by Race: 1980, accessed November 15, 2012, http://www2.census.gov/prod2/decennial/documents/1980a_caAB-03.pdf ; "1990 Census of Population and Housing, Age by Race and Hispanic Origin," accessed November 5, 2012, http://censtats.census.gov/pl94/pl94.shtml; "Census 2000 Summary File 1 (SF 1) 100-Percent Data," Los Angeles County, California, accessed November 5, 2012, http://factfinder2.census.gov/bkmk/table/1.0/en/DEC/00_SF1/DP1/0500000US06037.

Note: Starting in 2000, a "two or more races" category was utilized instead of single-race options only; this likely caused some superficial demographic changes in the data between 1990 and 2000.

Even more significant than the decrease in the black population in Los Angeles County overall were the neighborhood-to-neighborhood demographic shifts. Blacks left South Los Angeles, Inglewood, and Compton in search of better housing and to escape gang war zones. Because the African American population in the county overall did not significantly change, these individuals are likely to have moved to Latino neighborhoods, since Latino neighborhoods showed significant increases in their black population. In some of these neighborhoods, African Americans who had recently moved in were targeted. For instance, in Harbor Gateway, where Cheryl Green was killed, between 1990 and 2000 the neighborhood's African American population more than doubled, from 313 in 1982 to 835 in 2000.[55] Between 1980 and 1990, the mostly Latino city of Azusa, where several black families had been targeted, experienced a 238 percent increase in the black population. In the predominantly Latino neighborhood of Highland Park, where the Avenues gang was prosecuted for attacking African Americans, census records showed that the African American population had increased, albeit slowly. In 1990, there were 1,246 African Americans in Highland Park; the 2000 census records showed that 1,974 lived in the area.[56]

These increases did not mean that the African American population was threatening to overtake the number of Latinos in these neighborhoods. For instance, in Azusa, which experienced the 238 percent increase in the black population between 1980 and 1990, blacks were still just 4 percent, or 1,632 individuals out of a population of 40,819, which included 26,124 Latinos.[57] Nevertheless, there is reason to believe that even a small increase of African Americans in a neighborhood that was once exclusively Latino may have caused Latino gang members to worry that they were losing ground. According to one gang member, "in jail, people would comment, 'the blacks took over your neighborhood' . . . it's embarrassing because it's true." Evidently, African Americans moving in were associated with change in the neighborhood. Before blacks moved in, the neighborhood had been "kind of like a little TJ [referring to Tijuana]. . . . People would say, 'hey what's up?' Or offer a beer. You got tamales. Drugs. It was a great neighborhood for gang members."[58]

Moving beyond the Defensive Hate Crime Label: Gangs and Disadvantaged Neighborhoods

Identifying the attacks on African Americans simply as defensive hate crimes does not capture the full picture, however. There are also significant differences that characterize the incidents in Los Angeles. One major difference between incidents of anti-integrationist violence in white neighborhoods around the country and those directed at African Americans in predominantly Latino neighborhoods in Los Angeles is that in other areas of the country the attacks were committed by unaffiliated and, in the contemporary era, largely unorganized individuals. In Los Angeles, the attacks on African Americans were committed by organized groups, street gangs. Officials with the Justice Department said that the hate crime charges brought against Latino gangs were the first uses of civil rights statutes against an organized group since such charges had been brought against the various Ku Klux Klan organizations.[59] The gang aspect of these particular acts of anti-integrationist violence created significant challenges, some of which harken back to issues raised when the Ku Klux Klan was involved in hate crime activity.

Another piece of the story is that many of the incidents of anti-integrationist violence directed at African Americans in Los Angeles occurred in disadvantaged neighborhoods. For instance, in the mid- to late 1990s, Harbor Gateway, where several attacks on African Americans, including the murder of Cheryl Green, occurred, was an economically distressed neighborhood, populated largely by rundown bungalows and many Section 8–eligible apartment units. There was a paucity of city services, and landlords invested little in their properties. The area had no parks or schools nearby. Police patrols were scarce. Research on violence in economically distressed areas suggests that inner-city neighborhoods that lack the conventional status symbols like school achievement and jobs are where violent subcultures arise. In such locales residents begin to substitute acts of violence and intimidation, shows of nerve and courage, and displays of manhood and honor for traditional status markers.[60] In the violent subcultures that characterize many disadvantaged neighborhoods, status may be allocated on the basis of violent acts against outsiders in the neighborhood, who are sometimes members of other racial groups.[61] This code was espoused by young Latino men on the streets, as it reinforced manhood that had been denied by lack of opportunity to attain traditional status symbols.

In Harbor Gateway, attacks against African Americans can be interpreted not only as defensive hate crimes but also as typical reactions to the violations of the subculture norms requiring open displays of respect. Latino gang members frequently perceived African Americans living in the neighborhood as not respecting Latinos. As one gang member said, after they moved into Harbor Gateway, blacks were "writing on the walls, hurling bottles at us and telling on us at the same time."[62] In the neighborhood's violent subculture, lack of respect demands retaliation, not just against individual violators but against the entire community. The gang member continued, "that's kind of disrespectful . . . so [we are] going to shoot every black guy up there."[63]

In some cases in Los Angeles, purported lack of respect led to retaliation against individual African Americans who had been viewed as not respecting Latino primacy in the neighborhood. Take, for instance, Christopher Browser, the young African American man mentioned earlier in this chapter, who moved to Harbor Gateway in 1995. Browser frequently walked the streets of Highland Park carrying a boom box blasting rap—i.e., *black*—music. One gang member said that Browser was acting as if "the neighborhood was *his* neighborhood."[64] Trying to enforce deference, members of the Avenues gang repeatedly beat Browser, calling him "mayate"—Spanish slang for "nigger." They also tried to run him down with a car, robbed him, and threatened to kill him if he didn't leave. Seemingly resistant to their threats, Browser continued to play music in this manner for five years, until he was gunned down at a bus stop by gang members.[65]

Closely connected to the issue of respect is that of loyalty and honor. The code of honor demanded allegiance to the community and blanket refusal to betray that community by cooperating with the police. Violations of these norms of honor often had violent consequences.[66] Latino gang members saw blacks as more willing to go to the authorities than were Latino residents. Certainly some African Americans reported crimes committed by Latino gang members to the police. For example, black gang members were willing to cooperate with the police, which Latino gang members viewed as dishonorable. Latino gangs transformed this lack of loyalty into a crime for which all African Americans should pay.

Other issues having to do with the larger purpose of the enterprise affect members' activities. Part of the motivation for attacking African Americans (even those who had no gang affiliation) in Latino neighborhoods had to do with the presence of black gangs and competition for the drug trade. Though Latino and black gangs had once peacefully coexisted, that all changed in the early 1990s, when members of the then much smaller 204th Street gang began to interact with members of La Eme, a Mexican Mafia prison gang.[67] La Eme felt that African American gangs were competition and directed Latino gangs to stop fighting among themselves and expel any black members. In addition to eradicating blacks from the gang, the Mexican Mafia also ordered the 204th Street gang, according to the gang expert who testified at the murder trial of one 204th Street gang member, to "purify" the neighborhood.[68] Gang members paid attention to the Mexican Mafia's edicts because if a gang member went to jail, he or she might have to answer to La Eme.[69]

Carried out by smaller Latino gangs, the Mexican Mafia's racial policies began affecting African Americans' lives in Latino neighborhoods. Smaller gangs' obedience to the Mexican Mafia was entirely rational. Aside from individual gang members' desire to gain protection from the Mafia in the event they went to jail, there was a clear organizational incentive to engage in violence against blacks. Violence targeted at blacks—even individuals with absolutely no relationship to gangs— received kudos from the Mexican Mafia. As one Latino gang member related, when the 204th Street gang "lit off a grenade, or burned [a black person's] house down," La Eme representatives "would be like, 'that's what I'm talking about.'"[70]

Conclusion

There have been several major conflicts between non–gang-affiliated Latinos and African Americans in Los Angeles. These have occurred in the form of fights between blacks and Latinos in the first decade of the twenty-first century at several Los Angeles–area high schools, and wide-scale tension over Latino immigration into South Central, a Los Angeles neighborhood that was once occupied predominantly by African Americans. There is no evidence, however, that the violence described in this chapter—the targeting of African Americans in predominantly Latino neighborhoods by Latino gang members—was supported by the nonaffiliated Latino residents. Because gangs, which had a track record of committing violent attacks, were the perpetrators, it is unsurprising that there is little evidence of support from non–gang-affiliated neighborhood residents. Given how much loyalty mattered to gangs, it would have been hard for non–gang-affiliated Latinos to show public support for the targeted African Americans.

Even though the context is different when white residents attack minorities who are moving to white neighborhoods, Latino gang members' attacks on African Americans in Los Angeles have important lessons applicable to other contexts. Broadly speaking, when one ethnic group dominates a particular neighborhood, later entrants to the neighborhood may be seen as challengers to the dominant group's power and privilege. In the case of Latinos in Los Angeles, it was the incursions into Latino neighborhoods by African Americans that served to threaten members of Latino gangs. Seen this way, hate crimes become not just a mechanism for controlling the "face" of the neighborhood but also a powerful method of dealing with fear posed by the threat of change and ultimately reinscribing social dominance.

5

When Class Trumps Race

Explaining Perpetrator Motivation in Interclass Cases

Scholars discussing behavior that fits the anti-integrationist violence mold have focused closely on offenders' racial attitudes. It makes intuitive sense to assume that offenders would single out minorities for attack because they dislike them. In this chapter, I turn the lens to another defining characteristic of many acts of anti-integrationist violence that may offer clues to perpetrator motivation—socioeconomic class. Many incidents of anti-integrationist violence have occurred in working-class white neighborhoods, such as Canarsie and Bensonhurst in Brooklyn, and in South Boston. Highly publicized incidents occurring in these neighborhoods raise the specter that working-class whites may be more likely to resist minorities moving in than those living in middle-class or upper-class white neighborhoods. I also consider the socioeconomic class of those moving in. In several cases around the country, attempts to place public housing in middle- and upper-class white neighborhoods have been quite controversial. In both situations, one could argue that the perpetrators' actions are motivated by the targets' social class, or status, and not necessarily their race.

Working-Class Perpetrators from White Working-Class Neighborhoods

As chapter 2 highlights, anti-integrationist violence has been found in white neighborhoods in many different areas of the country. Previous chapters have focused on incidents of hate crime directed at minorities moving to working-class white ethnic neighborhoods. One particularly compelling explanation for violence toward African Americans committed specifically by working-class whites is the group position model of prejudice. This model asserts that a measure of a specific group's prejudice toward members of another group is captured by the extent to which members of other groups are viewed as a competitive threat.[1] Research has suggested that white working-class individuals' prejudice stems from a sense of competition with African Americans.

Predominately white blue-collar ethnic neighborhoods have come to be referred to as defended neighborhoods, described by the Chicago School sociologist Gerald Suttles as a residential area that "seals itself off through the efforts of delinquent gangs, by restrictive covenants, by sharp boundaries or by a forbidding reputation."[2] Suttles departs from earlier analyses of white ethnic neighborhoods by the sociologists Robert E. Park and Ernest W. Burgess, noting that though they often contain many members of the same ethnic group, defended neighborhoods do not need to be ethnically homogeneous to be stable.[3] Instead, stability comes from the geographic boundaries of the neighborhood. Residents of defended neighborhoods are often primed to react to a lurking threat. The threat has various forms, ranging from minority integration to urban decay.

A cohesive identity makes it easier to see outsiders as threatening. Ethnographers of blue-collar urban neighborhoods describe residents as having a very strong sense of place.[4] The residents know what they want to defend. The Beltway, a working-class neighborhood in Chicago, was such a place. According to the sociologist Maria Kefalas, "The people of the Beltway seem to share a collective understanding of how their place ought to look and, in a philosophical sense, how its residents ought to be. . . . Individuals who violate the landscape—and that includes other working-class whites—become the object of scorn and derision."[5] Often such neighborhoods act as a cohesive community where residents are tied to each other through large networks, common ethnic, racial, and class backgrounds, and community organizations. They also frequently interact with one another. Whether because of the ethnic ties within the community, the neighborhood's history, or the neighborhood's neat bungalows, residents maintain a very fierce pride about living in the area.

Several ethnographies have explored the issues of white identity in working-class white ethnic neighborhoods that are populated by immigrants and/or the children and grandchildren of immigrants who have Jewish, Irish, Italian, Polish, and other Eastern European backgrounds. These studies of working-class neighborhoods, particularly those located in very large cities such as New York, Boston, and Chicago, reveal that many of the residents saw themselves as possessing a common identity of whiteness that was at least in part created in response to the difference between themselves and outsiders.[6] In these places most residents shared a particular ethnic identity, race, and class, and those were ties that bound them to their neighbors and the rest of their community. Kefalas captures this in her description of the closed nature of identity in the Beltway: "Beltway is probably not the easiest place to live if you are gay, poor, neither working nor lower middle class, overly educated, unmarried, or not Catholic. Not 'fitting in' in the Beltway can make life fairly complicated, if not downright uncomfortable."[7]

Particularly in urban ethnic neighborhoods, individuals of different ethnic backgrounds or different classes were united in some sort of generic "whiteness" in response to the blackness of those moving in. Uniting around whiteness against blackness allowed both ethnic and class differences among groups of whites in the same neighborhood to diminish in importance. What really mattered to the residents of these neighborhoods was defending their neighborhoods against outsiders who were identified as nonwhites.

Defending Working-Class Neighborhoods

In order for violence to be associated with racial and ethnic minorities integrating white neighborhoods, the neighborhood must be defended—whites must resist minorities moving to the neighborhood with acts of violence. Beginning in 1998, social scientists began to use census and hate crime data to evaluate both group conflict and the defended neighborhood thesis. The first scholarly examination of the defended neighborhood thesis, by Donald Green, Dara Strolovitch, and Janelle Wong, examined police reports of racially motivated anti-minority crimes in the New York City area between 1987 and 1995.[8] Although ethnically diverse overall in 1990, New York was a good location to study because it contained several predominantly white neighborhoods, such as Sheepshead Bay in Brooklyn. According to Green and his colleagues, in 1990 Sheepshead Bay was 84 percent white, 7 percent Asian American, 6 percent Latino, and just 2 percent black.[9]

Green and his coauthors compared incidents classified and investigated as racially motivated bias crimes with census data showing racial change for Asian Americans, African Americans, and Latinos between 1980 and 1990 in a selection of predominantly white neighborhoods in Queens, Brooklyn, and the Bronx. To test whether a large percentage of whites in an area were threatened by minorities moving in, Green and his colleagues used census data to calculate the change in the black, Latino, and Asian American population proportions in the neighborhoods they were studying. Comparing this data with hate crime data in each of the areas being studied, Green and his colleagues found that anti-minority crime was correlated with increases in Asian American, Latino, and black migration to neighborhoods. It was not just that numbers of hate crimes increased as the number of minorities in the city as a whole grew. Green and his colleagues were careful to link increases in hate crime directly to change in the composition of formerly white neighborhoods. Increases in hate crime against each of the groups "hinged on the spatial arrangement of population growth, in particular, the extent to which newcomers cross into areas where whites have traditionally been numerically dominant."[10]

Following the work of Green, Strolovitch, and Wong, scholars tried to replicate the research in other cities, hoping to evaluate the reach of the defended neighborhood thesis—that many more bias crimes would occur in homogeneous white neighborhoods in the process of integration. Evaluating the defended neighborhood hypothesis in Sacramento, California, Ryken Grattet compared predominately white Sacramento neighborhoods that were integrating with more mixed neighborhoods and found that homogeneous white neighborhoods to which a large number of nonwhites moved had twice as many bias crimes as expected in comparison to neighborhoods not in the process of integration. In mixed neighborhoods, nonwhite in-migration in Sacramento was associated with a *lower* rate of bias crimes.[11]

Another study evaluating the defended neighborhood thesis in Chicago used similar data obtained from the city's police department's hate crime unit and compared both antiblack and antiwhite hate crimes in neighborhoods between 1997 and 2002. This research was different in that it also compared attachment to neighborhood by using research that probed individual neighborhood identity using community surveys. The author found that antiblack incidents were most common in traditionally homogeneous white communities to which blacks were moving, particularly when residents in such neighborhoods had lived there for a long time and possessed the ability to recognize outsiders.[12] Attempting perhaps to explain perpetrators' motives, the author, Christopher Lyons, offered a rationale for neighborhood hate crimes: "[U]nder conditions of change, hate crimes against blacks are a strategy for reasserting order, and maintaining racial divisions."[13]

Attempts to replicate the defended neighborhood thesis have also used national hate crime data collected in the Uniform Crime Reporting (UCR) *Hate Crimes Statistics*, which uses data collected by the US attorney general from state and local law enforcement. Using UCR data from 1998, 1999, and 2000, the sociologist Ami Lynch analyzed hate crime levels in neighborhoods around the country based on their dissimilarity indices computed from 2000 census data. Lynch's results demonstrated a significant relationship between hate crime and segregation. She found that cities located in the Northeast or the South, with higher rates of hate crime, an increased level of mobility, and more white segregation in 1990 had higher levels of white-black dissimilarity.[14] Cities with higher levels of hate crime thus had higher levels of housing segregation.[15]

Group Conflict in Defended Neighborhoods

Studying the dynamics of neighborhood interaction, social scientists have posited a number of theories to explain what happens when minorities' moves to white neighborhoods are resisted. Power and group conflict theory is predicated on the idea that as a group, whites do not wish to live in neighborhoods with minorities because they prefer to keep social distance between themselves and racial minorities.[16] A desire to protect these group interests makes whites worry about minorities moving to their neighborhood, especially when whites feel threats made to their dominance in a neighborhood.[17] Using this rationale, one can categorize acts of violence directed at minorities who are moving in as reactions to a perceived threat.

Residents of white neighborhoods that are integrated may feel threatened by a variety of factors. In many cases, by the 1980s many white working-class neighborhoods were on the decline, with residents facing rising unemployment, increasing poverty, and problems from drugs.[18] Residents also faced increased competition from in-migration of racial and ethnic minorities seeking both work and housing. The disappearing manufacturing sector and the restructuring of many cities' economies hit many inner-city white working-class neighborhoods and their residents quite hard. In Dubuque, Iowa, in the late 1980s, the unemployment rate soared to 10 percent, more than double the state's overall unemployment rate.[19] Some residents' resistance to the city's plan to diversify by bringing in minorities from the outside, expressed in the form of a number of cross burnings, may have been prompted by economic concerns. One unemployed firefighter commented, "I can't get a job and now I want someone else to come in and compete against me? Let's take care of those already here."[20] South Boston, discussed in the next section, was in the midst of a severe economic downturn as it faced minority integration. Frequently called the poorest white urban enclave in the country, South Boston saw a rash of drug overdoses and suicides in the late 1990s, adding to the poverty and unemployment the residents already faced.[21] This situation did not improve in the first decade of the twenty-first century. In 2009, the US economy faced one of the biggest recessions since the Great Depression, and unemployment achieved record heights, adding significantly to tension over jobs.

Living in neighborhoods facing difficult economic conditions with fewer employment prospects may have made working-class white men anxious to defend their position in the hierarchy. Their communities' racism, combined with feelings of competitiveness toward African Americans, made working-class whites more likely to greet newcomers to their neighborhoods with violence. Interviews with the perpetrators suggest that committing defensive hate crimes against newcomers has much to do with the inadequacies young men in lower-middle-class communities feel themselves. In Bensonhurst, an Italian neighborhood in southern Brooklyn, working-class white men would drink for several hours, then go on "missions" looking for individuals to beat up or harass in defense of the neighborhood. Their primary targets were

African Americans, though if none were available they would beat up Dominicans, Pakistanis, or Indians. Three of the youths offered a sense of their motivation:

> VINNIE: You go on missions to impress your friends. You get a name as a tough guy who's down with the neighborhood and down with his people.
> RONNIE: You prove you're a real Bensonhurst Italian who don't take no shit, who doesn't let the wrong kind of people into the neighborhood.
> ROCCO: You do it 'cause you want to be cool.[22]

These statements suggest that in addition to bolstering their own self-esteem, committing hate crimes against minorities bolstered the youth in their larger community and among their friends.

African Americans and other minorities were viewed as a threat not just because they were seen as competing for scarce jobs, but because their moving in symbolized a change in the white neighborhood residents' way of life. Many of the neighborhoods in which blacks have been targeted for violence—Brooklyn's Bensonhurst, Gravesend, Sheepshead Bay, and Canarsie—had once been dominated by second- and third-generation families of European immigrants, including Poles, Lithuanians, Germans, Italians, and Irish. By the 1990s, many of the residents lived in the neighborhood as a result of their own or their parents' flight from similar neighborhoods some thirty or forty years before, when African Americans, Asian Americans, and West Indians began to move in. Having previously fled minority entry, residents of these white working-class neighborhoods adopted a siege mentality and worried that they might again be put in a position where they felt that they needed to move. African Americans in working-class neighborhoods came to symbolize "a direct threat to the quality of the neighborhood life, as intruders who had the potential to ruin the stable, close-knit, safe, ethnic niche the white community had taken years to establish."[23] Racial attacks in working-class white neighborhoods became a way, in the minds of the attackers, to simultaneously prop themselves up and mount a vigorous defense of "their" turf and ethnic culture. In a sense, then, neighborhood defense was prompted as much by threat as by some white residents' attachment to their neighborhood.

Not Quite Brotherly Love: Philadelphia's
Working-Class White Neighborhoods

The same form of anti-minority sentiment that African Americans faced in and around Bensonhurst and other Brooklyn neighborhood in the 1990s was duplicated in several high-profile incidents in Philadelphia's working-class neighborhoods of Fishtown, Bridesburg, and Grays Ferry, which have long had a troubled racial history. These "river" communities were filled with aging, tiny row houses spread over three levels, with one or two rooms per level, where houses were shared with several families and sometimes divided up into rooming houses.[24] Working-class white neighborhoods like Fishtown, Bridesburg, and Grays Ferry remained white throughout the 1960s, 1970s, and 1980s, despite racial transitions in more affluent neighboring communities.

In an era of declining manufacturing, neighborhoods like Bridesburg, Fishtown, and Grays Ferry, which shared a manufacturing presence, were attractive to African Americans. Upon trying to move in, however, they were quickly rebuffed. Bridesburg, which is also known as Kirkbridesburg, was named for a ferry operator and bridge owner, Joseph Kirkbride, in 1843.[25] Boxed in by the highway, with a cemetery and several industrial businesses, Bridesburg was an isolated white working-class neighborhood located along the Delaware River, north of Frankford Creek. In the mid-1990s, several incidents were directed at minorities who had moved to the neighborhood. In one case, a black woman who moved to Bridesburg in the summer of 1995 had a living room window shattered by an M-80 firecracker and later found scrawled on a piece of paper stuck to her front door the words "Die Nigger." Another well-publicized case involved Bridget Ward, a black woman who was harassed the moment she moved to Bridesburg in 1996. As she was moving in, her next-door neighbor let her know that she did not belong in the neighborhood because she was black. That night, someone scrawled racist graffiti on her front door, windows, and front porch. Ketchup, perhaps to simulate blood, was left on both the front and back porches. As Ward walked about the neighborhood she was assaulted with racial epithets. She decided to move after a letter was sent threatening her family. News reports suggest that several of Ward's neighbors were happy to see her go. Dan Collins, a dock worker who lived just down the block from where Ward lived, told reporters when asked about Ward's leaving, "The fact is that you see other neighborhoods change and you see that minorities are the ones in them. We have a good thing here. Crime is low. There are no murders around here. We want to keep it that way. This is a little tight neighborhood."[26]

The incidents directed at minorities who had moved to Bridesburg were similar to those that had happened in nearby Fishtown, also a working-class white neighborhood on the Delaware River. In 1990, approximately 97 percent of Fishtown's almost ten thousand residents were white.[27] Many of the residents were descendants of Irish, Polish, and German Catholic immigrants, whose families had been in the neighborhood for several generations. Decidedly working-class in the mid-1990s, it was populated by office and factory workers, contractors, and salesmen, with the median household income just over $25,000.[28] Like several other working-class white neighborhoods in the mid-1990s plagued with poverty, drugs, unemployment, and a high dropout rate, Fishtown also had a legacy of racism. It was in this environment that in September 1994, a thirty-nine-year-old deaf black woman, Joan Smith, and her son were severely beaten by white neighbors who broke into their home. As Smith, who suffered two broken legs in the attack, and her son were beaten, the assailants shouted racial slurs.[29] This was not the first incident for the Smiths. A Molotov cocktail had been thrown through their windows soon after they had moved in.[30]

Another notable incident directed at a minority attempting to move to a working-class neighborhood in the 1990s in Philadelphia was the 1996 vandalizing of a house in a South Philadelphia neighborhood to prevent Samantha Starnes from becoming the first black to move to a block populated by two-story row houses.[31] At the trial on federal charges, one of the perpetrators testified that he and a neighbor had fired pellet guns at the windows and crammed the door locks with putty to send a "warning" to realtors who might be inclined to show the house to African Americans. The house, which was vacant at the time, was also flooded hours before Starnes was supposed to move in. Starnes elected not to occupy the house.

Bridget Ward, Joan Smith, and Samantha Starnes were hit very hard soon after they moved to working-class white neighborhoods in Philadelphia. What explains such resistance to women whose race (black) and gender (female) signaled vulnerability and lack of power? In addition, initially all were renters, rather than home purchasers. In these cases, as in the case of many minorities who move to working-class neighborhoods, these women's presence was resisted because they were signifiers; in fact, their own powerlessness was irrelevant to their attackers, who were already quite vulnerable. In these cases, the women were attacked because their moving in suggested the possibility of racial transition—white flight and the turn of their neighborhood from working-class white to black.

As a city, Philadelphia had a long tradition of racial transition. In the wake of World War II with an increase in mortgage capital and housing, Philadelphia's housing stock increased substantially. Much of the growth was in suburban, Levitt-style housing. Over time the population remaining in the working-class white neighborhoods within the city aged and grew smaller as many of the younger city residents sought both housing and employment outside the city. Demographers estimate that from 1960 to 1977, more than two hundred thousand whites left the city of Philadelphia. During this time period, only twenty thousand blacks left.[32]

Despite rapid racial transition of many white neighborhoods in West Philadelphia and North Philadelphia, some communities remained predominately white. This was true despite two factors that might have led to substantial decline in these neighborhoods. First, these were primarily industrial neighborhoods in a city dominated by white blue-collar workers. There had been significant industrial decline within the city; between 1955 and 1975 three out of every four industrial jobs were lost.[33] In addition, many of these neighborhoods were located in close proximity to large black populations. Nevertheless, tight ethnic neighborhoods, like Fishtown, Grays Ferry, Kensington, and Bridesburg, experienced less than average out-migration of white residents, and "blacks made few inroads."[34]

It was not for want of trying that blacks failed to permeate white working-class neighborhoods. The resistance to minorities moving to working-class neighborhoods in Philadelphia stemmed from a variety of factors, including racism, white residents' economic uncertainty, and finally the desire to close boundaries against the outside. The racist roots of the attempts to drive minorities out of working-class neighborhoods were clear from the slurs used by perpetrators, both during their acts of vandalism and when they were speaking to or about the targets. In the case of Edward Majors, who pled guilty to his role in preventing Samantha Starnes from purchasing a house in his South Philadelphia neighborhood, racial epithets were even used when he was testifying in the trial of the neighbor who had assisted him. Majors indicated that he did not want African Americans living next door. Majors also provided another explanation for his antipathy for blacks that was shared by others (working-class or not): an African American presence in the neighborhood depresses real estate property values.

Several crimes aimed at minorities who moved or attempted to move to working-class white neighborhoods were frequently well publicized and may have provided a disincentive for blacks to move to white neighborhoods. If such incidents were not enough, Philadelphia had a history of racially tense incidents involving attacks on blacks, which likely made both blacks and whites wary of interracial contact.[35] For instance, one well-publicized incident that caused significant racial tension involved two black men, Raheem and Warren Williams, who indicated that they were attacked and beaten by a group of white men leaving a parish church. The incident, which garnered national attention, spawned protests and prompted a march though Grays Ferry, attended by the mayor of Philadelphia and the Nation of Islam leader Louis Farrakhan.[36]

With respect to class in particular, examining anti-integrationist violence in Philadelphia may shed light on whether, and for what reason, such incidents may be more likely to occur in working-class neighborhoods. In 1980 whites living in Philadelphia neighborhoods where individuals had the highest level of education and occupational status were more likely also to be integrated. The political scientist Carolyn Adams and her colleagues tested 316 racial incidents reported to the Philadelphia Human Relations Commission in 1986 based on location and a variety of other factors, and found that the most important explanations for racial tension were the racial composition of the area—specifically, the percentage of whites in the area—and loss of manufacturing jobs.[37] White neighborhoods in which there had been a large number of jobs lost were more likely to have racial incidents. "When those communities are invaded or threatened by the migration of other racial or ethnic groups, their weakened economic competitiveness is transformed into community solidarity and conflict."[38] Minorities moving to working-class white communities like Fishtown, Bridesburg, and Grays Ferry were attacked because they were perceived as a threat.

No Housing Developments in Yonkers

In the early 1980s Yonkers, in New York's Westchester County, was a city of 188,000 people located just north of the Bronx. It was a racially divided city (and remained so, to some extent, twenty years later), with four ethnically distinct quadrants: Northeast, Northwest, Southeast, and Southwest. At the time, the vast majority of the city's nearly seven thousand public housing units were located in the southwest portion of the city. The majority of the city's African American residents lived in these housing projects, or in areas immediately surrounding the developments. None of the city's housing projects were located in the virtually all-white Southeast or Northeast Yonkers, which were heavily populated by Irish and Italian Americans. Yonkers public schools were similarly divided, with the vast majority being either almost exclusively white or almost exclusively minority. A suit brought by the federal government in the early 1980s, *United States v. Yonkers*, alleged that the city and the Yonkers school board had deliberately created the racial segregation in Yonkers public schools and housing. In 1985, Judge Leonard B. Sand of the US District Court in Manhattan ordered the city of Yonkers to remedy this by, among other things, locating two hundred units of public housing outside the city's southwest quadrant.[39]

In January 1988, the Yonkers city council met to approve the list of sites for the new housing. Nine hundred Yonkers residents appeared at the meeting. In a dramatic show of resistance during the five-hour meeting, white residents screamed and pleaded in an effort to avoid having the sites located in their neighborhoods. At one point in the meeting, after the mayor indicated that the city would follow the judicial decree ordering that the public housing be located in white neighborhoods, the crowd attempted to rush the stage. Several in the crowd had to be restrained by police officers.[40] Immediately after that city council decision, residents began protesting at City Hall. Council members' offices also received bomb threats and death threats. Residents organized a "Save Yonkers Federation" from a coalition of neighbor-hood associations. Over the next several months there were countless rallies opposing the townhouses, which residents argued would lower property values, cause crime, and lead to white flight.[41]

Despite residents' opposition, after many alterations of the plan, pub-lic housing was built in several working- and middle-class white neigh-borhoods in Yonkers. By 1993 construction was completed on the first two hundred low-income units.[42] In sharp contrast to the high-rise–style public housing located in black neighborhoods in Yonkers, the new units were scattered sites—much smaller buildings—that took the form in Yonkers of 800- and 1,000-square-foot single-family row houses. They were designed by the public housing architect Oscar Newman spe-cifically to fit into the neighborhoods in which they were placed.[43] The individual units had exposed brick fronts, bay windows, and front and back yards. Eighty percent of those who occupied the first units were black, 15 percent were Hispanic, and 5 percent were white.[44]

The legal battle to desegregate public housing in Yonkers dragged on for nearly three decades. The final settlement agreement was signed in 2007, when the city of Yonkers completed the last unit of low-income housing under the court order.[45] Despite the long-drawn-out legal battle, important measures of success were seen almost immediately. Compared to those who had remained in the old public housing in the southeast portion of the city, residents who moved to the new housing worried less about safety.[46] In addition, the families who moved expe-rienced fewer problems with abuse or violence, and were also twice as likely to find jobs.[47] Researchers statistically investigated the issue of the decline in property values after the units were built and found that no generalized price effect could be attributed to the development.[48] Few discernible price effects may have occurred because in Yonkers the developments triggered relatively little white flight.[49]

The fact that many of the white residents stayed after their neigh-borhood became more integrated doesn't necessarily mean that social integration had been achieved in Yonkers. Black and white residents interviewed several years after the move-ins indicated that, despite liv-ing in the neighborhood together, there was little mixing of old and new residents. One black resident likened the separation to a line in the middle of the street separating the public housing from the rest of the neighborhood. "It was a racial thing. . . . We were black, and they had the old ways. They weren't hostile; they weren't used to the idea of a housing project."[50]

For their part, though they agreed that their fears of neighborhood decline had largely not come to pass, the white residents who spoke to the press were not especially warm to the public housing residents' presence in the neighborhood. Some expressed resentment over the assistance provided to public housing residents. As one white resident who had organized her neighbors to fight the placement of a housing development a few blocks away explained, "We had to go out and earn the money to buy our houses. . . . They [the public housing tenants] were *given* these houses."[51] Ultimately, despite the expressed resentment and grudging acceptance, white residents of Yonkers were far more accepting of minorities than were many residents in two Irish and Italian working-class neighborhoods in nearby Boston.

Keeping Public Housing White in Boston

In some working-class defended neighborhoods, like Yonkers or Bensonhurst, African Americans lived nearby in public housing developments, so neighborhood defense was primarily concerned with keeping them out of the apartments or single-family housing in the neighborhood. In other neighborhoods, however, neighborhood defense was focused on keeping African Americans out of white housing developments inside the predominantly white neighborhoods. An illuminating example can be seen in Boston, where residents of two working-class white neighborhoods, South Boston and Charlestown, strongly resisted attempts to move minorities into segregated public housing units.

That public housing in these two neighborhoods remained white until the early 1990s was unsurprising. South Boston, a working-class predominantly Irish neighborhood, had a history of racial tension. In the mid-1970s, the neighborhood received national attention for its violent reaction to a federal judge's busing plan. In response to a suit by black parents, community leaders, and the NAACP, US District Judge W. Arthur Garrity's plan ordered, among other things, whites from Charlestown and South Boston to be bussed to schools in the predominantly black neighborhood of Roxbury, and African Americans to be bussed predominantly to white public schools in South Boston and Charlestown. In response to the judge's plan, white residents of both neighborhoods organized and protested. Hundreds marched on Beacon Hill, joining thousands gathered on the Boston Common singing, "[O] ur kids aren't going over there!"[52] One of the most violent of the incidents associated with busing occurred on the first day of school in September 1974, when crowds in South Boston attacked the school buses carrying African American children, throwing eggs, beer bottles, soda cans, and rocks. Windows shattered, and nine children were injured.[53] Tension left the schools by the late 1970s, but soon spilled over into the neighborhoods.[54]

In 1978, just four years after Judge Garrity's order desegregating Boston's public schools, Faith Evans, a black pre-med student at Brandeis University, agreed to move into the virtually all-white Mary Ellen McCormack housing project in South Boston. Evans moved in under police protection. Tenants in the complex were up in arms, and several hundred threatened a rent strike because Evans was allowed to move in. James Kelly, president of an active anti-busing organization called the South Boston Information Center, watched along with several other residents as Evans moved in, commenting, "She'll never be an acceptable member of the South Boston community. She'll always be the black person who's guarded." The twenty-year-old Evans lived in an apartment with her ten-month-old son for just eight months before her departure, which was attributed to harassment and the torching of a friend's car.[55]

South Boston wasn't the only place where the Boston Housing Authority had trouble moving minorities in the early 1980s. At the Fairmont Project in Hyde Park, a group of white youths systematically targeted each of the roughly two dozen black families living in the 400-unit housing development. Individual families would be harassed until they moved out, at which point the group would select another family for nightly torture, throwing stones and eggs. Minorities who had been moved to all-white housing projects in East Boston had their units firebombed in the early 1980s.[56] In 1984, five black families had been able to peacefully move into all-white housing projects in Charlestown, but only after the Housing Authority held a hundred community meetings and arranged a police roundup of known troublemakers prior to the move-ins.[57]

In 1988, nearly ten years after Faith Evans moved out of South Boston, city officials again attempted to integrate Boston's predominantly white housing developments. The desegregation occurred in response to a HUD report in the late 1980s that noted that because of the Boston Housing Authority's race- and national origin–based tenant selection process, there were no black residents in the three South Boston public housing projects.[58] The HUD report indicated that the Housing Authority had used similarly biased approaches for selecting tenants for developments in Charlestown.

After the HUD report, the city signed a voluntary compliance agreement, which stipulated that the city create a plan aimed at desegregating the largely white housing developments. To desegregate, the Housing Authority agreed to use a single list for all housing developments in the city. Applicants at the top of the list were allowed to take the first available apartment. The following year, in 1989, the city of Boston settled a lawsuit filed by the NAACP alleging that more than two thousand black and minority families had been discouraged from applying for housing in predominantly white developments.[59] The lead plaintiffs in the suit had been denied apartments in developments in South Boston and Charlestown.

White residents of South Boston and Charlestown referred to the BHA integration plan as "forced housing," echoing the earlier struggle around "forced busing." Community residents were dismayed with the plan to integrate the mostly white developments. At the time of the integration plan in 1988, minority families accounted for only 190 of approximately 2,300 households in South Boston public housing. Nevertheless, residents of South Boston claimed that they would have preferred the days when public housing in their neighborhood could be claimed more easily by their friends and relatives. "It's too bad, it couldn't stay the way it was. . . . why can't the kids from South Boston get these apartments?" asked one longtime public housing resident.[60]

Resentment over the integration of the housing developments led to some violence directed at new residents. Mary Bullock moved into the Old Colony housing development in April 1989 after a house fire. The family experienced a few incidents, but nothing serious enough to make her consider moving until several months after she moved in, when a brick was thrown at the window of the third-floor apartment.

Soon after, the apartment was sprayed with bullets. Two of the bullets came through the apartment's steel door and hit a wall within inches of where her eleven-year-old stepson was sitting. Other families experienced rock throwing and other less potentially serious incidents.[61]

Despite these incidents, the violence directed at those who had just moved into the housing projects did not reach the level that city officials feared. The absence of feared violence did not mean that white residents of Charlestown and South Boston were resigned to minorities moving to "their" projects. In 1990, two years after the integration, white tenant leaders at two South Boston housing projects held a community meeting attended by more than five hundred residents, many of whom were unhappy with the integration.[62] White residents did not just voice their concerns about integration at meetings. There was also violence. Racial incidents in South Boston more than doubled in the first year minority residents were living in the developments, from fifteen in 1988 to thirty-seven in 1989. Blacks who had moved to the housing development complained of vandalism, shots being fired through their windows, and racial epithets directed at them.

Public housing was integrated in Charlestown largely without incident. A few years after minorities had moved in to Charlestown, however, a cross was burned, and in a separate incident a Molotov cocktail was found outside a Puerto Rican woman's apartment. In 1996, one public housing development in South Boston, Old Colony, accounted for 49 percent of all police calls to public housing developments for bias-motivated crime.[63] In 1999 the Boston Housing Authority agreed to pay $650,000 in damages to thirteen black and Hispanic families who had alleged that their white neighbors harassed them at three South Boston and one Charlestown public housing developments between 1990 and 1996.[64]

Not Just the Working Class: The Latino Threat to Middle-Class White Neighborhoods

It is not fair to single out attacks made in working-class neighborhoods. For instance, chapter 2 describes a number of attacks leveled at minorities in suburban and upscale neighborhoods. Some of these incidents may have occurred because residents of middle-class neighborhoods also felt threatened by the presence of minorities. For instance, increasing numbers of attacks on Latinos in Suffolk County, New York, between 1999 and 2010 may have occurred because the large influx of Latinos represented a growing threat to white residents. After the town of Farmingville in Suffolk County and surrounding communities experienced a significant increase in Latino immigration—in some cases towns went from having no Latinos to having a population of 15 percent—some town residents began to direct hate crimes at Latinos.[65] Latinos were harassed and assaulted near their homes. Their homes and apartments were pelted with eggs, defaced with racial slurs, and pierced with gunshots.[66]

In an interview with an investigator for the Southern Poverty Law Center, one Farmingville Latino described his problems living in a white neighborhood in Suffolk County. Orlando, a twenty-two-year-old immigrant from Guatemala, was confronted by his neighbor as he was celebrating his birthday with friends in 2008. The man who confronted Orlando lived down the street, was drunk, and "came to cause trouble."

> One of my friends went to talk with him so there would not be any problems but [the neighbor] started to offend us, saying we were immigrants and we should not be in America, because we were stealing work from Americans, a lot of things like that. One of my friends tried to hold him back, and [the neighbor] hit him in the head with a flashlight. My friend's head had opened up in a wound. I went to try and help him and [the neighbor] then hit my head as well. Then he ran.[67]

Many of the townspeople in the middle-class neighborhoods in Suffolk County were upset with the rise in immigration because many of the Latinos were day laborers who gathered in groups on street corners waiting for work. Violence toward Latinos was the answer for some townspeople. County legislator Michael John D'Andre of Smithtown spoke out at a public hearing on immigration in August 2001, promising that if his town experienced an influx of Latino day laborers, residents will "be up in arms; we'll be out with baseball bats."[68] Similarly, in March 2007, county legislator Elie Mystal of Amityville commented about day laborers, "If I'm living in a neighborhood and people are gathering like that, I would load my gun and start shooting, period. Nobody will say it, and I'm going to say it."[69]

Some of the behavior targeting Latino immigrants in Suffolk County was organized. In 1998, a militant nativist group called Sachem Quality of Life (SQL) was formed to secure the deportation of all undocumented immigrants, which would, in the words of member Dave Drew, "restore" the town of Farmingville. In addition to rallies and lobbying, the group protested at the homes of Latinos and showed support for physical attacks on immigrants. In July 1999, SQL succeeded in getting the town of Brookhaven to pass a "Neighborhood Preservation Act" that limited the number of people occupying rental homes.[70] It is unclear how many attacks on immigrants the group was responsible for, but a few days after one of the group's anti-immigration forums, a member of SQL was arrested for threatening a local immigrant family.[71]

Status/Class: Is It Because Movers Are Too *Poor* for the Neighborhood?

At the opposite end of the class spectrum, at least with respect to the class of offenders, is violence directed at poor minorities who move to middle-class and more affluent communities. Harassment of public housing residents, who are disproportionately minorities, also could be motivated by the class of the individual targeted. In general, studies examining black-white interaction in neighborhoods indicate that integration is most successful when blacks and whites are of equal social status.[72] The equal status hypothesis suggests that when black public housing residents move to white suburbs with more affluent residents, there would not be a high level of social interaction, and integration would be met with significant resistance and potentially with violence.

Individuals living in white neighborhoods have long fought attempts to locate government-subsidized affordable housing in their neighborhoods. In 1968, the US Department of Housing and Urban Development, led by George Romney, HUD secretary under Richard Nixon, attempted to implement Operation Breakthrough. This program sought to integrate the suburbs by locating a large number of new units of low- and moderate-income housing in suburban spaces, many of which had little or no affordable housing.[73]

Perhaps because Operation Breakthrough tied water and sewer grants to suburban communities' allowing the construction of affordable housing, George Romney—who strongly favored the creation of affordable housing for the purpose of racial integration—was optimistic about public response to the program. In many locations, however, the carrot of increased funding was not enough to quell residents' displeasure, and there was wide-scale suburban opposition to the program from areas all over the country. Among other potential problems with the developments, residents were worried about racial divisions and decreasing property values. Distressed residents filed suit to prevent construction (Wilmington, Delaware; Seattle, Washington), signed petitions by the hundreds (Houston, Texas), and protested on construction sites (Kalamazoo, Michigan).

In the late 1960s and early 1970s, those opposed to Operation Breakthrough were clearly worried that the newly built developments would house poor minorities who were coming from the ghetto. One especially recalcitrant suburb was Warren, Michigan, a working-class suburb of Detroit. Though 30 percent of its workforce was African American in 1970, less than 1 percent of its residents were black. After the Warren city council vetoed plans for one hundred units of low-income housing and Warren city officials failed to meet program goals, the city was faced with a loss of $3 million in federal funding in 1970, and $14 million in subsequent years.[74] The city of Warren continued to resist; an eight-day petition drive protesting the building of housing developments collected nearly fifteen thousand signatures. After the petition drive, Warren's working-class residents voted in a city referendum to put an end to the community's $10 million urban renewal program if the program was tied to housing integration.[75]

The opposition to public housing in Warren was quite clearly not just an opposition to low-income residents but also a reflection of the residents' distaste for racial integration. The absence of African Americans in Warren was not a coincidence. In addition to the paucity of low-income housing, the city was marked by incidents of housing-related racial harassment when black residents had attempted but failed to purchase homes in Warren. Warren, along with other suburban communities like Redford and Wayne, had a long-standing reputation for being one of the suburban boundaries in the Detroit metropolitan area that was hardest for minorities to cross.[76] Minorities who moved into those suburbs routinely experienced arson, broken windows, and threats from their defensive white neighbors.[77]

Race versus Class: Is It Because They're Black?

Some of the current literature on segregation is predicated on the idea that opposition to minority neighbors stems from prejudice and racial discrimination.[78] As we saw in chapter 3, several studies have attempted to evaluate white preferences by showing cards depicting hypothetical neighborhood arrangements with different numbers of black residents. One early study of neighborhood preferences in the mid-1970s that drew respondents from the Detroit suburbs indicated that while the majority of blacks preferred a neighborhood with a 50/50 mix of blacks and whites, whites were less tolerant of integration.[79] Only 44 percent of whites indicated that they would feel comfortable with a neighborhood in which whites were slightly in the majority; when blacks are in the majority the number of whites comfortable with the neighborhood drops to 26 percent.[80] Replicating the study nearly twenty years later in Los Angeles, where Latinos and Asian Americans were interviewed in addition to blacks and whites, researchers found that African Americans were the least preferred out-group neighbor.[81] Other studies surveying whites and blacks who lived in Atlanta and Boston in the early 1990s found that roughly 35 percent of whites living in Atlanta would be comfortable with a neighborhood where whites were in the minority (eight black houses and seven white), and in Boston only 40 percent of whites surveyed said they would be comfortable with this mix.[82]

Class versus Race: Is it Because the Movers Are Poor?

The opposition of whites to majority-black neighborhoods may have more to do with class than race. Ingrid Gould Ellen's research suggests that whites are opposed to majority-black neighborhoods because of negative race-based stereotypes about such neighborhoods.[83] Ellen identifies five factors that increase the extent to which whites are comfortable in neighborhoods that are even 40 percent or 50 percent black. She argues that whites are likely to remain in communities that (1) have a history of racial stability; (2) are distant from large minority communities; (3) have lots of rental property; (4) have a very secure set of stabilizing amenities, like a university and a military base; and (5) are located in a metropolitan area with a small minority population, even when the minority population approaches 50 percent.

Unsurprisingly, opposition to building low-income housing has not waned. Perhaps in response to long-standing difficulty erecting the housing, some policy makers have suggested that public policy around housing for the poor abandon the explicit goal of racial integration, and focus instead on deconcentrating poverty. The conventional wisdom is that "physical, social, and economic conditions in the neighborhood contribute in important ways to the life chances of individuals, especially children and youth."[84] For these reasons, policy makers have continued to try to deconcentrate poverty by placing small buildings of affordable housing, sometimes called scattered sites, in neighborhoods that contain many more economically stable residents. In this way poor residents not only have the benefits that these neighborhoods offer— less crime, more parks and other amenities, and better schools—but also have different neighbors. Research shows that in areas of concentrated poverty a variety of social ills—such as violence, crime, substance abuse, and joblessness—are exacerbated.[85] Some evidence suggests that such behavior decreases when the percentage of disadvantaged neighbors drops below 20 percent.[86]

Significant public protest directed at the creation of affordable housing in non-poverty areas has occurred in cities around the country as diverse as Buffalo, Dallas, Chicago, Minneapolis, Oakland, Denver, Baltimore, Philadelphia, and Pittsburgh.[87] Opposition to the location of affordable housing in some neighborhoods is premised on the idea that undesirable neighbors moving in will pose a threat to the neighborhood residents' quality of life, security, and property values.[88]

The Deconcentration of Poverty in Chicago

Attempts to deconcentrate low-income households in Chicago were prompted by the terms of settlement of the *Gautreaux* lawsuit in 1976. The lawsuit, filed in 1966 on behalf of lead plaintiff Dorothy Gautreaux and all other Chicago Housing Authority (CHA) tenants and prospective tenants, alleged that the CHA (funded by and with the knowledge of HUD) had discriminated against the plaintiffs by locating almost all of the public housing sites in black neighborhoods and by assigning tenants on a racial basis in violation of the Fourteenth Amendment. The district court ruled in the plaintiffs' favor on a summary judgment in 1969 and directed the CHA to build its next seven hundred family units in predominantly white areas of Chicago. After that it was to locate at least three-quarters of its new family public housing inside the city of Chicago or Cook County. The Supreme Court ultimately held that the district court had the ability to adopt some form of remedy that applied to the entire Chicago metropolitan area.

By the mid-1990s, the placement of low-income residents in Chicago neighborhoods was restricted both by the opposition of neighborhood residents and by the availability of land in acceptable census tracts. At that point, there were only twenty-two census tracts that contained a high enough level of whites to be appropriate locations under the terms of the *Gautreaux* settlement.[89] Once a site was identified, the process of negotiation began. Community meetings were held; alderman support was sought. In some cases the very existence of subsidized housing in a neighborhood faced opposition. Such was the case in 1996, when the CHA and its court-appointed receiver, the Habitat Company, attempted to purchase a three-unit building in Hiawatha Park, a nearly all-white neighborhood on the city's North Side. In response to the plan, hundreds of residents turned out at community meetings to protest. The residents claimed that their opposition to low-income housing in their neighborhoods had to do with property values.[90]

Much of the press describing opposition by residents in Hiawatha Park also mentioned opposition to the placement of low-income residents in a predominantly black neighborhood on the city's South Side, Kenwood Oakland. There was opposition to the building of low-income housing in Kenwood Oakland, but the situation in the two neighborhoods was radically different. In Hiawatha Park, white residents by the hundreds opposed purchase of a single three-unit building to house, at most, three low-income families in their neighborhood. In Kenwood Oakland, black residents protested the building of an additional 241 units of low-income housing in their neighborhood.

Residents expressed fear that the additional units, added to an existing 1,000 units, would make the neighborhood "a dumping ground" for low-income residents.[91]

In the end, 2,700 scattered site units were built under *Gautreaux*. This was enough to house ten thousand persons, just a fraction of the thirty thousand families entitled to desegregated housing as a result of the order. Several hundred units were erected in black neighborhoods and several hundred units were built in Latino neighborhoods.[92] Units originally built in white neighborhoods eventually became located in black neighborhoods as whites moved out.[93] Middle-class protests kept scattered sites out of mostly white areas. In the end, very few scattered site units were constructed in the predominantly white northwestern and southern parts of the city.[94]

When Race Trumps Class

Though most of the incidents in this chapter focus on minorities who were moving to working-class neighborhoods or minorities who were poor and moving to more affluent neighborhoods, non-poor minorities moving to middle-class and more affluent neighborhoods have also been targeted because of their race. In suburbs and other middle-class and upscale neighborhoods in places like Seattle, Boston, Orange County, Florida, Chicago, Philadelphia, and St. Petersburg, Florida, the violence directed at minorities who have moved to all-white neighborhoods is similar to that occurring in working-class neighborhoods.[95] Just as in poor neighborhoods, in "nice" neighborhoods of cities and suburbs, crosses are burned on minorities' front lawns, houses are burned to the ground, and families are subjected to telephone threats and vandalism. The individuals targeted are engineers, city workers, retired persons, and professionals.

When anti-integrationist violence occurs in upscale neighborhoods, there may be a few distinctive features. In some cases, the minority who is targeted may offer a reward for the capture of the perpetrator. In 2004 when a number of incidents, including an attempted cross burning, were targeted at the Defoes, a black family living in an upscale subdivision in Gilbertsville, Pennsylvania, the family offered a reward of $5,000 for the capture of the culprit. As in other cases, upscale neighborhoods are anxious to dispel any taint of racism caused by the perpetrator's actions. The attempted cross burning prompted a unity walk by two hundred local residents. Three municipalities in the area offered an additional reward of $7,000 for the capture of the individual responsible for attempting to burn a cross on the Defoes' lawn. In this case, the vigilance paid off. The community's response to the attempted cross burning led to an in-state police manhunt resulting in the arrest of a local resident, Richard D. Rick Sr., just four months after the attempted crime. Rick was charged with ethnic intimidation, terroristic threats, arson, attempted criminal mischief, criminal trespass, and disorderly conduct for the incident directed at the Defoes.[96]

In cases involving middle- and upper-middle-class residents like the Defoes, perpetrators and their supporters cannot argue that the minorities moving in are any different, save for their race, from their white neighbors. Sometimes minorities are attacked when doing ordinary middle-class things like maintaining their property. Despite the minority targets' similarity to their white counterparts, the message in these cases is crystal clear: the minorities are not wanted in the neighborhood, at least by the perpetrators.

In one notable case, that involving the Hunters Brooke development, minorities' homes may have been attacked because they were more affluent than those of the white perpetrators. Hunters Brooke was an exclusive subdivision located in Maryland twenty-five miles south of Washington, DC. Eventually five men were caught and charged with the arson that occurred in December 2004. Two of the individuals involved in the crime admitted targeting the development because many of the buyers were black.[97] In this case, it may not have been wariness about the decline of the neighborhood as a result of African Americans moving in, but rather anger at the fact that they were able to do so. Prosecutors suggested that the individuals who set the fire may have been envious of people who could afford half-million-dollar homes. Jeremy Paraday, one of the men who pled guilty to the Hunters Brooke arson, admitted that he had singled out the development because many of the buyers were black. Mark Potok, of the Southern Poverty Law Center, commented that the actions of the perpetrators may have been motivated by their resentment of the black residents of Hunters Brooke.

Echoing what he imagined to be the thoughts of the perpetrators, Potok suggested they thought to themselves, "I'm white. I ought to be doing better. . . . Look at these black families moving in. They're very upper middle class. You know, they have sort of all the latest accoutrements, and that ain't right."[98]

It's certainly possible that the men who decided to burn down the development resented the upper-middle-class blacks who were able to purchase a home there. One of the individuals involved in setting the fires who made racist statements to investigators was a former Hunters Brooke security guard and had apparently been seen looking at the homes and preparing to move in. Presumably, if the perpetrators were members of the working class, there were other rich white neighborhoods that they chose not to target. For working-class or less well-off whites to elect to target an upscale development because upper-class blacks can afford to live there and they cannot is indicative of a defined racial hierarchy in which it is unacceptable for blacks to be successful while whites are not.

Conclusion

As we have seen thus far throughout the book, those who commit acts of anti-integrationist violence are resistant to minorities, especially African Americans, living in their communities. As chapter 3 details, some minorities are more acceptable than others. This chapter evaluates several different explanations for acts of violence against minorities moving to the neighborhood. There is significant resistance to minorities, particularly African Americans, moving to very different types of neighborhoods. Examining perpetrators' motivations in the previous chapter, I explored Latino resistance to African Americans moving to Latino neighborhoods in Los Angeles. In this chapter, I describe working-class whites' rejection of African Americans and middle-class rejection of poor African Americans. So what matters most in identifying opposition to minority move-ins? Interestingly enough, each of these situations—Latino resistance to African American newcomers, working-class whites' opposition to minorities, and middle-class whites' rejection of poor minorities—poses similar challenges for integration.

Despite the different class situations and racial constructs involved (in the case of the Latinos), each of these neighborhood contexts—working-class white neighborhoods, middle-class suburban neighborhoods, Latino neighborhoods in Los Angeles—is a space where a minority presence represents a distinct threat. For each of the groups who face minority integration, stereotypes of poor African American neighborhoods loom large. Blacks—irrespective of class—who are moving call to mind the worst of the ills of black ghettos: crime, poverty, and drugs. According to this reasoning, once a single person of color, usually a black or Latino, moves in, neighborhood decline follows. If a few minorities do manage to carve out a tiny space in the neighborhood, the neighborhood's ills become associated with their presence. For instance, one resident of a working-class white ethnic neighborhood in Brooklyn that was defended against minorities moving in described the negative impact of the newcomers' presence:

> I think most of our crime can be traced back to the influx of Puerto Ricans. I think most of the bombed out areas, I mean I walk up past Grand Avenue on Union Avenue and see these, what were gorgeous buildings at one time were taken over by Puerto Ricans and now they're not there. I mean they're so completely bombed out, who'd live in them. . . . I think they're just destructive people.[99]

Blaming crime on minority presence is a combination of scapegoating and stereotyping. As chapter 3 noted, a few scholars have argued that white neighborhood preferences result from whites' stereotyping of black neighborhoods, rather than blacks as individuals.[100] As the previous chapter indicates, the survey research on black-Latino relations and the violence directed at African Americans in Latino neighborhoods in Los Angeles suggests that a similar phenomenon may exist among Latinos.

Suggesting that working-class and middle-class whites and Latinos have similar feelings and concerns about integration of their neighborhoods does not mean that all the groups have the same amount to lose, or that their concerns stem from the same places. In fact, the specter of potential "danger" differs quite dramatically depending on the group making the assessment. Working-class whites and middle-class and poor Latinos are often the most literally tied to their neighborhoods. For economic reasons, they are likely unable to leave in the event of neighborhood decline. Not only do middle- and upper-class suburban residents have more economic flexibility to move should fears become reality, at least one study of low-income housing suggests that such fears are groundless.[101]

6

Responding to Neighborhood Hate Crimes

Many perpetrators of anti-integrationist violence, like those who commit other types of hate crimes, are never caught. If the perpetrators are caught, the government's response to anti-integrationist violence may involve a variety of actors, ranging from police officers investigating the crime to judges involved in sentencing. This chapter explores the challenges of a viable legal response to anti-integrationist violence. The mechanics of responding to anti-integrationist violence can be read through the story of one black family, the Joneses, who moved to a working-class white neighborhood in St. Paul, Minnesota, in the spring of 1990. The Joneses' experience is unusual only because one of the skinhead perpetrators, Robert A. Viktora (originally described in court records as R.A.V.), who burned a cross on their lawn, challenged his conviction in the Supreme Court, but their case is an excellent vehicle for exploring both the problems and the possibilities of state response.[1] In addition, the Joneses' story is also a fairly typical modern-day story of anti-integrationist violence.

Moving On Up

Similar to other black families who make the choice to move to white neighborhoods, Russ and Laura Jones sought to escape the black neighborhood they lived in. They were a bit ambivalent about moving to a white neighborhood on the east side of St. Paul. Though their new neighborhood did not have the crime or drugs of downtown, it was a working-class neighborhood that had only a few blacks. Laura Jones called it infamous in the black community. Russ Jones said that the atmosphere on the east side of St. Paul was clear—they "didn't like black folks."[2] The

Joneses liked the houses on the east side of town, though, and chose a house on the very edge of the area, hoping they wouldn't have problems.

The Joneses' fears of bad experiences in their new neighborhood were quickly realized. Within weeks of the family's move into their new house, the tires on their car were slashed. The next month, the tailgate of their brand-new station wagon was broken. A few weeks after that, as they walked from the house to the car, their son was called a "nigger." Then, on June 21, 1990, roughly three months after they moved into the house, at about 2:30 a.m., the Joneses were awakened by the sound of footsteps in their yard. Russ Jones looked out of the bedroom window and saw a cross burning. Like other targets of anti-integrationist violence, Laura Jones knew the significance of the burning cross, and it frightened her. "If you're black and you see a cross burning, you know it's a threat, and you imagine all the church bombings and lynchings and the rapes that have gone before, not so long ago. A cross burning is a way of saying, 'We're going to get you.'"[3]

Two hours later, at 4:30 a.m., Laura Jones awakened to the noise and glow of another burning cross.[4] This time, the cross had been burned in front of the apartment building across the street from the Joneses. A third cross had been burned in front of a nearby apartment building in which several minorities lived.

Police later arrested seventeen-year-old Viktora and eighteen-year-old Arthur Miller III. Viktora lived with Miller across the street from the Joneses. According to court records, the previous night, Viktora, Miller, and several other young white men had gathered at Miller's home discussing how disgusted they felt at the presence of an African American family in the neighborhood. Miller proposed burning a cross, saying, "Let's go burn some niggers."[5] The men went to the basement and taped together chair legs to form a crude cross. They placed it in the Joneses' fenced backyard, poured paint thinner on it, and set fire to it.

The Mechanics of Dealing with Neighborhood Hate Crime

In cases of neighborhood hate crime, as in other crimes, the very first governmental actor that the individual targeted by the harassment encounters is the police. If the targeted person calls 911, dispatch may send a patrol officer from the neighborhood to the scene to speak with the resident. In the best-case scenario, the responding officer gathers evidence, arrests any perpetrators at the scene of the crime, gets the names of witnesses, and writes a summary report. The responding officer is also responsible for providing assistance to the victim. If anyone on the scene is injured, the officer may call for medical assistance. The officers' behavior when dealing with the individual targeted by bias-motivated violence can be important. Significant research has shown that those targeted by hate crime feel especially vulnerable, and law enforcement officers have an important role to play in reassuring those attacked that the perpetrator will not return.[6] Reassurance is especially needed in anti-integrationist violence, where individuals are attacked at their homes, a place usually considered a sanctuary. Moreover, in these types of cases, there may be few places to turn for support from the community. The individuals attacked are not only one of the few if not the only persons of their race living in an area, but also newcomers to the community. The Jones case highlights this. After the second cross burning, Laura Jones recalled, "[W]e felt very vulnerable. We were the only black family there, and because our house is on the corner, we felt like we were sitting out in the open."[7]

Though reassurance is the "best practice" for responding officers, some may not behave in that manner when responding to victims of anti-integrationist violence. The Joneses, for example, were not reassured by the responding officers. After the burning cross was discovered, the Joneses called the police, who, they said, arrived at the house in about ten minutes. The police asked them a few questions, and then packed up to leave. Reflecting on the officers' behavior later, Laura Jones said the police seemed as if they did not really know what to do, and said they had no suspects because there were no witnesses. Police experience investigating hate crimes is critical to their ability both to investigate the crime and to provide support for the targets. In the Jones cases, the investigating officers did not behave in a manner that suggested they had any experience investigating bias crime. The officers who responded to the cross burning on the Joneses' lawn saw no need to take the cross as evidence. The officer was preparing to leave, and when Russ Jones asked the officer what he should do with the cross, the officer told him to "just throw away" the smoldering cross. Russ Jones had to dismantle and dispose of the cross himself after the officers left.[8]

Procedurally, the police response in the Joneses' case was the average that a target of bias crime can expect when he or she calls the police. In the typical bias crime case to which police are called, after the responding officer—generally a patrol officer from the geographic area in which the crime has occurred—has left the scene, if he or she thinks that it is warranted, he or she may file an incident report describing the crime. Most jurisdictions leave the filing of incident reports up to the discretion of the responding officer. If the officer decides not to file a report, unless there is some follow-up by an agency or the targeted individual, no official investigation will take place. If the report is filed, it will be forwarded to detectives, who then decide whether to investigate the crime. If the incident is deemed worthy of investigation by precinct detectives, they will gather evidence—contact or try to find witnesses, re-interview the individual targeted, and, if they discover the perpetrator, make an arrest. Along with the duties of investigation, in jurisdictions with hate crime statutes, police may also assess incidents and classify them as hate crimes, if warranted.

The process of investigating anti-integrationist violence is complicated by three factors. First, harassment of this type is frequently low-level crime—harassment or vandalism—and is thus a type of crime that police have little incentive to investigate. Second, even if a department does allocate personnel, such investigations are often time-consuming because perpetrators frequently strike at night, when there are few witnesses. The third and final complicating factor applies to neighborhoods where community members support the actions of the perpetrator and may resist officers' attempts to investigate such crimes.[9]

As chapter 2 indicates, while organized opposition to minorities moving into white neighborhoods is rare in the contemporary era, it can occur in small, close-knit ethnic communities. Such was the case in Gertown and Hillsdale, two working-class ethnic neighborhoods in "Center City," a medium-sized city, which staunchly opposed the investigation of anti-integrationist violence.[10] Both were working-class white neighborhoods and had a history of resistance to minority integration. When minorities began to move to the neighborhood in the late 1980s, crimes were directed at minority newcomers, and bias crimes occurring in these two neighborhoods became most of the work for Center City's hate crime unit, the Anti-Bias Task Force (ABTF).[11]

In contrast to the contemporary pattern described in chapter 2, residents in Gertown and Hillsdale immediately organized to resist investigation of bias crimes directed at minority newcomers. The resistance took a variety of forms. Community newspapers encouraged residents not to speak to the police, and the community developed a code of silence surrounding incidents. This was especially frustrating for investigators because crimes directed at minorities were often committed by strangers whom the target could not identify. Moreover, even though crimes often took place at night, the two neighborhoods were small and close-knit, so detectives in the ABTF were aware that in all likelihood community members knew who had committed the crimes. As a further obstructionist mechanism, members of the neighborhood used elected officials to put pressure on the unit through higher-ups in the department. The community's goal was to reorient the unit's priorities so that it focused more time on crimes involving white victims. All of this pressure complicated the unit's job and increased the amount of time it took to investigate cases.[12]

Legal Remedies for Anti-Integrationist Violence

One is entirely free not to like one's neighbors. However, committing a crime against a newcomer because you do not like people of their race living in your neighborhood is prohibited by the general criminal law and may also violate state and federal fair housing or other civil rights law, and state or local hate crime laws, which often prohibit violence on the basis of race, religion, or sexual orientation. With respect to anti-integrationist violence, behavior directed at racial and ethnic minorities integrating white neighborhoods may be punished under a variety of federal and state laws. The various remedies, federal and state, are described below.

Federal Remedies

CIVIL RIGHTS ACTIONS

Violence directed at individuals pursuing their rights to housing constitutes the majority of cases of racial violence prosecuted by the Department of Justice.[13] The most common federal civil rights statutes that may be used to prosecute anti-integrationist violence are found in Section 241 of Title 18 of the US Code.[14] Section 241, passed during Reconstruction after the Civil War, punishes conspiracies to "injure, oppress, threaten, or intimidate any person in any State, Territory, or Commonwealth, Possession or District in the free exercise or enjoyment of" rights protected under the US Constitution and federal law.[15] In other words, Section 241 makes it a federal crime for two or more people to conspire to injure, threaten, or intimidate any person who is exercising his or her constitutional or statutory rights.

Federal civil rights law under Section 241 is most commonly recognized for its use in prosecuting the Ku Klux Klan and in famous civil rights cases, such as the 1964 murders of the civil rights workers Michael Schwerner, James Earl Chaney, and Andrew Goodman.[16] It has also been used to punish anti-integrationist violence. For example, Section 241 has been used in many instances to punish those who burned crosses in attempts to drive black families from their homes.[17] In cases prosecuted under Section 241, the prosecution must demonstrate that the victim was engaging in a federally protected right with which the perpetrators interfered.[18] This may be challenging in some hate crime cases,[19] but not in those involving anti-integrationist violence, because such incidents are directed at individuals in and around their homes. When Section 241 is used to punish anti-integrationist violence, the federally protected activities include one's right to use property or housing under Title 42 Section 1982 of the US Code. Title 42 Section 1982 mandates that "all citizens . . . shall have the same right, in every State and Territory, as is enjoyed by White citizens thereof to inherit, purchase, lease, sell, hold, and convey real and personal property."[20]

United States. v. Callahan serves as a representative case of the use of Section 241 to prosecute anti-integrationist violence.[21] In this case Vincent J. Callahan was charged under Section 241 with having conspired with two others to burn down a house that had just been vacated by Charles Williams and Marietta Bloxom, a black couple, and their daughter. The violence directed at Williams and Bloxom was part of a concerted effort to drive blacks from the neighborhood. In mid-November 1985, Williams and Bloxom had moved to Elmwood, a working-class white neighborhood in Philadelphia. About a week after Williams and Bloxom moved in, four hundred demonstrators gathered outside their home, shouting racial slurs and demanding the couple leave.[22] Frightened, the family decided to do just that. Ironically, they were in the process of moving out when the house was set on fire. Two and a half weeks after Williams and Bloxom moved in, Gerald and Carol Fox, an interracial couple, and their children moved in three blocks from the Williams-Bloxom house. The Foxes were also subjected to racial slurs, epithets, vandalism, and demonstrations by local residents urging the Foxes to leave.[23]

THE FEDERAL FAIR HOUSING ACT

Remedies protecting housing rights are a crucial part of civil rights law. Because of the housing-based context of anti-integrationist violence, the most common federal remedy is prosecution under Section 3631 of the Federal Fair Housing Act (FHA). The Fair Housing Act, enacted as Title VIII of the Civil Rights Act of 1968, was created to provide fair housing throughout the United States.[24] As a broad remedy, it prohibits a variety of discriminatory housing practices, including extralegal violence.[25] The part focused particularly on violence is the "Prevention of Intimidation" subchapter, which contains Section 3631. Modeled after Section 245 of Title 18 of the US Code, with language that tracks that of 245(b),[26] Section 3631 is just one section of the Fair Housing Act used to prosecute acts of anti-integrationist violence. Section 3631 provides imprisonment or fines if an individual,

> whether or not acting under color of law, by force or threat of force willfully injures, intimidates or interferes with, or attempts to injure, intimidate or interfere with—
>   (a) any person because of his race, color, religion, . . . or national origin and because he is or has been selling, purchasing, renting, financing, occupying, or contracting or negotiating for the sale, purchase, rental, financing or occupation of any dwelling.

The maximum allowable penalty for a violation of Section 3631 is life in prison. Section 3631 also allows victims various other remedies under the Fair Housing Act, including the ability to sue to obtain damages or an injunction for violations of Section 3617 (described below), a section of the FHA that also prohibits interference, intimidation, or coercion in the exercise of one's federal housing rights. The broad protections against interference under the FHA have been used to prosecute racial violence in a variety of contexts. For instance, Sections 3617 and 3631 of the FHA have been used to prosecute a variety of violent acts, including cross burnings,[27] firebombings and arson,[28] vandalism, assault,[29] and threats[30] targeted at racial and ethnic minorities and whites in the exercise and enjoyment of their fair housing rights.

Though incidents of anti-integrationist violence may take a variety of forms, ranging from violent assaults to verbal harassment, many of the cases prosecuted under the FHA involve extremely violent conduct. When the facts in the case satisfy the requirement for conspiracy, the Justice Department also prosecutes cross burning and other forms of bias-motivated interference with housing rights under Section 241 of Title 18 of the US Code as a conspiracy to interfere with housing rights. Because move-in violence so regularly involves multiple perpetrators, charges brought under the FHA's Section 3631 are routinely accompanied by charges brought under Section 241 of Title 18 of the US Code.[31] Like Section 241, Section 3631 seems to be generally well received by courts as a means of addressing anti-integrationist violence, since many of the successful prosecutions result in convictions under both statutes.

There is some evidence from the federal court decisions that judges see move-in violence as a serious problem, worthy of punishment. Rather than erecting barriers that will make it hard for the government to prove that racism motivated the defendant, in *United States v. Nix* the court held that the government is not required to show that a defendant's actions are entirely racially motivated to prove a violation of Section 3631. As long as a defendant's actions are at least partially influenced by the race of the victim, a Section 3631 conviction can result.[32] In a case with similar implications under Section 241, the Sixth Circuit held that a defendant's choice of racially charged actions of cross burning and spray-painting racial slurs on victims' properties precluded his argument that his actions were aimed at a particular group of black youths with whom defendant had an earlier altercation, rather than at African Americans in general.[33] Courts have also been supportive of various sentencing enhancements for defendants convicted of intimidation or interference with housing rights under Section 3631.[34] They have similarly been willing to set aside sentences that are too lenient,[35] or to deny sentencing reductions for those convicted of violating Sections 3631 and 241.[36]

Any reading of the Fair Housing Act's legislative history suggests that the act was an attempt to pave the way for significant nationwide housing integration. As the brief legislative history provided in chapter 2 suggests, the FHA was created to address the extralegal violence that serves as a barrier to integration. As chapter 3 demonstrates, despite the use of the FHA, segregation among African Americans (the most segregated racial group in the country) has declined but still remains high, with residential segregation among African Americans in many major cities identified as severe.[37] As so many of the cases brought under the FHA reveal, when minorities move to white neighborhoods and crimes are committed against them, they leave.[38] Thus, forty years after the passage of the FHA, extralegal violence still serves as a barrier to housing integration.

DIVINING INTIMIDATION UNDER THE FHA

Section 3617 of Title 42 makes it unlawful for persons to coerce, intimidate, or threaten others in the exercise or enjoyment of their fair housing rights.[39] As detailed above, in the past the FHA has been used to prosecute "typical" acts of move-in violence—violent harassment aimed at minorities and others who moved to and were living in white neighborhoods. Until recently, few cases have defined either the precise conduct that constituted intimidation,[40] or whether the act could be applied to individuals who are not still in the process of acquiring—that is, those who have already purchased—housing. A series of recent court decisions addresses these issues in a manner that raises the concern that the FHA may be being interpreted in ways that significantly blunt its ability to address anti-integrationist violence.

Though the decision was subsequently reversed on appeal, *Ohio Civil Rights Commission v. Akron Metropolitan Housing Authority* in the Court of Common Pleas in Summit County, Ohio, may serve as somewhat of a cautionary tale for courts' interpretation of the Fair Housing Act as a remedy in anti-integrationist violence cases.[41] The case involved Fontella Harper, an African American who lived in a housing development operated by the Akron Metropolitan Housing Authority (AMHA). Harper had lived in the development for ten years when Beverly Kaisk, a Caucasian woman, moved to an apartment two doors away from Harper.

Harper maintained that shortly after the Kaisks moved in, Kaisk and her two children began to harass the Harpers and their African American visitors, calling them "niggers" and "black bitches." Such incidents, according to Harper, were not isolated and included physical confrontation and threats of violence. Harper complained to the AMHA, to no avail.

In its defense against the suit, the AMHA contended that it bore no responsibility for the hostile environment. Rather, the hostile environment, if it existed, was created by the Kaisks. The defendants placed heavy reliance on *Lawrence v. Courtyards at Deerwood Ass'n*. In *Lawrence*, African American homeowners sued their homeowners' association after it refused to get involved when they experienced racially motivated harassment soon after they moved to the residential development.[42] The homeowners' association refused to intervene, claiming that it was unwilling to "become involved in a personal dispute between neighbors." In *Lawrence*, the court granted the association's motion for summary judgment on the interference claim because it indicated that the defendants had no duty to stop the neighbors' conduct, and the association had not engaged in threatening behavior toward the homeowners.[43]

In *Ohio Civil Rights Commission*, the court granted the defendant's motion for summary judgment. In deciding that the alleged harassment was not sufficiently severe, Judge Stormer noted that when in the past courts have allowed claims for racial discrimination under the FHA, they limited its application to "only the most extreme or violent conduct":

> On one side lie cross-burning, fire bombing and other similarly overt discriminatory acts designed to intimidate, coerce, or interfere with housing rights. On the other side lie unfortunate skirmishes between neighbors, tinged with discriminatory overtones or occasional discriminatory comments. Nothing in the text of the FHA or the case law interpreting it indicates that Congress intended to federalize the latter type of dispute.[44]

The Ohio judge's decision reflected a lack of appreciation for the context and effects of move-in violence. Though many move-in attacks are physically violent, frequently acts of neighborhood terrorism begin with incidents of harassment—vandalism or the use of slurs and epithets—that have a low offense level but are nevertheless terrifying to those targeted. By lumping harassment in the category with ordinary neighbor disputes, Judge Stormer failed to recognize the power that the use of slurs may have in the context of the racial integration of neighborhoods. If Judge Stormer's reasoning represents a trend, the ability of the Fair Housing Act to serve as a remedy in cases of anti-integrationist violence is seriously undermined. If other courts begin requiring cross burning or firebombing in order to secure relief under the FHA, there may be two negative effects. First, it may inadvertently send a message that the perpetrators have carte blanche to racially harass, so long as a cross is not burned or the victim's house is not firebombed. Second, it may send the message that hate crime targets should stay as events escalate.

There have been other troubling developments for those who might use the Fair Housing Act to punish anti-integrationist violence. In one case from 2004, *Halprin v. Prairie Single Family Homes of Dearborn Park Association*, the Seventh Circuit placed severe limitations on who could utilize the Fair Housing Act.[45] Rick Halprin, who was Jewish, moved to the Dearborn Park subdivision in Chicago, Illinois, with his wife. Soon after the Halprins moved in, the president of the neighborhood association allegedly wrote "H-town" (short for "Hymie town") on the Halprins' property. As is typical in cases of move-in violence, vandalism followed: landscaping was damaged and holiday lights were cut down. The Halprins' attempts to find the perpetrator(s) were thwarted and the Halprins were further harassed.

Though the harassment the Halprins experienced was typical of many other successful move-in violence cases brought under the Fair Housing Act, in affirming the dismissal of their case under Section 3604, Judge Posner maintained that the FHA did not apply to the Halprins' situation. He noted that of Sections 3603, 3604, 3605, and 3606, the only relevant one was Section 3604, which applied to the act of selling or purchasing a home. "The language indicates concern with activities, such as redlining, that prevent people from acquiring property. . . . Our plaintiffs, however, are complaining not about being prevented from acquiring property but about being harassed by other property owners."[46] In other words, because the Halprins were harassed after they moved in rather than before they acquired the property, they were not eligible for relief under the FHA. Posner concluded, "[W]e do not think Congress wanted to convert every quarrel among neighbors in which a racial or religious slur is hurled into a federal case."[47]

In assessing the reach of *Halprin*, it is important to note that the Seventh Circuit's view regarding post-acquisition harassment in *Halprin* was not universally followed. In upholding the conviction of a defendant who burned the home of an Asian American family against a commerce clause challenge in *United States v. Nicholson,* the court specifically rejected the argument that the applicability of these statutes hinged on whether or not the purchase of the home had already been completed:

> Congress has the power under both 18 U.S.C. Section 241 and 42 U.S.C. Section 3631 to protect housing rights not only at the time of purchase and at the time of sale, but also against violent interference during the time between purchase and sale. A person who wishes to intimidate a minority victim from purchasing a home cannot insulate himself from Federal liability by intimidating the victim the day after the victim closed on a home.[48]

In 2009, five years after *Halprin*, in *Bloch v. Frischholz* the Seventh Circuit Court of Appeals clarified the issue of post-acquisition harassment decided in *Halprin*.[49] *Bloch* examined whether condominium owners in Illinois could bring a claim against the condo association under the Fair Housing Act for racial and religious discrimination alleged to have occurred long after the plaintiffs moved in. The Blochs, who are Jewish, alleged that the condo association discriminated against them by repeatedly removing several mezuzot from outside the family's apartments.[50] In reversing the lower court's decision to grant the defendant's motion for summary judgment, the appeals court noted that *Halprin* did not prohibit all post-sale actions brought under the Fair Housing Act. Rather, the court of appeals reiterated the extremely stringent standard established in *Halprin*—that the Fair Housing Act covers post-acquisition discriminatory behavior "that makes a dwelling unavailable to the owner or tenant, somewhat like constructive eviction." In *Bloch*, constructive eviction was determined to be an appropriate analogy because once the mezuzot were removed, the Blochs' apartments became unavailable for occupation by observant Jews. Thus, the court decreed that the plaintiffs had offered enough evidence to allow a trier of fact to decide whether they had suffered intentional discrimination.

Though there have been some favorable interpretations, in other cases courts have read the Fair Housing Act in a manner that may limit the FHA's use in move-in violence cases. If courts continue to interpret the FHA in this manner, there are important consequences for the racial balance of neighborhoods. The high standard the Seventh Circuit Court of Appeals reiterated in *Bloch*, for instance, can make it extremely difficult for many victims of anti-integrationist violence to pursue Fair Housing Act claims. This is especially the case if the individual neglects to move out, or suffers the type of harassment that is so typical in many move-in violence cases— vandalism or low-level assaults. Because such incidents are traumatizing, though not necessarily graphic like a cross burning, courts may find that their post-acquisition harassment was only, in the words of Judge Posner in *Halprin,* a mere "quarrel among neighbors,"[51] and therefore cannot rise to the level that triggers the Fair Housing Act's post-acquisition coverage.

State Remedies

STATE AND LOCAL HATE CRIME STATUTES

In addition to federal penalties under which anti-integrationist bias-motivated violence may be punished, states and localities around the country have passed special hate crime legislation criminalizing bias-motivated incidents. The dual sovereignty rule allows incidents to be prosecuted under both state and federal law.[52] Thus, though most hate crimes may be punished under federal law, most hate crime prosecutions (like most prosecutions in general) occur at the state, rather than the federal, level.[53]

Nearly all states have some form of hate or bias crime law.[54] There are several different types of state hate crime statutes. The most common type of state bias crime statutes are bias-motivated violence and intimidation laws, in which "ethnic intimidation" and "malicious harassment" make the commission of a hate crime a separate offense.[55] In such cases, if a crime is already defined in the state's criminal code and has been committed with racial animus or if the defendant has selected the victim based on particular characteristics—most commonly race, color, religion, and national origin—then the defendant has committed a hate crime.[56]

Several states use hate crime penalty enhancement statutes and laws that treat bias motivation as an aggravating factor in sentencing.[57] In states with a special penalty enhancement statute or an aggravated penalty statute, if a crime has been determined to have been motivated by bias, the defendant will receive an increased sentence.[58] States may also have statutes that define hate crimes in ways similar to federal legislation, as civil rights violations.[59] Finally, in situations in which crosses are burned, perpetrators have been charged under state cross burning statutes.[60]

Several state remedies addressing bias-motivated violence have come under constitutional scrutiny. The first of these occurred in 1993 in *R.A.V. v. St. Paul*, when the Supreme Court struck down as violative of the First Amendment a St. Paul hate crime ordinance used to punish a cross burning.[61] The very next year, in *Wisconsin v. Mitchell*, the Court upheld a hate crime penalty enhancement statute.[62] In doing so, the Court limited the effect of *R.A.V.* by allowing states to create statutes aimed at the *act* of intentional selection of a victim because of his race.

STATE CRIMINAL LAW

Anti-integrationist violence commonly includes cross burning, vandalism and other property damage, and low-level assaults. Such incidents are common law crimes and may be prosecuted under the state criminal law. There are, unfortunately, two barriers to the prosecution of these types of crimes under the "ordinary" criminal law. The first barrier is one of police response and investigation. When they are not classified as hate crimes but rather as simple assaults and vandalism, hate crimes fall into the category of low-level crimes.[63] Because of their low offense level, police officers have little desire to investigate.[64] Even cross burnings have been mischaracterized as malicious mischief, vandalism, or burning without a permit.[65] In some jurisdictions, police have been reluctant to take hate crime victims' complaints seriously. If police do not file an official police report or investigate, such crimes are unlikely to be charged. Even if the police are committed to investigation, if the crime occurs in the middle of the night without witnesses, they may feel powerless to help victims or bring charges.[66]

Even if the police decide to investigate and a perpetrator is found, use of the ordinary criminal law may still present difficulties. The Jones case described at the beginning of this chapter presents an excellent example of how the ordinary criminal law may not work to address the complexities involved in prosecuting incidents of move-in violence.

There were no witnesses who saw the cross placed on the Joneses' front lawn.[67] The perpetrators were discovered when one of them was overheard bragging to his friends about the cross burning. The four perpetrators, one adult and three juveniles, were then charged with various crimes. In thinking about how best to charge the juveniles, the prosecutor in the case evaluated several statutes: trespass, arson, vandalism, and terroristic threats.[68] Trespass, arson, and vandalism were eliminated because some of the elements of the crime were missing.[69] For instance, the prosecutor indicated that a vandalism charge would not have been possible because of a missing statutory element—there was no destruction of property, not even a burned spot on the Joneses' grass.[70] The prosecutor decided to charge one of the juveniles under Minnesota's recently passed bias crimes ordinance because the adult had already pled guilty to a misdemeanor and received probation.[71] After Robert A. Viktora hired a First Amendment lawyer, the statute was challenged and eventually struck down by the US Supreme Court.

CHALLENGES AT THE LOCAL LEVEL: PROSECUTING HATE CRIMES IN CHICAGO

State hate crime statutes are good options so long as prosecutors wish to bring charges and victims agree to come forward. Chicago serves as an example of some of the challenges of prosecuting hate crimes because there is heavy institutionalization supporting the prosecution of hate crimes. Offenders in Chicago may be prosecuted under the Illinois Hate Crime Act, which proscribes a variety of crimes, including assault, battery, aggravated assault, trespass, vandalism, and harassment committed by reason of an individual's "actual or perceived race, color, creed, religion, ancestry, gender, sexual orientation, physical or mental disability, or national origin."[72] Violations of the statute are a class IV felony for the first offense and a class II felony for a second or subsequent offense. The Illinois Hate Crime Act also requires that offenders not convicted of a crime or not sentenced to prison terms be ordered to perform two hundred hours of community service. The hate crime probation program is a system in which crime offenders who are not sentenced to serve prison terms have probation sentences related to the crime they have committed. In other words, offenders spend time serving the community they have harmed.

In Chicago, as in several other cities, there is a statute that allows plaintiffs to file civil suits requesting relief in the form of money damages. For plaintiffs to recover, using the statutes requires dedicated civil rights counsel, experienced in hate crime cases. In Chicago, the Lawyers' Committee for Civil Rights Under Law helped a number of plaintiffs recover damages in hate crime cases, some of which were move-in violence cases.[73] For instance, the Lawyers' Committee was counsel to Clevan Nicholson, who was with Lenard Clark when he was attacked in Bridgeport in 1997. Nicholson received a $500,000 damage award as a result of a lawsuit filed against one of the white assailants.[74] The Lawyers' Committee also filed a federal suit on behalf of Andre Bailey and Sharon Henderson, the couple who had a cross burned on their lawn in Blue Island in the Chicago suburbs, as described in chapter 2. A federal jury awarded the couple $720,000 in damages.[75]

Victims of anti-integrationist violence have the best theoretical chance to receive redress when there are, as in Chicago, a variety of community-based sources responsible for responding to bias-motivated violence in integrating areas in the city. Chicago has a massive law enforcement community organized around enforcing the Illinois Hate Crime Act. These institutions include the Cook County state attorney's office, responsible for prosecuting a crime; police officers in the Civil Rights Section of the Chicago Police Department, the first hate crime unit in the country, founded in 1948, responsible for investigating a crime; and staff members of the Chicago Human Rights Commission responsible for providing support for victims of bias crimes.

Prosecutors in Cook County, Illinois, have a significant commitment to prosecuting hate crime cases. Indeed, in the 1990s the state attorney's office created a manual, "A Prosecutor's Guide to Hate Crime," aimed at showcasing proper methods of prosecution in this particular area. After the white supremacist Benjamin Smith shot and killed Ricky Byrdsong, who had been Northwestern University's first black basketball coach, the Cook County state attorney Richard Devine agreed to increase his office's focus on hate crime, including working with police departments to provide training, and dedicating more of his own office staff to investigating and prosecuting hate crimes.[76] All of this was designed to help secure a greater number of convictions in hate crime cases.

Despite the city's massive institutionalization in the area of hate crime, the enforcement of hate crime law in Chicago may not have been adequate to address the city's problems of anti-integrationist violence. Aggressive enforcement of hate crime law tends to increase the numbers of hate crimes, because hate crimes are considered significantly underreported. In Chicago between 1996 and 2008, hate crimes reported to the Chicago Police Department *decreased* or remained the same in eleven out of the thirteen years, and only increased over the previous year for two years, 1997 and 2001. In fact, rather than going up, between 1996 and 2008 the number of hate crimes reported by the Chicago police *fell* by 59 percent, from 175 reported incidents in 1996 to just 72 reported incidents in 2008 (see table 6.1). In each year, African Americans were the majority of victims of racially motivated crimes.

Chicago's experience of declining hate crime would not be so curious if it were matched nationally. It is not (see table 6.2). Statistics collected from around the country over the same time period show that, rather than decreasing, in seven of the thirteen years hate crime increased. In

Table 6.1

Reported Hate Crimes, Chicago, 1996–2008

Year	Reported Incidents	% Change, 10-Year Average	% Change from Previous Year
1996	175	—	-20
1997	212	-3	+21
1998	204	-6	-4
1999	202	-6	-1
2000	182	-16	-10
2001	215	0	+18
2002	128	-40	-40
2003	128	-36	0
2004	122	-35	-4
2005	90	-50	-26
2006	80	-52	-11
2007	72	-54	-10
2008	72	-49	0
1996	175	—	-20

Source: Chicago Police Department

the years that there were decreases in the national figures, the decreases were smaller and less frequent than the decreases in Chicago. Significant events like well-publicized hate crimes often spur copycat crimes or cause backlashes or retaliation. For instance, after the World Trade Center was attacked in 2001, many cities experienced a rise in the number of bias-motivated attacks against Arab Americans. Copycat or retaliation-based bias crimes often lead to a temporary increase in the number of bias crimes identified by law enforcement in a particular locality. Such was not the case in Chicago, however. Chicago also seems to be immune to the general trend of significant events spurring copycat crimes. Though 1997 was one of the two years when hate crime increased in the city, no significant increases were reported in Bridgeport after the beating of Lenard Clark. When hate crimes increased nationwide in 2001, there was an increase in Chicago, though the size of the increase was much smaller.

It is unclear what to make of the steadily and fairly dramatically decreasing number of reported hate crimes in Chicago. When in 2000 reported hate crimes were down by 10 percent, having also fallen the

Table 6.2

Reported Hate Crimes, United States, 1996–2008

Year	Reported Incidents	% Change from Previous Year
1996	8,759	+9
1997	8,409	-4
1998	7,755	-8
1999	7,876	+2
2000	8,063	+2
2001	9,730	+20
2002	7,462	-23
2003	7,489	+.3
2004	7,649	-.5
2005	7,163	-6
2006	7,722	+8
2007	7,624	-1
2008	7,783	+2

Source: US Department of Justice

previous year, the head of the City of Chicago Human Relations Commission, Clarence Wood, hypothesized that the decrease was attributable to two things: better education and also victims of hate crimes declining to report out of frustration at the actions of police or the court system.[77] Interviews with victim advocates in the area echo Wood's view:

> JB: What is your interaction with the CPD Hate Crime Unit?
> WILLIAM: It is relegated to doing nothing. They [the detectives] find reasons not to count hate crime. Remember the case with the blind man. He was assaulted and the perpetrators called him a "blind motherfucker." They caught them, but they weren't charged with a hate crime.[78]

"Michael," another victim advocate who had also worked with the Chicago police hate crime unit, explained that if an individual was charged with both a hate crime and a more serious offense, then the more serious offense would go forward and the hate crime charge, as a lesser offense, would fall away. Thus, the hate crime unit's work preparing hate crime cases would be lost. "It would be better if there was an option to charge people with hate crime 1 (five to ten years) or hate crime 2 (ten to twenty years)," he said.[79]

The declining numbers of hate crimes reported to the police, along with the tendency for the charges to be dropped, suggest that hate crimes law as it currently stands may not be the best avenue of redress for targets of anti-integrationist violence in Chicago. Statistics on the percentage of the identified hate crime cases that are actually prosecuted are difficult to obtain, but the *Chicago Defender* reported that the police had made arrests in 106 of the 175 reported hate crimes in 1996. Hate crime charges were sought in only 19 of 106 cases for which arrests were made.[80] The difficulty of proving and potentially investigating such cases may be the reason for the paucity of charges. "What makes hate crime so unique is that it is the only crime where prosecutors have to prove why the crime happened," noted Joan O'Brien, who at the time was in the municipal division of the Cook County state's attorney's office. "Every other crime, we don't have to prove the motivation, even in a murder case."[81]

STATE CROSS BURNING STATUTES

In anti-integrationist violence cases in which the perpetrator burns a cross, states may use cross burning statutes as a remedy if such a statute is available. State cross burning statutes originated in the 1950s as a reaction to the use of the burning cross by the Ku Klux Klan. Such statutes may penalize cross burning in a variety of ways, either as a section of a statute that criminalizes the use of symbols in an intimidating manner[82] or as part of a statute that prohibits malicious intimidation.[83] One example of move-in violence prosecuted under a state cross burning statute is *State v. Talley*. Talley, along with two other individuals, was prosecuted for having burned a cross on his own lawn in the presence of a mixed-race family who had planned to move to his neighborhood. Talley had complained that "having niggers next-door" would ruin his property values. He was prosecuted under Washington State's malicious harassment statute, which specifically punished cross burning.[84]

Like other types of hate crime statutes, cross burning statutes have also been challenged on First Amendment grounds. In the wake of the Supreme Court's decision in *R.A.V.*, Washington State's court and a few other state courts struck down their cross burning statutes.[85] In 2003, in *Virginia v. Black*, the Supreme Court once again evaluated the constitutionality of statutes prohibiting cross burning. In this case, the Supreme Court considered an appeal by the Commonwealth of Virginia from a decision of the Virginia Supreme Court striking down Virginia's cross burning statute.[86] Though the respondents in the case, Barry Black, Richard Elliot, and Jonathan O'Mara, had all been convicted under the statute for burning a cross, the circumstances of the cross burnings were somewhat different. Black had presided over the burning of a cross at a Ku Klux Klan rally. O'Mara and Elliot were convicted for having burned a cross on the lawn of a black neighbor who had recently moved to the neighborhood.

In its decision in *Black*, the Supreme Court found Virginia's statute unconstitutional, not because it criminalized cross burning per se, but rather because, under the Virginia statute, the act of burning a cross was prima facie evidence of the intent to intimidate. In other words, the Court allowed states to outlaw cross burning performed with intent to intimidate. Though state statutes that criminalize cross burnings undertaken with intent to intimidate were upheld, after *Black* states may not take the fact that a cross was burned as prima facie evidence that this requirement has been met. In other words, there must be an independent determination based on the facts in the case indicating whether in burning a cross the defendant manifested an intention to intimidate the targets.

Cases in which a cross is burned on the front lawn of the only black family in an all-white neighborhood, especially when it is done soon after they have moved in, are situations in which the intent of the perpetrators seems very clear. Nevertheless, after *Black*, the Supreme Court's requirement of evidence of intent to intimidate may hamper the state's ability to successfully prosecute this type of move-in violence. For instance, a number of cross burning cases involve joking and/or drunken perpetrators who, after the fact, may insist that they never intended to cause harm.[87] Even if the cross burner is drunk or the cross has been burned as a joke or prank, in cases in which it has been burned on the lawn of the only black family in the area, it may nevertheless send a clear message—that the family should leave the neighborhood. It is not clear whether under *Black* the conviction of the cross burner in such a case would pass constitutional muster.

The Failure of Law

Despite the wide variety of legal remedies, anti-integrationist violence remains largely unaddressed. In federal cases, the responsibility for prosecuting hate crimes falls to the Justice Department, whose interest in bringing cases, commentators note, can vary with the politics of the administration.[88] For instance, a study by the Southern Poverty Law Center revealed that between 1987 and 1989, the Justice Department initiated prosecution in just thirty-one cases involving racial violence.[89] Though the precise number of actual hate crimes between 1987 and 1989 is unknown, in 1990 Congress passed the Hate Crime Statistics Act, mandating that the FBI collect data on hate crimes. FBI statistics on hate crime in 1991, the first year in which the agency collected data from law enforcement agencies nationwide, reported that nearly three thousand racially motivated hate crimes had occurred.[90] If the number of actual hate crimes in the late eighties was anywhere near the number reported to the FBI in 1991, the Justice Department may have neglected many opportunities to prosecute hate crimes.

The lion's share of the blame for failure to prosecute acts of anti-integrationist violence falls to the states. In most hate crime cases, prosecution falls generally to the states, where there may also be difficulties. Though most states do have some sort of legislation, there are frequently problems with enforcement. For instance, those targeted by anti-integrationist violence may not know much about the available remedies, or that such behavior is even illegal. It therefore falls to police and prosecutors to find and then investigate these cases. The low visibility of many of the acts that constitute this type of violence means that it may be difficult for such crimes to be recognized by either state or federal authorities.

Even when such acts are prosecuted, civil rights law, irrespective of the statute used, may not be a magic bullet for victims. It does not make them whole, even when they "win." Linda and Isaiah Ruffin, whose story is recounted in chapter 2, could not have asked for better legal results. They were targeted by two cross burnings directed at them three weeks after they moved to their dream house in a small town in northern Alabama in 1991. They had selected the rural community of Horton because they wanted to move their children away from the crime in Cleveland. For targets, they were lucky in that the perpetrators were caught, tried, and convicted. The seven Ku Klux Klan members responsible for the attack were convicted of depriving the Ruffins of their civil rights and received sentences ranging from eight months to eight years. In 1994, the Ruffins were awarded $900,000 in damages. After the jury verdict, Isaiah Ruffin said he wished he had never taken the case to court. "After what I've been through, I wouldn't do it again. . . . It cost me too much. I've had a hell of a sacrifice and it hasn't ended yet."[91] Ruffin remained in the community after the cross burning, though not in the house, which the family lost after they were unable to sell it. Ruffin's wife returned to Cleveland with their children after a second cross was burned at the family's home the summer after the first cross burning. Reflecting on his family's sacrifice and all of the stress it caused, Isaiah Ruffin lamented, "It'll never be over. . . . How can it be behind us when it destroyed a marriage of 18 years? The investment we made in our house was totally lost. My children are emotionally messed up."[92]

In addition to the emotional trauma caused by the events, the legal system may not be able to provide redress for the isolation that targets may feel if their neighbors support the perpetrator. As was described in the earlier chapters, open support for the perpetrator of racial violence is rare. A more common situation is when neighbors are silent, neither condemning the perpetrators' actions nor supporting it. The lack of open support for the family, as one of very few if not the only minorities in the area, further compounds both the isolation and the pain of the perpetrators' actions. For instance, in the Bailey-Hendersons' experience described in chapter 2, Andre Bailey commented on the pain caused by his neighbors' silence. They were the first blacks to their particular block. After his next-door neighbor burned a cross on the family's lawn, "No one came over to support us or tell us that we were welcome here despite what happened," Bailey said two years after the event.[93] The Bailey-Hendersons' neighbors may have been reluctant to stop for a variety of reasons. A woman who grew up in the house next door to the Bailey-Hendersons commented, "This kind of thing is going to happen anywhere there's a change. I don't think it's right what happened, but people get scared, worried their property values will go down."[94]

The Utility of Violence as a Tool to Prevent Integration

It is difficult to ascertain the precise impact of the violence directed at minorities integrating white neighborhoods since the passage of the Fair Housing Act in 1968. Chapters 2 and 5 describe widespread opposition by white working-class neighborhoods, particularly New York's Yonkers and Canarsie, to minority integration. In these cases, white residents opposed to housing integration were unable to keep their neighborhoods from changing racially. By 1992, the townhouses were built and eventually two hundred families moved from the projects to seven scattered sites located in white neighborhoods. In 2000, Northeast Yonkers, the predominantly Irish and Italian American neighborhood that had been almost exclusively white in the 1980s, was only about 72 percent white, with Hispanics, Asian Americans, and blacks making up the balance.[95]

The change in Canarsie was much more dramatic and began occurring in the mid-1980s. By the 2000 census, Canarsie was a far different place than it had been in the mid-seventies. In the 1990s, many immigrants from the Caribbean—Jamaica, Haiti, and Trinidad and

Tobago—moved to Canarsie. As one might have expected given the massive resistance to black entry, whites left Canarsie en masse when blacks began to move in. As one Caribbean resident who bought his house when there were just a handful of black families on the block said of the white people who had so quickly departed, "I guess they see black people coming," he chuckled, "and they run away from black people."[96] Between 1990 and 2000, Canarsie's white population plummeted to just over one-third of residents. In fact, between 1990 and 2000, Canarsie's racial makeup changed more than any other neighborhood in New York. Canarsie's black population, which had been just 10 percent in 1990, grew to 60 percent in 2000.[97]

Minority integration could not be permanently halted despite the anti-integrationist violence of the 1970s and 1980s, the most deadly case of which occurred in 1985 in Cleveland, Ohio, when a black family's home in the predominantly white Slavic Village was firebombed. Generally, the acts of anti-integrationist violence do not take the lives of its targets, but in this tragic case it did. The home was occupied by the Gants, who were the only black residents on the street. At about 1:45 a.m. on Sunday, June 2, 1985, the Gants' house erupted into flames. According to court records, a firebomb had been thrown through the center front window of the house. Seven of the residents of the house escaped unharmed, but Mabel Gant, a sixty-seven-year-old grandmother, was unable to get out, and died in the fire. In their investigation of the firebombing, the FBI and the Cleveland police department searched Kenneth J. Lowery's basement and found firebombs, Mason jars, lids, and wicks. The FBI also found witnesses who said that Lowery had yelled, "Go home niggers," at the Gants' house and, "I'm going to burn those niggers out." Lowery, the main suspect in the crime, was never convicted of the crime itself. He was, however, eventually convicted of perjury for statements he made to the FBI in connection with the crime.[98]

Even a crime as violent as a firebombing that resulted in the death of an elderly woman could not stop the inevitable pace of minority integration. In 1980, 3 percent of the population in Slavic Village was African American, substantially lower than the African American population in the city of Cleveland as a whole, which at that time was 46 percent African American. In 1990, 95 percent of the residents in Slavic Village were white, compared with 42 percent in the city of Cleveland as a whole. By 2000, the demographics of Slavic Village had changed significantly from the time of the bombing, and 26 percent of the residents were African American.[99]

Over the long term, violence directed at minorities integrating white neighborhoods has not been able to stop the demographic shifts that white residents opposed to minority integration fear. Most troubling, however, are the shorter-term consequences of these actions. Post-move violence and harassment cause minorities, who often have some trepidation about renting or purchasing houses in white neighborhoods, to regret or cancel their purchases. In cases in which individuals elect to stay, their lives and the lives of their children are forever changed. Such was the case with one city worker who moved to a predominately white neighborhood in Chicago in the mid-1980s. He and his wife were Puerto Rican, and his family moved to the neighborhood because they, like so many other minorities who move to white neighborhoods, were trying to achieve the American dream of owning a home. Their dreams of a brighter future in their new neighborhood were dashed when Mr. Garcia met his next-door neighbor.

> The first thing that happened was the encounter with the woman. . . . [M]y wife went down the stairs, opened the door, again fully expecting that, you know, probably a welcome, that's what we were . . . expecting. And super surprised when the statement that she made, which was to the effect of . . . that her and her family did not appreciate having niggers living next door to them.[100]

For the next twelve years, though the Garcias tried to ignore their next-door neighbors, they were continually harassed. Mr. Garcia described the harassment:

> [T]here were quite a few instances. You know, me walking down the path over to my walkway, and the door opening, and the n-word being yelled out the door. . . . there goes that monkey, that kind of stuff. My kids . . . both the Mrs. and my daughter being called "spic whores." My son being called "little nigger." And my younger son, Diego, was very fair skinned, being that, they called him the "little white nigger." Diego was maybe five years old, so, you know, those are wounds that don't heal.[101]

Conclusion

Despite the long-standing impact on his children (also noted by many other targets of anti-integrationist violence), Mr. Garcia was comparatively fortunate. He was living in Chicago, which had a substantial hate crime infrastructure: hate crime law, lawyers working on anti-integrationist violence, and prosecutors devoted to filing charges in these types of cases. Faced with civil rights charges, the Garcias' tormentor agreed to sell his house and move away from the neighborhood.

Unfortunately, many targets of bias-motivated violence in their homes are not so lucky. Hate crime law and the Fair Housing Act remain underutilized remedies.[102] Though it is impossible to say precisely how many individuals are intimidated while exercising their housing rights, it seems clear that there are many more incidents appropriate for charges than there are in which charges are filed. In 2009, to help address some of the problems that state and local jurisdictions experience with hate crime investigations, Congress passed the Matthew Shepard and James Byrd, Jr. Hate Crimes Prevention Act.[103] The Shepard/Byrd Hate Crimes Prevention Act expands federal authority to engage in hate crime investigations if local authorities decline to be involved, and provides additional funding to help states and localities investigate and prosecute hate crime. It is not clear that this new remedy has helped close the enforcement gap, however. In 2010, the first year the law was in force, the FBI reported that law enforcement agencies had identified 6,624 hate crimes.[104] The first conviction under the act did not occur until May 2011.[105]

Of the close to seven thousand hate crimes identified by law enforcement in 2010, just under half (3,725) were racially motivated.[106] Hate crime experts suggest that large percentages of such crimes occur in and around the victims' homes.[107] One possible reason for the paucity of bias crime and fair housing cases in light of such a large number of reported crimes may be that in cases of move-in or other types of anti-integrationist violence, criminal charges may be seen as the most obvious and, for prosecutors, the easiest types of remedies. If families do not know that they have civil rights relief available to them, they may not press for such relief. More importantly, cases of anti-integrationist violence are physically threatening and have drastic effects on the families at whom they are directed. In the wake of incidents, families may often move away or, if they have not yet moved in, nullify their purchase or rental of the living space in the neighborhood where the incident occurred. In a new house and a different neighborhood, individuals may feel disinclined to revisit the crime by pursuing civil rights actions.

Move-in violence directed at minorities who have just moved to neighborhoods is so threatening because it self-consciously invokes a well-known history of violence directed at minorities who "stepped out of line." In the Reconstruction South, for instance, minorities who transgressed social boundaries were lynched. Though it has been decades since blacks were lynched, moving to white neighborhoods may feel to some minorities as if they are crossing some sort of invisible color barrier. Contemporary incidents, even if there are proportionally few of them, reinforce the notion that minorities who move to white neighborhoods are breaking some sort of color barrier. If an incident happens, it becomes hard not to see it as a message that the minority family does not belong. It is therefore not surprising that many minorities victimized by move-in violence leave the neighborhood.

There may, however, be a way to prevent minorities from leaving in the wake of move-in violence. If the incident does not represent the feelings of others in the neighborhood, neighbors can and should communicate this to the family. If a city has a specialized police unit to investigate hate crimes, such incidents should be investigated, even if as vandalism they would not normally garner much attention. In other words, in sharp contrast to the perpetrator's intended message, everything should be done to demonstrate to the family that they moved to a place where they do in fact belong.

Conclusion

The Reality of Anti-Integrationist Violence and Prospects for Integration

Blacks, Latinos, Asian Americans, and other ethnic minorities choose to move to white neighborhoods for many of the same reasons that whites do: attractive houses, good schools for their children, better proximity to employment, and access to services. As previous chapters have shown, however, some minorities' dreams of a better life quickly turn to a nightmare of racial epithets, vandalism, cross burnings, and even arson and firebombing. The harrowing nature of contemporary anti-integrationist violence and the promise of integration are captured by two stories, both of which occurred in Vidor, Texas.

As chapter 2 describes, in the early 1990s Vidor, Texas, was a nearly all-white town. It had a reputation as a Ku Klux Klan stronghold. Few, if any, blacks lived there until 1993, when East Texas housing authorities were ordered by the court to desegregate the Vidor housing complex. As part of the plan, two black women and their families, and two single black men moved to a housing development in Vidor. The women were harassed and threatened by local residents and moved out within two weeks. The two men, fifty-eight-year-old John DeQuir and thirty-seven-year-old Bill Simpson, stayed a bit longer. Simpson, who was the last to leave, moved to the development in February 1993 and left in September 1993.

Like other low-income individuals who move to housing developments, Simpson moved to Vidor out of necessity. An imposing figure at seven feet tall and three hundred pounds, Simpson had broken his leg, leaving him unable to work. Explaining why he moved to a place with a reputation as a Klan stronghold, Simpson said, "I never wanted to be a hero, I just needed a place to stay. I was living on the street in Beaumont."[1] "I wanted to live a quiet honest life."[2] But his life in Vidor was anything but quiet. Hounded by racial epithets, obscene gestures, and threats, Simpson began to fear for his life. "I've had people who drive by and tell me they're going home to get a rope and come back and hang me," Simpson said.[3]

On September 1, 1993, Simpson left Vidor and moved eight miles away to Beaumont, Texas. Beaumont was much more integrated than Vidor, with a population that was 38 percent black. Like many poor minorities, Simpson moved not to a white neighborhood, but rather to the type of neighborhood he could afford. Like the type of neighborhood in which he had grown up, it was a black neighborhood in a high-crime area. Simpson's new neighborhood contained drug dealers, prostitutes, crack houses, and a violent crime rate more than twice the level of the rest of the region. Within hours of moving back to Beaumont, Simpson fell victim to one of the perils of being poor and living in a high-crime area. At 10:30 p.m., Simpson was shot five times with a nine-millimeter pistol. The robbery yielded $2.14, all Simpson had in his pocket.

While more tragic and ironic than the stories of most minorities who attempt to move to white neighborhoods, Bill Simpson's story has much in common with the stories of those who are "crimed out" of white neighborhoods. Like the targets of anti-integrationist violence described in the preceding chapters, Simpson was seeking a better life when he moved to Vidor. Simpson found the resistance he faced in Vidor extremely threatening, despite its "low offense" level. Minorities who face violent resistance to their presence are often terrified by behavior similar to what Simpson experienced—verbal assaults, threats, and vandalism. It is not just the actions of the perpetrators that targets have to worry about, but rather the fact that their race makes them always vulnerable to attack.

Threatened by this violence in a space where they are already so unprotected, targets often leave the neighborhood. When targets of anti-integrationist violence leave, they often return to neighborhoods similar to those they originally came from—less integrated, poorer places with more crime and fewer social services. Returning to similar neighborhoods, they are subject to the same risks from crime, and other negative consequences of living in a poor neighborhood. After Simpson's death, a police spokesman commented that Bill Simpson had been "a victim of a lot of what we're seeing in Beaumont—random robberies."[4]

The crime in poor black neighborhoods makes minorities willing to face white neighborhoods known for their racism. Donise Jackson and her five children, who moved from Port Arthur to Vidor after it had been cleaned up in the wake of Simpson's death, commented that given their options, Vidor was a better place for her and her children in spite of its problems. In Vidor she had the opportunity to take high school equivalency classes and receive job training. Vidor offered Jackson the chance to find employment. In Port Arthur, on the other hand, Jackson and her children lived amid the stench of the oil refinery emissions in one of the poorest neighborhoods. "I feel like this is the best place for me and my children," Jackson said of Vidor.[5]

Jackson's move to Vidor is the other half of the Vidor story, which may say something about prospects for integration after anti-integrationist violence has been addressed. In the wake of the failed integration of the Vidor public housing projects, in September 1993 HUD Secretary Henry Cisneros seized control of the Orange County (Texas) Housing Authority, demanded the resignation of its director, and vowed that blacks would again live in Vidor.[6] Security was increased, including an eight-foot-tall wire fence and a twenty-four-hour police guard shed. More than $1 million was spent on improvements, including a new laundry facility, air conditioning, job training, high school equivalency classes, and shuttle van transportation for residents. Federal marshals provided added security. The first black families moved in to the complex in the predawn hours of January 13, 1994. By September 1994, one-third of the housing project's seventy-four units were inhabited by black families.[7]

Though the housing project itself was integrated, it is not clear how deep or how lasting the integration of Vidor will be. After all, Vidor was not all that different from several other southeast Texas towns. In 2000, census records showed just eight black residents of Vidor, out of a population of 11,440. Though blacks were 12 percent of the population of Texas in 2000, Vidor and two other southeast Texas towns, Lumberton and Mauriceville, had fewer than ten black residents.[8] Data from the 2010 census show that 95.7 percent of Vidor's residents were white and 5.1 percent were Latino.[9]

The more limited integration that Vidor experienced is not to be taken lightly. In several other cities, including Chicago and Yonkers, there have been attempts to integrate white neighborhoods by relocating former public housing residents. While these efforts do not constitute the "full integration" that I describe below, there are substantial benefits that accrue to the minorities who are able to access these programs. These individuals are far better situated economically than if they remain in segregated neighborhoods.

Segregation, Integration, and Violence

One of the biggest surprises about anti-integrationist violence is its universal nature. As chapters 2 and 3 demonstrate, anti-integrationist violence is not just limited to Ku Klux Klan strongholds or small towns in Texas. Such violence occurs in the Northeast, the South, the West, and the Midwest, in small towns, rural areas, and big cities. One can find incidents in working-class neighborhoods as well as upscale suburbs.

The diversity of spaces in which anti-integrationist violence occurs as well as the fact that such violence still exists despite vast increases in tolerance and ethnic heterogeneity makes it harder to explain the contemporary existence of crimes directed at minorities who move to white neighborhoods. The simplest explanation for why anti-integrationist violence is occurring at the same time and in the same nation that twice elected a black president, is that though many whites may be willing to support a black politician, in particular circumstances, a majority of whites still remain reluctant to share their neighborhoods with people of color, particularly African Americans.

For perpetrators and those who support their behavior, all-white neighborhoods are private spaces. It is clear that the desire to keep African Americans out of these spaces is much deeper than measures of racial tolerance suggest. Whites of a variety of backgrounds do not wish to live in neighborhoods where African Americans live. In survey research as well as experimental designs, African Americans are the least preferred neighbors.[10] Anti-integrationist violence is symptomatic of that underlying feeling. Whites who harass minorities who move to white neighborhoods are fairly clear that they want minorities to leave their neighborhood. We see this in their language in cases when they talk to targets, or see it in their writing in cases of graffiti.

The "Integration Nightmare"

Beliefs concerning the negative effects of nonwhite integration on property values are long-standing, having been enshrined in real estate appraisal manuals at least as early as 1932.[11] The fear that African Americans moving in will decrease property values is a fear that cuts across lines of class and even ethnicity. For instance, even among other people of color, such as Asian Americans and Latinos, African Americans are the least preferred neighbors. "The blacks are moving in, all whites will abandon the neighborhood, at which point property values will plummet and the neighborhood will go to hell" is what I term the "integration nightmare" that everyone regardless of class, race, or experience imagines. Regardless of its lack of factual basis, the integration nightmare becomes the justification for not wanting black people ever to be one's neighbors.

Larger than life, the integration nightmare is invoked frequently when integration is foisted on unwilling whites. One vivid manifestation of the nightmare is found in this response to a *Philadelphia Weekly* article criticizing the intense level of racial segregation in Philadelphia in 2010. The article had suggested that segregation had been caused at least in part by white flight. In response, the letter writer invoked the integration nightmare to explain why he, for one, wants no part of racial integration:

> Between my wife and I, we work 3 jobs in one household so we can live as far as possible from Section 8 housing. Keep your brave new world, liberal views to yourself. I don't want Section 8 anywhere near me. I don't want anyone receiving any type of government assistance living near me. Do you need to hear it again? I don't care what their excuses or reasons are to receive that money. Nobody puts a gun to their heads and says "take this money or your dead." I pay THOUSANDS of dollars a year in Federal, State, City and property taxes to keep it away from my neighborhood. I'll say it. They don't deserve to live in or near my neighborhood. When are we going to stop this "free money" mentality? I don't care how horrible their neighborhood is. You made your bed now sleep in it. Remember, neighborhoods are made up of those that live in them.[12]

The integration nightmare is an imagined story that stems from a combination of racism, stereotypes, and worries that blacks will move in and fail to care for their property. While it is true that "white flight" has occurred in cities and suburbs across the country, there are three important things to note about the phenomenon.

First, in foreseeing rapid racial turnover after minorities move in, white residents are imagining that nonwhite integration proceeds down just one path. As chapter 5 indicates, that assumption is empirically false. Many neighborhoods around the country have integrated slowly and modestly. Second and more important, white flight is not caused by the minorities, but rather by whites who panic and flee the neighborhood. In other words, it can be controlled by white residents who refuse to panic. Third, the nightmare exaggerates the effect of African Americans moving to white neighborhoods.

When crimes are directed at minorities moving to the neighborhood because of the worry that the neighborhood will "turn," perpetrators assume that the neighborhood will be transformed by the arrival of a single black person or other minority. This assumption is wildly speculative, particularly in the majority of cases where the target is of the same or even higher class than the perpetrator. In fact, arrival of middle-class African Americans or Latinos may have less effect on middle-class white neighborhoods than does the arrival of a poor white person. Some research even suggests that minorities moving to a neighborhood increase property values.[13]

One way to address anti-integrationist violence is to recognize when the integration nightmare is being deployed. It is important for white neighborhood residents to understand that the fear of someone black moving to a white neighborhood originated with stories of rapid neighborhood racial turnover and is fueled by other types of racial separation. That most white people live in overwhelmingly white neighborhoods is just one marker of separation. Most white children attend predominantly white schools. If the schools are not entirely white, then the classrooms in which white students learn are. Activities outside school are predominately white; social and religious events are often segregated. There is little socialization across color lines. When a family of color moves to the white neighborhood, they are likely stepping into an area in which people have little or no contact with anyone like them.

Thus whites have little real-world experience on which to base the idea that racial integration is safe.

Context matters. Housing integration takes place in neighborhoods, which are collections of homes. Homes are where Americans need and want to feel safe. The integration nightmare is so destabilizing because it seems to threaten whites' safety and/or investment in their homes. The absence of cross-racial interaction means that whites and others cannot use their life experiences to predict what sort of experience they will have with an African American neighbor. The nightmare of rapid racial turnover, though destabilizing in its implications, may be comforting in its familiarity.

The integration nightmare is so all-encompassing that it can prevent whites from seeing blacks as good neighbors, or even any sort of neighbor at all. This was the experience of sixty-one-year-old Jean-Joseph Kalonji, an immigrant from Zaire whose son Bruno purchased a foreclosed home in Newtown County, near Atlanta, in April 2012. After closing, the Kalonjis were advised by their real estate agent to change the locks on the house. While Jean-Joseph and his wife were doing this, they were confronted by two white men, who they later learned lived next door. The men were armed with automatic weapons and told them to get out of the house. When the Kalonjis insisted they had purchased the home, the neighbors did not believe them, and so called the Newtown County sheriff's office. The Kalonjis did not have closing papers with them, so the deputies arrested them and charged them with loitering and prowling. The elder Kalonji, who had fled persecution in his native Zaire, said that the experience brought back painful memories. "There, they put me down with the gun to my head, and come here, the same," he said.[14]

The Kalonjis were relatively lucky. Sometimes the assumption that the black person is not a neighbor but is instead a criminal has tragic consequences. Such was the case at the Retreat at Twin Lakes, a gated community in Sanford, Florida, one evening in February 2012. Twenty-eight-year-old George Zimmerman, a neighborhood watch volunteer, encountered Trayvon Martin, an unarmed black high school student who was in the development to visit his father's girlfriend. Martin was returning from a convenience store with iced tea and candy. Ironically, the gated community Zimmerman was protecting was quite integrated.

Twenty percent of its residents were African American, 23 percent Hispanic, 49 percent non-Hispanic white, and 5 percent Asian American.[15] Despite the fact that Martin fit in the neighborhood demographically, Zimmerman called 911 to report Martin as a "suspicious" person. Zimmerman pursued, confronted, and then fatally shot the unarmed Martin. Though Martin was a slight, unarmed teenager, the authorities who responded to the incident after Martin had been shot accepted that he was "suspicious," and initially declined to charge Zimmerman.[16]

Why Care about Anti-Integrationist Violence?

The first reason to care about anti-integrationist violence is that evidence indicates that such acts affect housing integration in this country. Though it is impossible to measure the precise degree to which integration is affected by anti-integrationist violence, this conclusion has two linked pieces of support. The first is anecdotal, based on experiences of individuals who have moved to white neighborhoods. Though the precise number is hard to quantify, as chapters 2 and 6 detail, both newspaper accounts and the record in civil rights and Fair Housing Act cases demonstrate that when confronted with cross burnings, racist vandalism, arson, firebombings, and the like while living in a white neighborhood, many racial and ethnic minorities feel threatened and elect to leave the neighborhood.

In addition to this anecdotal evidence, two strands of research support the idea that when violent acts directed at minorities who have moved to white neighborhoods are publicized, they have a ripple effect and (unsurprisingly) deter other minorities from moving in. Research indicates that African Americans live in neighborhoods that are blacker than one might expect given both their income and their willingness to live in white neighborhoods.[17] Part of the explanation could be that blacker neighborhoods are chosen because middle-class African Americans fear harassment in white neighborhoods. This theory is supported by results from the Multi-City Study of Urban Inequality (MCSUI). The MCSUI surveyed minorities in Detroit, Los Angeles, Boston, and Atlanta, exploring whether they felt welcome in predominantly white communities in each of the cities. They found that if minority group members perceive themselves as unwelcome in particular communities, then these feelings affect actual residential patterns.[18] Violence is perhaps the ultimate marker for lack of welcome, so hearing about harassment of other African Americans might well operate as a disincentive for African Americans to choose white neighborhoods.

Why Segregation Matters

Segregation—particularly black-white segregation—in the United States exists at levels that social scientists and demographers take pains to explain. As chapter 3 highlights, census data from the first decade of the twenty-first century reveal that the average white person lives in a neighborhood that is 77 percent white, and conversely, the average black person lives in a neighborhood that is only 34 percent white and as much as 48 percent black.[19] Since 1990, very little progress has been made in decreasing the high levels of residential segregation between blacks and whites.[20] Decreases in the actual rate of neighborhood segregation have proceeded at an almost glacial pace since 2000.[21]

The level of residential segregation matters because research demonstrates that there is some relationship between neighborhood segregation and other types of social outcomes. Using data from 2005 to 2009, researchers have found that the national black-white dissimilarity rate for African Americans is 62.7.[22] This means that approximately 63 percent of African Americans would have to move to a predominately white census tract to be evenly distributed among whites. Such a high level of racial segregation is especially costly to African Americans, America's most segregated ethnic group. Many though not all of African Americans who are highly segregated by race are also poor.

There have been two types of mobility programs attempting to alleviate poverty. The first focused on race (moving individuals from black neighborhoods to white neighborhoods), while the second focused just on class (individuals were moved from poor black neighborhoods to less poor neighborhoods). Research on these two types of programs suggests that it matters whether one focuses on class or race. The *Gautreaux* mobility programs, described in chapter 5, which attempted to alleviate poverty by moving carefully selected individuals who are African American to predominately white suburbs, demonstrated significant success in improving the movers' and *their children's* employment and economic outcomes. Scholars collected data on where the mothers and their children who were part of the first *Gautreaux* program lived in the late 1990s, approximately two decades after their initial move. They determined that the program cut neighborhood poverty rates by more than half.[23] By contrast, the second program, Moving to Opportunity (MTO), which focused on class, not race, was not as successful as *Gautreaux* had been at improving the movers' educational and employment outcomes. Though later research comparing MTO programs in other cities did show that some MTO movers made improvements in important physical and mental health outcomes, there were no improvements in economic self-sufficiency.[24] In other words, those who had taken advantage of the MTO program were not more likely than the control group to have decreased their use of welfare, to be enrolled in better schools, or to be employed.[25]

When One Group "Owns" the Best Neighborhoods

Beyond the issue of life chances of African Americans as a group, there are civil rights and social justice reasons to try to alleviate America's high level of housing segregation, particularly when it is caused by the type of violence described in the previous chapters. The failure to address anti-integrationist violence sends a message that whites "own" particular neighborhoods and have the right to use extralegal violence to keep these spaces white. The assumption of ownership of a neighborhood violates both legal norms that prevent discrimination and social norms that insist upon racial equality. If the Fair Housing Act and the Fourteenth Amendment mean anything, individuals should have the ability (and not just the theoretical right) to live anywhere they choose, free from harassment.

Another significant social justice reason is that, in many ways, housing segregation is a government-created problem. As chapter 1 describes, over the last century the federal government created policies that encouraged and supported segregated white neighborhoods. Most important in this regard were policies that led to the creation of segregated white suburbs. The federal Home Owners Loan Corporation (HOLC) created a series of procedures for guaranteeing loans that were racially discriminatory and "all but eliminated black access to the suburbs and government mortgage money."[26] The Federal Housing Administration recommended the use of racially restrictive covenants on new suburban homes—like those created in Levittown—almost two years after the Supreme Court decision declaring their enforcement unconstitutional.[27]

Such procedures have a significant impact on the ability of African Americans to build wealth. Racial covenants prevented returning black GIs from buying affordable homes in Levittown. Those minorities who could afford to buy property in the large cities in the postwar period were also disadvantaged because in addition to a preference for underwriting suburban mortgages, the HOLC rating system meant that individuals who purchased in racially mixed neighborhoods were unable to secure government mortgages. The experience of blacks who did not have federal government support is strikingly different from that of whites who were able to secure title to land in the twentieth century, and thus "were much more likely to finance education for their children, provide resources for their own and their children's self-employment, or secure their political rights through political lobbies and electoral processes."[28] This racialized legacy of government support for whites has contributed to the significant wealth gap between blacks and whites.[29]

What Happens If We Fail to Integrate?

Segregation has costs, some of which are significant, for whites as well as minorities. The law professor Sheryll Cashin observes that whites pay a significant premium to live in white neighborhoods with "good" schools.[30] In Detroit, the premium whites pay to live in a white neighborhood may be as high as 43 percent, which is the difference between the average cost of a home for a white person compared to that of a black person with the same income.[31] According to Cashin,

> This phenomenon of overpriced or out of reach whiteness pervades real estate markets throughout the country. The problem seems magnified, however, in the metropolitan areas where there is a tale of two races as in Washington, DC, Atlanta, Detroit, and Chicago. Real estate markets in areas with large black populations seem to mirror white people's worst

fears. Buying your way into a well buffered, "premium" white neighbor-hood is the best defense against perceived crime and bad schools.[32]

Chasing the neighborhoods with the best schools can lead to personal bankruptcy and foreclosure, particularly in a climate of economic downturns. For suburban dwellers, chasing white neighborhoods may subject them to the stress of long commutes, less time with family, and the social isolation of children.[33]

One immediate consequence of the failure to integrate is that the African American poor stay poor. Home building and home value are a significant part of many Americans' wealth. The poor's confinement to neighborhoods where they are unable to build wealth and are separated from resources is a problem not just for them but for the rest of society. The proliferation of crime caused by the absence of jobs cannot be con-tained by poor neighborhoods. Raising the drawbridge will not work: even the best security systems cannot keep out an increasingly desper-ate poor population. This fact is something that wealthy South Africans have learned. If the class of poor people is large enough, one cannot make a security system powerful enough to prevent the rich from being victimized by poor criminals. Even if Americans were willing to pay the human cost of attempting to wall off an entire group, it is doubtful that most Americans would elect to shoulder the personal cost of increased vulnerability and rising crime that middle-class South Africans con-front on a daily basis.

The idea that whites wholly own white spaces and have a right to keep minorities out is deeply entrenched in particular neighborhoods. This, after all, was the ideology that allowed blacks to be attacked just for walk-ing through white neighborhoods in Brooklyn in the 1980s, as discussed in chapter 2. Increasing diversity has not eliminated the assumption by some whites that they own particular areas. Examples since 2005 include the bands of armed whites in Algiers Point, Louisiana, who bragged about shooting black refugees who crossed into their neighborhood in the aftermath of Hurricane Katrina, and attacks waged by whites against Latinos living in Shenandoah, Pennsylvania.[34] In the latter case, one of the most violent attacks involved the beating death of Luis Ramirez, a Latino man who had been accosted in a park by a group of white teenag-ers who told him, "Hey, you better get out of this neighborhood!"

The existence of all-white neighborhoods and neighborhoods consisting largely, if not entirely, of people of color seems to invite violence, particularly if it occurs after members of stigmatized groups have crossed into "white" territory. The idea that whites have a right to keep their neighborhood white is part of the reason that, despite increasing tolerance and increasing national and political diversity, so many whites (even those unwilling to engage in violence) do not wish to share their neighborhoods with minorities, particularly African Americans.

Curbing Anti-Integrationist Violence

Some level of anti-integrationist violence may be inevitable, since white neighborhoods have amenities which some whites will always want to protect by restricting access.[35] Carefully crafted legal and social remedies can make it possible to lessen both its frequency and the impact of this violence, however. This will require refocusing our energies in the civil rights arena, since addressing housing-related violence has not been a significant focus of civil rights advocacy in recent years. In housing law, when we talk about minorities' access to white neighborhoods, the focus has been primarily on barriers to entry in the form of discrimination. The assumption of many is that violence is no longer a factor. However, violence and discrimination remain a reality for too many minorities integrating white neighborhoods. As chapter 6 demonstrates, there are myriad legal remedies that may be aimed at the problem of violence in the context of housing. If an individual burns a cross on the lawn of a minority family, then he or she can be prosecuted under federal law or state hate crime law. In particular jurisdictions, the family may be able to seek monetary damages against the perpetrator. The availability of remedies is critical to addressing integration-related violence. Every jurisdiction that wants to truly address the problem of residential segregation should have remedies aimed at addressing integration-related violence.

As in other contexts, however, legal remedies are only as good as the institutions that are charged with enforcing them. Arson, firebombings, cross burnings, racist graffiti, and vandalism often take place in the middle of the night. Thus, the prosecution of anti-integrationist violence as a hate crime requires targeted effort and careful investigation.

Most jurisdictions do not have specialized investigative units dedicated to tracking down the person who scrawled "Nigger go home" on a black person's garage. In jurisdictions that do not have dedicated personnel, and even in some that do, most acts of anti-integrationist violence are treated as low-level crimes such as vandalism, racial harassment, and the like. Many police do not consider it a serious crime. Prosecutors often share this assessment.

Jurisdictions that want to effectively combat anti-integrationist violence need to have prosecutors, police officers, and victim advocates who take seriously the problem of anti-integrationist violence and respond to actions that may initially look like "vandalism" or other crimes that the police tend to ignore. This will require specialized training for individuals at every level of the process, from police officers to prosecutors, and dedicated personnel charged with investigating and prosecuting these sorts of hate crimes. An effective response will require not just the commitment of resources but also the belief by all local officials that such crimes are worth pursuing because they are important violations of civil rights. Of all the institutional requirements, this last bit is the hardest. Often acts of anti-integrationist violence look like petty crimes—vandalism or other property damage. To support minorities' right to live in all of the city's neighborhoods, local officials must understand that a cross burning is not just an arson.

Addressing the Negative Effects of Anti-Integrationist Violence

By far the most harmful effect of anti-integrationist violence is the disincentive that such violence creates. In the wake of violent incidents, minorities may leave the white neighborhoods to which they have moved after they are targeted. Hearing of such incidents, other minorities may decide not to relocate to a particular neighborhood. Just protecting the legal right of minorities to live unmolested in white neighborhoods has not eradicated, and is likely never to eradicate, anti-integrationist violence. The specter created by the integration nightmare casts a very long shadow, and the prospect of violating the law will not deter all perpetrators. If after the crime there is no support for the targeted family, many targets are likely to feel better able to protect themselves and their families by leaving the neighborhood.

The decision to leave a white neighborhood after an act of anti-integrationist violence is more straightforward if the target does not feel part of the community. Even before such crimes occur, many minorities who move to white neighborhoods report that they found the neighborhood to be a forbidding place where they did not feel welcome. In fact, minorities who move to white neighborhoods report a general failure of their neighbors to include them in communal activities or make them feel generally as if they belonged. When a cross is burned on their lawn, "Nigger go home" is written on their garage, or rocks are thrown through their car windows, the new neighbors' feeling of isolation and vulnerability skyrockets.

Rather than being blindsided when such incidents occur, it would be better if the community saw the arrival of minorities to their neighborhood as having the potential for anti-integrationist violence and laid the groundwork to address these crimes in advance. The best way to prevent the negative effects of anti-integrationist violence is for community members to reach out to minority newcomers before any act of violence occurs. Residents might do this by affirmatively welcoming minority newcomers to the neighborhood, inviting them to participate in neighborhood activities if such activities exist, and if such activities don't exist reaching out to them personally "across the fence" and in the public spaces of the neighborhood—on the streets, while doing yard work, and while walking back and forth to public transportation.

Such affirmative contact will have multiple benefits. The first is that white neighbors may learn that their new minority neighbor is, in essence, someone who is very much like them. Second, increased contact will express to the newcomer (and to would-be perpetrators) that the newcomer is a legitimate part of the community. Finally, if an ugly hate crime does occur, the notion that the target is a real community member will have a ring of truth to it. Not only will it make it more likely that legal remedies are pursued against the perpetrator, but also the target who has been attacked is part of a community, rather than just one family living in a sea of strangers. This is likely to make the target feel less alone, and the act of anti-integrationist violence may feel less frightening. It is harder to alienate a person who has already felt the warm embrace of community.

The Prospects for Integration

Once neighbors have worked to control anti-integrationist violence, is a greater degree of housing integration possible? Most likely. Integration can take various forms. For instance, from Vidor, Texas, to Yonkers, New York, government programs have taken carefully selected public housing residents and enabled them to move to majority-white neighborhoods. This is a resource-heavy way of making integration happen. In Vidor and Yonkers, public housing was built in majority-white neighborhoods. These neighborhoods had to be convinced to accept the public housing. As studies show, moving from a majority-black environment to a majority-white one is not without its challenges. Residents need to be aware of what they are getting into and supported once they arrive. Satisfying these requirements may lead to lasting integration. If the goal is one of getting minorities and whites to live in the same neighborhood, that goal is entirely within reach, even in the most difficult of circumstances.

Places like Vidor and Yorkers stand as an example of blacks' and whites' ability to live side by side without violence. This limited version of integration is certainly better than cities with minority neighborhoods and white neighborhoods that are closed to minorities. If minorities and whites live in the same neighborhoods, even if they do not interact, at the very least, African Americans are afforded many of the same amenities to which whites have access—safe neighborhoods, better schools, and the opportunity to build wealth through increasing the value of their homes. From a legal perspective, it means that the Fair Housing Act and civil rights law truly ensure access for everyone in the community, not just for whites.

Not Just Elbows Together

A more compelling and more challenging version of integration would be one in which minorities and whites do not just live together, but also have interaction. I call this "complete integration." It is the difference between schools that have integrated classrooms, where minorities and whites sit side by side and work together on activities, and schools where tracking means that minority students see the other students only in the cafeteria and on the sports fields.

Complete integration is a multigenerational project that will take years to complete, provided we actually begin serious work on it. I again cite Vidor as an example of the pitfalls that we face. Though Vidor is no longer all-white, it is not yet fully integrated. Some individuals reported a few positive experiences in Vidor, while others were more cautious about expressing any praise for the area. One resident of Vidor told the *Dallas Morning News* in 2001, "Sometimes I feel like I am in the camp of the enemy. I have to be careful and go undetected. . . . I'm not an idealist. I'm a black person, and there are certain boundaries I cannot cross."[36]

Complete or full integration requires not just living in the same area—which will be no small feat, given the negative experiences of some minorities moving to white neighborhoods—but also meaningful interaction. By meaningful interaction, I mean real interracial interaction: talking to each other, worshiping together, sharing stories, and connecting. This requires integrating a variety of spaces that are currently separate. Interacting, however, requires hard work across racial lines. We are, quite simply, "a country of strangers" who rarely converse across racial lines.[37] As Attorney General Eric Holder famously noted, in all things race we are a nation of cowards. Part of the reason we are so hesitant may be that we fear offending, and fear making mistakes. Pushing through these fears, however, is the only way we can break through the barrier to full integration and become the society that America claims it wants to be.

The outreach that stems the worst effects of anti-integrationist violence may have wider and much more profound implications as well. If sufficiently practiced, there is a chance that initial interaction from white neighbors at the critical point at which a person of color moves into a white neighborhood could lead to meaningful social interaction and full integration—not just "elbows together and hearts apart," as Martin Luther King Jr. phrased it.[38] Full integration involves not just whom one sees in the neighborhood, but also with whom one socializes, over the dinner table, at sports and community events, and the like. Interaction during downtime or "private life" has been called the last race problem.[39] The segregation of white private life is the last civil rights barrier. If African Americans and other minorities can break through that barrier to have a place in whites' private lives, then the neighborhoods to which they move will finally be fully integrated.

NOTES

INTRODUCTION

1. For a discussion of this and other incidents of anti-integrationist violence in Chicago in the late 1950s, see Amanda I. Seligman, *Block by Block: Neighborhoods and Public Policy on Chicago's West Side* (Chicago: University of Chicago Press, 2005), 167.

2. Niraj Warikoo, "Two Men Schemed to Drive Black Family out of Home, Indictment Says," *Detroit Free Press*, January 12, 2006.

3. Jack Levin and Jack McDevitt, *Hate Crimes: The Rising Tide of Bigotry and Bloodshed* (New York: Plenum, 1993), 246.

4. John R. Logan and Brian J. Stults, "The Persistence of Segregation in the Metropolis: New Findings from the 2010 Census," Census Brief prepared for Project US2010, http:www.s4.brown.edu/us2010.

5. Howard Shuman et al., *Racial Attitudes in America: Trends and Interpretations* (Cambridge: Harvard University Press, 1997), xi.

6. Logan and Stults, "The Persistence of Segregation."

7. Ibid.

8. Camille Charles, "The Dynamics of Residential Racial Segregation," *Annual Review of Sociology* 29 (2003): 167–207.

9. Thomas J. Sugrue, *The Origins of the Urban Crisis: Race and Inequality in Postwar Detroit* (Chicago: University of Chicago Press, 1996), 195.

10. Stephen Grant Meyer, *As Long as They Don't Move Next Door: Segregation and Racial Conflict in American Neighborhoods* (Lanham, MD: Roman and Littlefield, 2000), 6.

11. Johnson v. United States, 333 U.S. 10 (1948).

12. Payton v. New York, 445 U.S. 573 (1980); United States v. Karo, 468 U.S. 705 (1984); Kyllo v. United States, 533 U.S. 27 (2001).

13. Stanley v. Georgia, 394 U.S. 557 (1969).

14. Federal Bureau of Investigation, Criminal Justice Information Services Division, Table 1: Incidents, Offenses, Victims, and Known Offenders by Bias Motivation (2010), accessed October 15, 2012, http://www.fbi.gov/about-us/cjis/ucr/

hate-crime/2010/tables/table-1-incidents-offenses-victims-and-known-offend-
ers-by-bias-motivation-2010.xls.

15. Federal Bureau of Investigation, "Crime in the United States," accessed October
15, 2012, http:// http://www.fbi.gov/about-us/cjis/ucr/crime-in-the-u.s/2010/
crime-in-the-u.s.-2010/tables/10tbl01.xls.

16. "Man Convicted in 2002 Taylor Hate Crime Fire," *Detroit Free Press*, April 21,
2007, A6.

17. Ibid.

18. Ibid.

CHAPTER 1

1. Thomas J. Sugrue, *Sweet Land of Liberty: The Forgotten Struggle for Civil Rights in
the North* (New York: Random House, 2008), 201.

2. Lawrence B. De Graaf, "The City of Black Angels: Emergence of the Los Angeles
Ghetto, 1890–1930," *Pacific Historical Review*, August 1970, 324.

3. Stephen Grant Meyer, *As Long as They Don't Move Next Door: Segregation and
Racial Conflict in American Neighborhoods* (Lanham, MD: Roman and Littlefield,
2000), 5.

4. Howard N. Rabinowitz, *Race Relations in the Urban South, 1865–1890* (Athens:
University of Georgia Press, 1996), 97–98.

5. Ibid., 98.

6. Henry L. Taylor, "The Spatial Organization and the Residential Experience:
Black Cincinnati in 1850," *Social Science History* 10, no. 1 (1986): 61.

7. Ibid., 64.

8. Sugrue, *Sweet Land of Liberty*, 201.

9. Ira Berlin, *Many Thousands Gone: The First Two Centuries of Slavery in North
America* (Cambridge: Harvard University Press, 1998), 29.

10. Rabinowitz, *Race Relations*, 112.

11. Ibid.

12. David Katzman, *Before the Ghetto: Black Detroit in the Nineteenth Century*
(Urbana: University of Illinois Press, 1973), 69.

13. Kenneth Kusmer, *A Ghetto Takes Shape: Black Cleveland, 1870–1930* (Urbana:
University of Illinois Press, 1976), 12.

14. Ibid.

15. James Loewen, *Sundown Towns: A Hidden Dimension of American Racism* (New
York: New Press, 2005), 29.

16. Ibid., 31.

17. Ibid., 50.

18. Ibid., 51.

19. Ibid., 64.

20. Stanley Lieberson, *Ethnic Patterns in American Cities* (New York: Free Press of
Glencoe, 1963), 122, table 38.

21. Joe William Trotter Jr., *Black Milwaukee: The Making of an Industrial Proletariat, 1915–45* (Champaign: University of Illinois Press, 1985), 23.

22. Ibid.

23. Allan H. Spear, *Black Chicago: The Making of a Negro Ghetto, 1890–1920* (Chicago: University of Chicago Press, 1967), maps 1–4.

24. San Francisco's racial zoning ordinance is described in *In re Lee Sing*, 43 Fed. 359 (N.D. CA 1890).

25. A. Leon Higginbotham, *Shades of Freedom: Racial Politics and Presumptions of the American Electoral Process* (New York: Oxford University Press, 1996), 120.

26. Ibid., 121.

27. Garrett Power, "Apartheid Baltimore Style: Residential Segregation Ordinances of 1910–1913," *Maryland Law Review* 42 (1982): 298.

28. Ibid., 310.

29. Buchanan v. Warley, 425 U.S. 60, 69 (1917).

30. Ibid., 20.

31. Meyer, *As Long as They Don't Move Next Door*, 105.

32. 245 U.S. 60, 82 (1917).

33. Leonard S. Rubinowitz and Kathryn Shelton, "Nonviolent Direct Action and the Legislative Process: The Chicago Freedom Movement and the Federal Fair Housing Act," *Indiana Law Review* 41 (2008): 674–75.

34. Harold X. Connolly, *A Ghetto Grows in Brooklyn* (New York: New York University Press, 1977), 21–22.

35. Becky M. Nicolaides, *My Blue Heaven: Life and Politics in the Working-Class Suburbs of Los Angeles, 1920–1965* (Chicago: University of Chicago Press, 2002), 156.

36. Ibid.

37. Douglas Henry Daniels, *Pioneer Urbanites: A Social and Cultural History of Black San Francisco* (Philadelphia: Temple University Press, 1991), 76.

38. Ibid., 99.

39. Charles Spurgeon Johnson, *The Negro War Worker in San Francisco: A Local Self-Survey* (American Missionary Association and Julius Rosenwald Fund, 1944), 3.

40. Ibid.

41. Meyer, *As Long as They Don't Move Next Door*, 16.

42. Ibid.

43. Ibid.

44. Philip A. Clinker and Rogers M. Smith, *The Unsteady March: The Rise and Decline of Racial Equality in America* (Chicago: University of Chicago Press, 1999), 115.

45. Ibid.

46. Ibid.

47. Ibid.

48. Nicolaides, *My Blue Heaven*, 156.

49. Power, "Apartheid Baltimore Style," 289, 295.

50. St. Clair Drake and Horace Clayton, *Black Metropolis: A Study of Life in a Negro City* (New York: Harbinger, 1970), 178.

51. Ibid.

52. Ibid.

53. James Wolfinger, *Philadelphia Divided: Race and Politics in the City of Brotherly Love* (Chapel Hill: University of North Carolina Press, 2007), 11.

54. Ibid.

55. Ibid.

56. Arnold R. Hirsch, *Making the Second Ghetto: Race and Housing in Chicago, 1940–1960* (Chicago: University of Chicago Press, 1983), 40–67.

57. Kevin Boyle, *Arc of Justice: A Saga of Race, Civil Rights, and Murder in the Jazz Age* (New York: Henry Holt, 2004), 24–25.

58. Meyer, *As Long as They Don't Move Next Door*, 33.

59. Ibid., 34.

60. Boyle, *Arc of Justice*, 348.

61. Sugrue, *Sweet Land of Liberty*, 204.

62. Charles Abrams, *Forbidden Neighbors* (New York: Harper and Brothers, 1955), 230.

63. Ibid.

64. Sugrue, *Sweet Land of Liberty*, 204.

65. Eric Avila, *Popular Culture in the Age of White Flight: Fear and Fantasy in Suburban Los Angeles* (Berkeley: University of California Press, 2004).

66. Nicolaides, *My Blue Heaven*, 193.

67. Kevin Kruse, *White Flight: Atlanta and the Making of Modern Conservatism* (Princeton: Princeton University Press, 2005), 60.

68. Meyer, *As Long as They Don't Move Next Door*, 55.

69. Ibid.

70. Glenn T. Eskew, *But for Birmingham: The Local and National Movements in the Civil Rights Struggle* (Chapel Hill: University of North Carolina Press, 1997), 66.

71. Meyer, *As Long as They Don't Move Next Door*, 88.

72. Ibid., 59.

73. Ibid., 62.

74. Ibid., 66.

75. Avila, *Popular Culture in the Age of White Flight*, 30.

76. Meyer, *As Long as They Don't Move Next Door*, 66.

77. David M. P. Freund, *Colored Property: State Policy and White Racial Politics in Suburban America* (Chicago: University of Chicago Press, 2010), 180.

78. Thomas J. Sugrue, *The Origins of the Urban Crisis: Race and Inequality in Postwar Detroit* (Princeton: Princeton University Press, 2005), 73.

79. Ibid., 74.

80. Avila, *Popular Culture in the Age of White Flight*, 31.

81. Hirsch, *Making the Second Ghetto*, 41.

82. Ibid.

83. Ibid., 53.
84. Rudy Pearson, "A Menace to the Neighborhood: Housing and African-Americans in Portland, 1941 to 1945," *Oregon Historical Quarterly* 102, no. 2 (Summer 2001): 158–79, 160.
85. Ibid.
86. Ibid.
87. Ibid.
88. Ibid., 166.
89. Ibid., 171.
90. Ibid., 173.
91. Freund, *Colored Property*, 179.
92. Scott Kurashige, *The Shifting Grounds of Race: Black and Japanese Americans in the Making of Multiethnic Los Angeles* (Princeton: Princeton University Press, 2008), 161.
93. Celia Rasmussen, "L.A. Then and Now: Dream Home Came with Racial Restrictions," *Los Angeles Times*, November 11, 2007.
94. Ibid.
95. Meyer, *As Long as They Don't Move Next Door*, 31. The cases included Corrigan v. Buckley, 271 U.S. 323 (1926); Sipes et al. v. McGhee, 316 Mich. 614, 25 N.W.2d 638 (Mich. 1947). In the Supreme Court, of course, *Sipes* counts as a "win."
96. "Victory on Sugar Hill," *Time*, December 17, 1945, 2.
97. 334 U.S. 1 (1948).
98. Ibid., 5.
99. 316 Mich. 614, 25 N.W.2d 638 (Mich. 1947).
100. 334 U.S. 1, 8 (1948).
101. Ibid., 20.
102. 334 U.S. 24 (1948).
103. 14 Stat. 27 (1866).
104. 334 U.S. 24, 34. (1948).
105. Sugrue, *Sweet Land of Liberty*, 209.
106. Ibid., 208–12.
107. Sugrue, *Origins of the Urban Crisis*, 222.
108. Ibid.
109. Sugrue, *Sweet Land of Liberty*, 200.
110. Nicolaides, *My Blue Heaven*, 191.
111. Kenneth T. Jackson, *Crabgrass Frontier: The Suburbanization of the United States* (New York: Oxford University Press, 1985), 238.
112. Freund, *Colored Property*.
113. Loewen, *Sundown Towns*, 254.
114. Jackson, *Crabgrass Frontier*, 241.
115. Ibid.
116. Florence Roisman, "Teaching about Inequality, Race, and Property," *Saint Louis University Law Review* 46 (2002): 684.

117. "Levittown, New York, Population by Race," accessed November 15, 2012, http://censusviewer.com/city/NY/Levittown.

118. Freund, *Colored Property*, 245.

119. Ibid., 246.

120. Ibid.

121. Hirsch, *Making the Second Ghetto*, 51.

122. Sugrue, *Origins of the Urban Crisis*, 208.

123. Ibid., 211.

124. Ibid., 59.

125. Ibid., 232–33.

126. Ibid., 233.

127. Ibid.

128. Will Cooley, "Moving On Out: Black Pioneering in Chicago, 1915 to 1950," *Journal of Urban History* 36, no. 4 (2010): 485–506, 498.

129. Arnold R. Hirsch, "Massive Resistance in the Urban North: Trumbull Park, Chicago, 1953–1966," *Journal of American History* 82, no. 2 (September 1995): 522–50, 522–24.

130. Ibid., 531.

131. Amanda I. Seligman, *Block by Block: Neighborhoods and Public Policy on Chicago's West Side* (Chicago: University of Chicago Press, 2005), 167.

132. Ibid.

133. "Bert Glass," in discussion with the author, June 20, 2006.

134. Ibid.

135. Ibid.

136. Ibid.

137. Eskew, *But for Birmingham*, 53.

138. Ibid.

139. Ibid., 54.

140. Kruse, *White Flight*, 43.

141. Ibid., 47.

142. Ibid., 55.

143. Ibid., 56.

144. Tracy E. K'Meyer, *Civil Rights in the Gateway to the South: Louisville, Kentucky, 1945–1980* (Lexington: University Press of Kentucky, 2009), 61.

145. Ibid., 62.

146. Catherine Fosl, *Subversive Southerner: Anne Braden and the Struggle for Racial Justice in the Cold War South* (Lexington: University of Kentucky Press, 2002), 136–42.

147. Ibid., 141.

148. Ibid.

149. Ibid., 147.

150. Ibid., 198. The experience of the Wades' purchase is also described in Anne Braden's memoir, *The Wall Between* (Knoxville: University of Tennessee Press, 1999).

151. Sugrue, *Origins of the Urban Crisis*, 62.
152. Hirsch, *Making the Second Ghetto*, 98.
153. Seligman, *Block by Block*, 25.
154. Sugrue, *Origins of the Urban Crisis*, 239.
155. Ibid., 241. Though at various points the Catholic Church has supported neighborhood integration—for instance, as part of Chicago's Catholic Interracial Council in the 1960s—there is some evidence that various actors in the individual Catholic parish churches saw minority integration as a threat to the cohesiveness of their parishes. For instance, in the early 1960s in West Garfield Park, the Chicago Archdiocese provided financial and logistical aid to United Property Group (UPG). The UPG was focused on keeping the West Garfield Park neighborhood white. In 1964 church officials withdrew support for the UPG. Seligman, *Block by Block*, 170–75. See also the discussion of Italian Catholics in Chicago in the 1930s and 1940s in Thomas A. Guglielmo, "Encountering the Color Line in the Everyday: Italians in Interwar Chicago," *Journal of American Ethnic History* 23, no. 4 (Summer 2004): 45-77, 53-54. There is also discussion of Catholic opposition to racial integration in John T. McGreevy, *Parish Boundaries: The Catholic Encounter with Race in the Twentieth Century Urban North* (Chicago: University of Chicago Press, 1996), 110.
156. Sugrue, *Origins of the Urban Crisis*, 235.
157. Ibid., 241.
158. Guglielmo, "Encountering the Color Line in the Everyday: 45–77.
159. Ibid., 48.
160. Ibid.
161. Ibid., 53.
162. Ibid., 54.
163. Ibid., 51.
164. Ibid., 53.
165. Sugrue, *Origins of the Urban Crisis*, 215.
166. Ibid.
167. Carolyn Adams et al., *Philadelphia: Neighborhoods, Division, and Conflict in a Postindustrial City* (Philadelphia: Temple University Press, 1991), 81.
168. Ibid.
169. Sugrue, *Origins of the Urban Crisis*, 216.
170. Ibid., 215.
171. Kruse, *White Flight*, 82.
172. Sugrue, *Origins of the Urban Crisis*, 241.
173. Kruse, *White Flight*, 68–69.
174. Seligman, *Block by Block*, 186.
175. Ibid.
176. Ibid., 188.
177. Phyllis Palmer, *Living as Equals: How Three White Communities Struggled to Make Interracial Connections during the Civil Rights Era* (Nashville: Vanderbilt University Press, 2008), 97.

178. Ibid., 102-3.

179. Ibid., 105.

180. 42 U.S.C. § 1982; *Hurd v. Hodge,* 334 U.S. 24 (1948).

181. Freund, *Colored Property,* 209.

182. Ibid.

183. Rubinowitz and Shelton, "Nonviolent Direct Action," 663.

184. Ibid., 675.

185. Ibid., 679.

186. Ibid., 680.

187. Ibid.

188. Ibid., 711.

189. Senate Report 90-721 (1967), reprinted in 1968 U.S.C.C.A.N. 1837, 1839.

190. 42 U.S.C. § 3631 (2000).

CHAPTER 2

1. Kevin Kruse, *White Flight: Atlanta and the Making of Modern Conservatism* (Princeton: Princeton University Press, 2005).

2. Amanda I. Seligman, *Block by Block: Neighborhoods and Public Policy on Chicago's West Side* (Chicago: University of Chicago Press, 2005), 175.

3. Verson C. Thompson, "Three Crosses Burned in Pr. George's; Three Crosses Burning in Pr. Georges Held Bizarre, but Serious," *Washington Post,* February 7, 1977, C1.

4. "Victimized Family Visited by Reagan," *New York Times,* May 4, 1982, B8.

5. On Bensonhurst, see Jonathan Rieder, *Canarsie: The Jews and Italians of Brooklyn against Liberalism* (Cambridge: Harvard University Press, 1985); and Howard Pinderhughes, "The Anatomy of Racially Motivated Violence in New York City: A Case Study of Youth in Southern Brooklyn," *Social Problems* 40 (1993): 478. On Yonkers, see Lisa Belkin, *Show Me a Hero: A Tale of Murder, Suicide, Race, and Redemption* (Boston: Little, Brown, 1999). On Cicero, see William Julius Wilson and Richard P. Taub, *There Goes the Neighborhood: Racial, Ethnic, and Class Tensions in Four Chicago Neighborhoods and Their Meaning for America* (New York: Random House, 2006).

6. Wilson and Taub, *There Goes the Neighborhood.*

7. Rieder, *Canarsie,* 84.

8. Ibid., 21.

9. Quoted in ibid., 22.

10. Ibid., 200.

11. Ibid., 201.

12. Ibid.

13. Southern Poverty Law Center, *"Move-In" Violence: White Resistance to Neighborhood Integration in the 1980s* (Montgomery: Southern Poverty Law Center, 1987).

14. Ibid., 2.

15. Gary Gateley, "Racial Incidents Beset Two Towns," *New York Times,* April 20, 1986, 8.

16. The experiences of Goffer and Franklin are described in Leonard Rubinowitz and Imani Perry, "Crimes without Punishment: White Neighbors' Resistance to Black Entry," *Journal of Criminal Law and Criminology* 92 (Fall 2001–Winter 2002): 404–5. Another firebombing of a black family who moved into a different white neighborhood in Chicago occurred just two weeks later, in November 1984. "Chicago Reports 2nd Racial Attack," *Washington Post*, November 21, 1984, A8.

17. "Black Homes under Attack in Toledo," *Chicago Tribune*, August 19, 1986.

18. William E. Schmidt, "Population Changes Bring Worries about Racism to Rural Georgia County," *New York Times*, February 20, 1985, A10. "Man Charged with Assault and Racial Clash in Cleveland," *Philadelphia Inquirer*, June 14, 1986, A6. Luix Overbea, "Boston Neighbors Get Together to Ease Racial Tensions," *Christian Science Monitor*, September 15, 1982. William K. Stevens, "White Philadelphian, 13, Is a Model to Those Combating Racist Incidents," *New York Times*, November 24, 1986, B14.

19. Douglas S. Massey and Nancy A. Denton, *American Apartheid: Segregation and the Making of the Underclass* (Cambridge: Harvard University Press, 1993), 91.

20. "Philadelphia Mayor Acts on Racial Strife," *Chicago Tribune*, November 3, 1985, 6C.

21. Ibid.

22. Steven A. Marquez, "Burnt Offering: VA Sells Elmwood House to White Neighbor," *Philadelphia Daily News*, February 22, 1986, 5.

23. Carolyn Adams et al., *Philadelphia: Neighborhoods, Division, and Conflict in a Postindustrial City* (Philadelphia: Temple University Press, 1991), 22.

24. Howard Pinderhughes, *Race in the Hood: Conflict and Violence among Urban Youth* (Minneapolis: University of Minnesota Press, 1997), 89.

25. Ibid., 92–93.

26. Donald P. Green, Dara Z. Strolovitch, and Janelle S. Wong, "Defended Neighborhoods, Integration, and Racially Motivated Crime," *American Journal of Sociology* 104, no. 2 (September 1998): 397.

27. Ibid., 373.

28. U.S.C. § 534 (HCSA) (1990).

29. Ami Lynch, "Hating the Neighbors: The Role of Hate Crime in the Perpetuation of Black Residential Segregation," *International Journal of Conflict and Violence* 1 (2008): 2.

30. Jack Levin and Jack McDevitt, *Hate Crimes: The Rising Tide of Bigotry and Bloodshed* (New York: Plenum, 1993), 246.

31. Federal Bureau of Investigation, Hate Crime Statistics, 2008. Table 12, Agency Reporting by State, accessed November 12, 2012, http://www2.fbi.gov/ucr/hc2008/jurisdiction.html.

32. Ibid.

33. Jeannine Bell, *Policing Hatred: Law Enforcement, Civil Rights, and Hate Crime* (New York: New York University Press, 2004).

34. Ryken Grattet, "The Urban Ecology of Bias Crime: A Study of Disorganized and Defended Neighborhoods," *Social Problems* 56, no. 1 (2009).

35. Michael A. Fletcher, "A Neighborhood Slams the Door: Racist Acts Drive Philadelphia Family out of White Area," *Washington Post*, May 18, 1996, A1; Joseph A. Slobodzian, "Neighbor Tells of Racial Vandalism," *Philadelphia Inquirer*, April 4, 1998, B1; "Black Woman, Son Assaulted, Four Are Jailed," *New York Times*, September 27, 1994, A4.

36. David Gambarcorta et al., "Advice about Racism Proved to Be Prophetic," *Philadelphia Daily News*, December 14, 2007, 6.

37. Ibid.

38. Danielle Gordon and Natalie Pardo, "Hate Crimes Strike Changing Suburbs," *Chicago Reporter*, September 1997, 1.

39. Abdon M. Pallasch, "Families Seeking Safety Find New Threats," *Chicago Tribune*, November 30, 1998, 1.

40. John Ritter, "Supporters Urge Berwyn Black to Rethink Move," *Chicago Sun-Times*, March 9, 1992, 5.

41. Teresa Puente, "Increasingly Diverse Areas Face Hate Crimes," *Chicago Tribune*, July 1, 1996, 1.

42. Gordon and Pardo, "Hate Crimes Strike Changing Suburbs."

43. Joseph Kirby, "Family May Remain in Berwyn After Local Outpouring of Support," *Chicago Tribune*, March 9, 1992, 3; Ian Demsky, "Police Seek Leads After Cross Is Burned in Goodlettsville," *Tennessean* (Nashville, TN), October 27, 2004, 2; Darryl E. Owens, "Racists Harass Winter Garden Home," *Orlando Sentinel Tribune*, July 9, 1991, B1.

44. "Three Suspects Sought in Cross Burnings," *Commercial Appeal* (Memphis, TN), April 2, 1994.

45. Jerry Seper, "New York City Reels over Series of Racial Attacks," *Washington Times*, January 16, 1992, A3.

46. "Around the Nation," *Houston Chronicle*, September 15, 2004, A8.

47. "Latest Cross Burning Scares Portland Woman," *Seattle Times*, June 25, 1992.

48. No incidents were reported in Alaska, Delaware, Hawaii, Idaho, Kansas, Montana, New Hampshire, New Mexico, North Dakota, South Dakota, or Vermont.

49. The highest number of incidents were identified in California (48), followed by Florida (40), Illinois (32), New York (26), Pennsylvania (24), Massachusetts (24), Missouri (24), and Ohio (23).

50. Darrell Glover, "The Hateful Truth: Racists Are Targeting Black Family," *Seattle Post-Intelligencer*, July 16, 1991, B1.

51. "Cross Burning: Family Calls for National Investigation," *Ft. Lauderdale Westside Gazette*, August 19–25, 2004, 1B. A similar incident involved a large cross burned into the lawn of a Jewish family in an upscale development in Lake Oswego, Oregon. Nia Carlson, "Cross Seared into Family's Lawn," *Oregonian* (Portland, OR), June 23, 2004.

52. Some incidents may fall into multiple categories, so this figure is different from the total number of incidents.

53. Suzanne P. Kelly, "'Minnesota Nice' Marred by Racism: Tension Underlies Increase in Number of Hostile Acts," *St. Petersburg (FL) Times*, March 22, 1992, 6B; Owens, "Racists Harass Winter Garden Home."

54. Victoria Agnew, "Slurs Painted on a Man's Home," *Charleston (SC) Post and Courier*, June 3, 1997.

55. Rick Bella and Bobby Allyn, "Move-In Day Finds Words of Hatred, Fire Threat," *Oregonian* (Portland, OR), September 3, 2010.

56. Darrell E. Owens, "Family Troubled by Racial Vandalism," *St. Petersburg (FL) Times*, July 10, 1991, 4B.

57. "Probation for Racial Slur," *Chicago Sun-Times*, February 15, 1996, 18.

58. Robert Perez, "KKK Warning Greets Biracial Couple," *Philadelphia Inquirer*, July 7, 1992.

59. Kathy Chaney, "Vandals Spray Paint Racist Message on Garage of Black Family in West Lawn," *Chicago Defender*, September 13, 2007.

60. David Weber, "West Roxbury Residents Rally against Racism," *Boston Herald*, September 27, 1996, 1.

61. Abby Vansickle, "Strangers Ease Sting of Racist Graffiti," *St. Petersburg (FL) Times*, July 30, 2004, 13; Douglas Crouse, "Coming Together against Bias: Groups Support Victimized Family," *Herald News* (Passaic County, NJ), June 4, 2006; Femi Cole, "Community Reaching Out to Family," *Green Bay Press-Gazette*, July 3, 1999, 1B.

62. Vansickle, "Strangers Ease Sting."

63. "Wise Calls Cross Burning Incident a Hate Crime," *Charleston Daily Mail*, August 3, 2004, 2A; Jane Kwiatkowski, "Two Hundred Attend Rally to Show Support for Victims of Racial Attack," *Buffalo News*, April 5, 1998, 1C.

64. In the vast majority of cases in which perpetrators are identified, the perpetrator is male.

65. Russell Walker, "Bigotry Kindling for Tremont Arson Fires?" *Cleveland Call and Post*, August 22–28, 2007, 1A.

66. Lu-in Wang, "The Transforming Power of 'Hate': Social Cognition Theory and the Harms of Bias Related Crimes," *Southern California Law Review* 71 (November 1997); Jack McDevitt et al., "Consequences for Victims: A Comparison of Bias- and Non-Bias–Motivated Assaults," *American Behavioral Scientist* 45 (December 2001).

67. Joshua Partlow, "Graffiti Near Arson Target Probed as a Possible Slur," *Washington Post*, November 2, 2005.

68. Stefani G. Kopenec, "Two White Men Admit to Burning Black Family's Wichita Falls Home," *Austin American Statesman*, August 6, 1996.

69. "No Room for Hatred in Diverse Deltona," *Orlando Sentinel*, April 25, 2004, K3.

70. McDevitt et al., "Consequences for Victims," 711.

71. Ibid., 709.

72. Ibid.

73. Ibid.

74. Johnson v. Smith, 878 F. Supp. 1150, 1155–56 (N.D. Ill. 1995).

75. Williams v. Derifield, No. 04 C 5633, 2005 WL 3455867 (N.D. Ill. Dec. 13, 2005).

76. Ibid., 7.

77. United States v. Stewart, 65 F.3d 918 (11th Cir. 1995).

78. Bart Jones, "One Year Later: Farmingville Firebomb," *Newsday*, July 6, 2004.

79. "Courage Protect the Black Family," *Charleston Gazette*, February 10, 1999, 4A.

80. Maria Newman, "Victim of Hate Crime Calls High Court Ruling a 'Slap in the Face,'" *New York Times*, June 27, 2000, B5.

81. Apprendi v. New Jersey, 530 U.S. 466 (2000).

82. Newman, "Victim of Hate Crime."

83. Apprendi, 530 U.S. 466.

84. Newman, "Victim of Hate Crime."

85. Ibid.

86. United States v. Long, 935 F.2d 1207, 1211 (11th Cir. 1991).

87. United States v. Myers, 892 F.2d 642 (1990).

88. State v. Talley, 858 P.2d 217, 220 (Wash. 1993).

89. "Despite Vandals, Blacks Move into White L.I. Neighborhood," *New York Times*, October 2, 1991.

90. Christina L. Esparza, "Vandals Strike Home: Glendora Police Investigate Possible Hate Crime," *San Gabriel Valley Tribune*, April 8, 2004.

91. Michelle Hunter, "Racist Symbols Appear in Metairie Yard: Black Family Stunned by 'This Garbage,'" *New Orleans Times-Picayune*, June 10, 2008.

92. Wyn Craig Wade, *The Fiery Cross: The Ku Klux Klan in America* (New York: Simon and Schuster, 1987), 185.

93. Ibid., 263–64, 279, 290. For more discussion of the history of cross burning, see Jeannine Bell, "O Say, Can You See: Free Expression by the Light of Fiery Crosses," *Harvard Civil Rights–Civil Liberties Law Review* 39, no. 2 (Summer 2004): 343–45.

94. Wade, *The Fiery Cross*, 329.

95. "Latest Cross Burning Scares Portland Woman."

96. Jingle Davis, "Cross Purposes: Why Was Symbol Burned on Woman's Front Yard?" *Atlanta Journal and Constitution*, March 28, 2000.

97. "Cross Burning: Family Calls for a National Investigation."

98. "Racial Incidents Probed," *Pittsburgh Post-Gazette*, November 25, 1997, B4; Kwiatkowski, "Two Hundred Attend Rally"; Tom Murphy, "Police: Teenager Tried to Burn Crosses on Lawns and Self-Described Skinhead Also Scratched Racist Emblems on Mailbox, Police Say," *Syracuse (NY) Post-Standard*, September 6, 1998, B1; Jackie Paul, "Racial Vandalism Targets Black Family in Highland," *Riverside (CA) Press-Enterprise*, March 13, 1999, B1.

99. Paul, "Racial Vandalism."

100. Gregory Freeman, "Burned Out, Home Defaced, Man Will Not Pass Along 'Baton of Hatred,'" *St. Louis Post-Dispatch*, January 15, 1993, 1C.

101. Mari A. Schaefer, "Hate-Crime Incident in Collingdale," *Philadelphia Inquirer*, July 17, 2008.

102. Mike Tharpe and Jeannye Thornton, "Death in Black and White: White Bigots Hounded Bill Simpson; Police Say Black Thugs Killed Him," *US News and World Report*, June 13, 1994.

103. Young v. Pierce, 628 F. Supp. 1037 (E.D. Tex. 1985).

104. "2 Blacks Leaving Vidor Blame Racism: HUD Concerned about Housing Project," *Dallas Morning News*, August 27, 1993, 34A.

105. Pam Easton, "Vidor's Black Population Reaches Eight, Census Shows: Town Trying to Move Past Integration History," *Dallas Morning News*, July 16, 2001, 13A.

106. Susan Fahlgren, "Klan, Town Battle Court-Ordered Desegregation of Housing Complexes," *Los Angeles Times*, January 10, 1993, 4.

107. Ibid.

108. "Blacks Battle Hate in All White Enclave," *Orlando Sentinel*, January 12, 1995, A8.

109. Bruce Tomaso, "Hard Ground: Desegregation Advocates Aren't Sure Battle Can Be Won against Town's Lingering Racism," *Dallas Morning News*, August 2, 1993, 1A.

110. "Racial Tension Smolders in City Once Tagged 'Selma of the North,'" *Los Angeles Times*, November 24, 1991, A1.

111. Ibid.

112. James Harney, "Iowa City Confronts Racism, but Racism Refuses to Die," *USA Today*, November 18, 1991, 10A.

113. Ibid.

114. Ibid.

115. "Cross Burned in Dubuque," *New York Times*, November 13, 1991.

116. Weber, "West Roxbury Residents Rally against Racism."

117. Luz Delgado, "Black Family in North End Is Met with Racist Graffiti," *Boston Globe*, July 31, 1992.

118. Ibid.

119. Ibid.

CHAPTER 3

1. Jane Hill, *The Everyday Language of White Racism* (Malden, MA: Wiley-Blackwell, 2008), 29.

2. Jack Levin and Jack McDevitt, *Hate Crimes Revisited: America's War on Those Who Are Different* (Boulder: Westview, 2002), 11.

3. Ibid.

4. Ibid., 91.

5. Ibid., 78.

6. Ibid., 78–79.

7. Ibid., 79.

8. Ibid.

9. Russell Walker, "Bigotry Kindling for Tremont Arson Fires?" *Cleveland Call and Post*, August 22–August 28, 2007, 1A.

10. Ibid.

11. John Logan et al., "Ethnic Diversity Grows, Neighborhood Integration Lags Behind," Lewis Mumford Center, April 3, 2001, http://mumford.albany.edu/census/WholePop/WPreport/MumfordReport.pdf/.

12. Segregation figures for 2005–2009 are drawn by Logan and Stults's pooling of the American Community Survey (ACS). See John R. Logan and Brian J. Stults, "Racial and Ethnic Separation in the Neighborhoods: A First Look at Changes since 2000," Census Brief prepared for Project US2010, December 14, 2010, http:www.s4.brown.edu/us2010.

13. Ibid., 7.

14. Numbers that provide the average experience for African Americans or for any other group do not describe the extent to which members of any group lack contact with members of other races. For African Americans, a group that is so segregated, capturing the degree of contact with others is especially important. With a range of between 0 and 100, the exposure of a group to itself is captured by the Index of Isolation. An isolation score of 77 for whites means that the average white person lives in a neighborhood that is 77 percent white. Also quantified using a score ranging from 0 to 100, the exposure of one group to another is assessed using the Index of Exposure. An exposure score of 8.3 for black-white exposure suggests that the average black lives in a neighborhood that is 8.3 percent white. Ibid., 4.

15. Ibid., 5.

16. Ibid.

17. Rachel L. Swarns, "Vaulting the Racial Divide, Obama Persuaded Americans to Follow," *New York Times*, November 5, 2008; Bob Herbert, "Take a Bow, America," *New York Times*, November 8, 2008, A27; Adam Nagourney, "Obama Elected President as Racial Barrier Falls," *New York Times,* November 4, 2008, A1.

18. Lydia Saad, "One-Third in U.S. See Improved Race Relations under Obama," *GALLUP Politics*, August 24, 2011, accessed June 20, 2012, http://www.gallup.com/poll/149141/one-third-improved-race-relations-obama.aspx.

19. Ibid.

20. Gregory S. Parks and Matthew W. Hughey, eds., *The Obamas and a (Post) Racial America?* (New York: Oxford University Press, 2011), 31.

21. Ibid.

22. Ibid., 34.

23. Kathleen Schmidt and Brian Nosek, "Implicit (and Explicit) Racial Attitudes Barely Changed during Barack Obama's Presidential Campaign and Early Presidency," *Journal of Experimental Social Psychology* 46 (2010): 308–14.

24. Luigi Esposito and Laura L. Finley, "Barack Obama, Racial Progress, and the Future of Race Relations in the United States," *Western Journal of Black Studies* 33, no. 3 (2009).

25. Ibid., 170–71.

26. Vincent L. Hutchings, "Change or More of the Same? Evaluating Racial Attitudes in the Obama Era," *Public Opinion Quarterly* 73, no. 5 (2009), 919.

27. Ibid., 923.

28. Ibid., 928.

29. Howard Shuman et al., *Racial Attitudes in America: Trends and Interpretations* (Cambridge: Harvard University Press, 1997), xi.

30. Ibid., 311.

31. Ibid.

32. Ibid., 312.

33. Sheryll Cashin, *The Failures of Integration: How Race and Class Are Undermining the American Dream* (New York: Public Affairs, 2004), 44.

34. Ibid., 42.

35. Cashin suggests that fewer than 4 percent of Americans live in the stable integrated neighborhoods she describes.

36. Camille Zubrinsky Charles, *Won't You Be My Neighbor? Race, Class, and Residence in Los Angeles* (New York: Russell Sage, 2006); Maria Krysan, "Whites Who Say They'd Flee: Who Are They, and Why Would They Leave?" *Democracy* 39 (November 2002): 675–96, 675.

37. The MCSUI as a whole surveyed both households and employers. In this section, I discuss only the section on households. Alice O'Connor, "Understanding Inequality in the Late Twentieth Century Metropolis: New Perspectives on the Enduring Racial Divide," in *Urban Inequality: Evidence from Four Cities*, ed. Alice O'Connor, Chris Tilly, and Lawrence D. Bobo (New York: Russell Sage, 2001), 14.

38. Ibid.

39. Camille Zubrinsky Charles, "Processes of Racial Residential Segregation," in O'Connor, Tilly, and Bobo, eds., *Urban Inequality*, 233.

40. Ibid., 236.

41. Ibid.

42. Ibid.

43. Ibid., 237.

44. Ibid., 236.

45. Ibid., 237.

46. Charles, *Won't You Be My Neighbor?*, 134.

47. Ibid., 135.

48. Ibid.

49. Ibid.

50. Ibid.

51. Krysan, "Whites Who Say They'd Flee," 679.

52. See, e.g., United States v. Stewart, 65 F.3d 918 (11th Cir. 1995); United States v. J.H.H., 22 F.3d 821 (8th Cir. 1994); United States v. Montgomery, 23 F.3d 1130 (7th Cir. 1994); United States v. Lee, 6 F.3d 1297 (8th Cir. 1993); United States v. Long, 935 F.2d 1207 (11th Cir. 1991); United States v. Anzalone, 555 F.2d 317 (8th Cir. 1997).

53. See United States v. Hartbarger, 148 F.3d 777 (7th Cir. 1998); United States v. Smith, 161 F.3d 5 (4th Cir. 1998); United States v. May, 359 F.3d 683 (4th Cir. 2004); United States v. Gilbert, 884 F.2d 454 (9th Cir. 1989); United States v. Hayward, 6 F.3d 1241 (7th Cir. 1993); United States v. Wood, 780 F.2d 955 (11th Cir.), *cert. denied*, 476 U.S. 1184 (1986); United States v. Johns, 615 F.2d 672 (5th Cir.), *cert denied*, 449 U.S. 829 (1980); United States v. Sheldon, 107 F.3d 868 (4th Cir. 1997) (unpublished); Munger v. United States, 827 F. Supp. 100 (N.D.N.Y. 1992); United States v. Ramey, 24 F.3d 602 (4th Cir. W.Va., May 17, 1994) .

54. See, e.g., United States v. Hartbarger, 148 F.3d 777, 780 (7th Cir. 1998); United States v. Redwine, 715 F.2d 315, 318 (7th Cir. 1983).

55. Waheed v. Kalafut, 1988 WL 9092 (N.D. Ill.) (unpublished).

56. See, e.g., Stirgus v. Benoit, 720 F. Supp. 119, 123 (N.D. Ill. 1989); United States v. J.H.H., 22 F.3d 821.

57. See, e.g., United States v. Hartbarger, 148 F.3d 777; United States v. McInnis, 976 F.2d 1226 (9th Cir. 1992); United States v. Pospisil, 186 F.3d 1023 C.A.8 (Mo.) (1999); Stirgus v. Benoit, 720 F. Supp. 119, 123; Johnson v. Smith, 810 F. Supp. 235, 238–39 (N.D. Ill. 1992); Egan v. Schmock, 93 F. Supp. 1090, 1092–93 (N.D. Cal. 2000); Ohana v. 180 Prospect Place Realty Corp., 996 F. Supp. 238, 239–43 (E.D.N.Y. 1998); Stackhouse v. DeSitter, 620 F. Supp. 208 (N.D. Ill. 1985).

58. United States v. J.H.H., 22 F.3d 821 (1994).

59. United States v. Nichols, 149 F. App. 149 (4th Cir. 2005) (unpublished).

60. Another prominent example of a similar situation is the beating death of Vincent Chin, a Chinese American. Chin was killed in 1982 by two out-of-work Detroit autoworkers who blamed Asian Americans for their employment difficulties.

61. U.S. Dist. LEXIS 3362.

62. *Milwaukee Journal Sentinel*, October 24, 2001.

63. *Milwaukee Journal Sentinel*, February 13, 2002. In a similar vein, see also Commonwealth v. Stephens, 515 N.E.2d 606 (1987).

64. United States v. Magleby, 241 F.3d 1306 (10th Cir. 2001).

65. United States v. Gresser, 935 F.2d 96 (6th Cir. 1991).

66. Despite the use of these slurs, an FBI investigation turned up no evidence that either of the men eventually convicted of the crime, Timothy Singer and Gresser, were affiliated with the Ku Klux Klan.

67. United States v. Myers, 892 F.2d 642 (7th Cir. 1990).

68. United States v. Mahan, 190 F.3d 416, 419 (6th Cir. 1999).

69. Ibid., 419–20.

70. United States v. Vartanian, 245 F.3d 609, 611–13 (6th Cir. 2001). The defendant also threatened to destroy the agent's car, find the defendant's family, chop them into little pieces, and bury them in the backyard where nobody would ever find them.

71. Scire v. United States, 1997 WL 138991 (E.D.N.Y. 1997).

72. See, e.g., United States v. J.H.H., 22 F.3d 821 (1994); United States v. Myers, 892 F.2d 642 (7th Cir. 1990); Ohana v. 180 Prospect Place Realty Corp., 996 F. Supp. 238, 239–43 (E.D.N.Y. 1998).

73. For a description of the facts in this case, see the government's brief, United States, Appellee, v. Tuffarelli, 1996 WL 34422561 (C.A.2) (Appellate Brief).

74. State v. Talley, 858 P.2d 217, 220 (Wash. 1993).

75. Reynolds Farley et al., *Detroit Divided* (New York: Russell Sage, 1997), 199.

76. Ibid.

77. Hill, *The Everyday Language of White Racism*, 27.

78. Ibid., 26.

79. United States v. May, 359 F.3d 683, 685 (4th Cir. 2004); United States v. Magleby, 241 F.3d 1306, 1308–9 (10th Cir. 2001); United States v. Sheldon, 107 F.3d 868 (4th Cir. 1997); United States v. Wood, 780 F.2d 955, 956–59 (11th Cir.), *cert. denied*, 476 U.S. 1184 (1986); United States v. Johns, 615 F.2d 672, 674 (5th Cir.), *cert. denied*, 449 U.S. 829 (1980); Commonwealth v. Mitchell, 1993 WL 773785 1992; People v. Mackin, 730 N.W.2d 476, 477 (Mich. 2007).

80. United States v. Hayward, 6 F.3d 1241, 1243–44 (7th Cir. 1993), *overruled by* United States v. Colvin, 353 F.3d 569 (7th Cir. 2003); United States v. Wood, 780 F.2d at 956–59; Bryant v. Polston, 2000 WL 1670938.

81. United States v. Gilbert, 884 F.2d 454, 455–56 (9th Cir. 1989).

82. Johnson v. Smith, 878 F. Supp. 1150 (N.D. Ill. 1995).

83. Charles, "Processes of Racial Residential Segregation," 230.

84. Ibid.

85. Ibid., 231.

86. Shanshan Lan, "Beyond Black and White: Race, Class, and Chinese Americans in Multiracial Chicago," *Chinese America: History and Perspectives* 21 (2007): 83.

87. The first damage award in an ethnic intimidation case in Chicago was won as a result of a lawsuit brought on behalf of Mack Green, a black South Side resident who was attacked by a white Bridgeport resident after his tow truck broke down in Bridgeport in 1988. William Grady, "$475,000 Award Raises the Stakes of Racial Attack," *Chicago Tribune*, August 3, 1990, 1.

88. In 2007, the population of Bridgeport was 26 percent Asian American, 30 percent Latino, 41 percent white, and less than 1 percent black. Ibid.

89. Ka Vang, "Bridgeport's Mural Brushes Up an Image," *Chicago Tribune*, August 8, 1997, 3; Ryan Strong, "Bridgeport 10 Years Later," *Chicago Defender*, July 27, 2005.

90. "Marge Jones," interview with the author, June 14, 2006.

91. "Sandy Smith," interview with the author, June 13, 2006.

92. "Annie Michaels," interview with the author, June 9, 2006; "Josephine Smalls," interview with the author, June 27, 2006; and "Charles Kim," interview with the author, October 23, 2006.

93. Strong, "Bridgeport 10 Years Later"; Natalie Pardo, "Hate-Crime Patterns Highlight Parks," *Chicago Reporter*, December 1996.

94. Maurice Possley and Peter Kendall, "Clark Case Leaves Us Tension on Both Sides: Reaction Mixed to Verdict in Racial Attack on Boy," *Chicago Tribune*, September 20, 1998, 1; Vang, "Bridgeport's Mural Brushes Up an Image."

95. Pardo, "Hate-Crime Patterns Highlight Parks."

CHAPTER 4

1. Corina Knoll, "Racial Hatred Runs African-American Family Out of Dream Home," *Los Angeles Times*, June 4, 2009.

2. Jack Levin and Jack McDevitt, *Hate Crimes: The Rising Tide of Bigotry and Bloodshed* (New York: Plenum, 1993), 113; Jeannine Bell, *Policing Hatred: Law Enforcement, Civil Rights, and Hate Crime* (New York: New York University Press, 2004); Southern Poverty Law Center, *"Move-In" Violence: White Resistance to Neighborhood Integration in the 1980s* (Montgomery: SPLC, 1987), 2.

3. Earl Ofari Hutchinson, *The Latino Challenge to Black Americans* (Los Angeles: Middle Passage Press, 2007), 17.

4. Ibid., 19.

5. Edward T. Chang and Jeannette Diaz-Veizades, *Ethnic Peace in the American City: Building Community in Los Angeles and Beyond* (New York: New York University Press, 1999), 125.

6. Daniel Widener, "Another City Is Possible: Inter-Ethnic Organizing in Contemporary Los Angeles," *Race/Ethnicity: Multidisciplinary Global Context* 1, no. 2 (Spring 2008): 189–219.

7. Shana Bernstein, *Bridges of Reform: Interracial Civil Rights Activism in Twentieth-Century Los Angeles* (Oxford: Oxford University Press, 2011), 9.

8. Widener, "Another City."

9. Karen Umemoto and C. Kimi Mikami, "A Profile of Race-Bias Hate Crime in Los Angeles County," *Western Criminology Review* 2, no. 2 (2000), http://wcr.sonoma.edu/v2n2/umemoto.html.

10. Ibid.

11. "FBI Investigating Alleged Harassment of Two Families," *Los Angeles Times*, December 8, 1992.

12. Teresa Watanabe, "Crimes Rooted in Hatred Increase," *Los Angeles Times*, July 25, 2008.

13. Vicki Torres, "Hate Crimes Ruin a Dream Neighborhood," *Los Angeles Times*, November 29, 1992.

14. "FBI Investigating Alleged Harassment of Two Families."

15. Torres, "Hate Crimes Ruin a Dream Neighborhood."

16. Umemoto and Mikami, "A Profile of Race-Bias Hate Crime," 16.
17. Ibid.
18. Ibid.
19. Ibid.
20. Ibid., 18.
21. Ibid.
22. Torres, "Hate Crimes Ruin a Dream Neighborhood."
23. Joe Mozingo, "Highland Park Gang Trial Paints a Landscape of Hate," *Los Angeles Times*, July 25, 2006.
24. Ibid.
25. Joe Mozingo, "Four Latino Gang Members Are Convicted of Anti-Black Plot," *Los Angeles Times*, August 2, 2006.
26. Ibid.
27. Mozingo, "Highland Park Gang Trial."
28. People v. Avila, 2005 WL 2065211 (Cal. App. 2 Dist.).
29. Ibid.
30. People v. Martinez, 2003 WL 195006 (Cal. App. 2 Dist).
31. Green had not been specifically targeted. Three other teenagers were shot and seriously wounded in the same attack.
32. Sam Quinones, "How a Community Imploded," *Los Angeles Times*, March 4, 2007.
33. Sam Quinones, "Fear Still Lingers for Many in Harbor Gateway," *Los Angeles Times*, December 30, 2007.
34. Ibid.
35. Quinones, "How a Community Imploded."
36. Torres, "Hate Crimes Ruin a Dream Neighborhood."
37. Ibid.
38. Stephanie Chavez, "Three Firebombs Proved as Hate Crimes," *Los Angeles Times*, December 8, 2001.
39. Dennis Chong and Duke Hong Kim, "Beyond Black-and-White: The Experiences and Effects of Economic Status among Racial and Ethnic Minorities," in *New Race Politics in America*, ed. Jane Junn and Kerry L. Haynie (New York: Cambridge University Press, 2008), 39.
40. Lawrence D. Bobo et al., *Prismatic Metropolis: Inequality in Los Angeles* (New York: Russell Sage, 2000), 530.
41. Camille Zubrinsky Charles, *Won't You Be My Neighbor? Race, Class, and Residence in Los Angeles* (New York: Russell Sage, 2006), 23.
42. Lawrence D. Bobo, "Racial Attitudes and Relations," in *America Becoming: Racial Trends and Their Consequences*, ed. Neil J. Smelser, William Julius Wilson, and Faith Mitchell (Washington: National Academy Press, 2001), 277.
43. Ibid.
44. Ibid., 278.

45. Tatcho Mindiola Jr., Yolanda Flores Niemann, and Nestor Rodriguez, *Black-Brown Relations and Stereotypes* (Austin: University of Texas Press, 2002); Charles, *Won't You Be My Neighbor?*

46. Charles, *Won't You Be My Neighbor?*

47. Hutchinson, *Latino Challenge*, 26.

48. Ibid., 27.

49. Ibid.

50. Sam Quinones and Richard Winton, "Azusa Gang Indictment: 51 Charged in Azusa Gang's Terrorizing of Blacks," *Los Angeles Times*, June 8, 2011.

51. Watanabe, "Crimes Rooted in Hatred Increase."

52. Donald P. Green, Dara Z. Strolovitch, and Janelle S. Wong, "Defended Neighborhoods, Integration, and Racially Motivated Crime," *American Journal of Sociology* 104, no. 2 (September 1998): 372–403; Ryken Grattet, "The Urban Ecology of Bias Crime: A Study of Disorganized and Defended Neighborhoods," *Social Problems* 56, no. 1 (2009): 132–50; Christopher J. Lyons, "Defending Turf: Racial Demographics and Hate Crime against Blacks and Whites," *Social Forces* 87, no. 1 (September 2008): 377.

53. Eric Avila, *Popular Culture in the Age of White Flight: Fear and Fantasy in Suburban Los Angeles* (Berkeley: University of California Press, 2004), 30.

54. Ibid., 28–30.

55. Quinones, "How a Community Imploded."

56. Mozingo, "Highland Park Gang Trial."

57. Torres, "Hate Crimes Ruin a Dream Neighborhood."

58. Quinones, "How a Community Imploded."

59. Brentin Mock, "A Blackout," *Southern Poverty Law Center Intelligence Report* 124 (Winter 2006): 51.

60. Ross L. Matsueda, Kevin Drakulich, and Charis E. Kubrin, "Race and Neighborhood Codes of Violence," in *The Many Colors of Crime: Inequalities of Race, Ethnicity, and Crime in America*, ed. Ruth D. Peterson, Lauren J. Krivo, and John Hagan (New York: New York University Press, 2006), 334.

61. Ibid., 339; Green, Strolovitch, and Wong, "Defended Neighborhoods," 372–403; Howard Pinderhughes, *Race in the Hood: Conflict and Violence among Urban Youth* (Minneapolis: University of Minnesota Press, 1997).

62. Mozingo, "Highland Park Gang Trial."

63. Ibid.

64. Ibid. (italics mine).

65. Ibid.

66. Matsueda, Drakulich, and Kubrin, "Race and Neighborhood Codes of Violence," 337.

67. "La eme" is Spanish for the letter *m*.

68. People v. Martinez, 2003 WL 195006 (Cal. App. 2 Dist).

69. Quinones, "How a Community Imploded."

70. Ibid.

CHAPTER 5

1. Herbert Blumer, "Race Prejudice as a Sense of Group Position," *Pacific Sociological Review* 1, no. 1 (Spring 1958): 3–7; Lawrence Bobo and Vincent Hutchings, "Perceptions of Racial Group Competition: Extending Blumer's Theory of Group Position to a Multiracial Social Context," *American Sociological Review* 61 (1996): 951–72.

2. Gerald D. Suttles, *The Social Construction of Communities* (Chicago: University of Chicago Press, 1972), 21.

3. Ibid., 27.

4. Howard Pinderhughes, *Race in the Hood: Conflict and Violence among Urban Youth* (Minneapolis: University of Minnesota Press, 1997); Maria Kefalas, *Working-Class Heroes: Protecting Home, Community, and Nation in a Chicago Neighborhood* (Berkeley: University of California Press, 2003); Jonathan Rieder, *Canarsie: The Jews and Italians of Brooklyn against Liberalism* (Cambridge: Harvard University Press, 1985); Judith DeSena, *Protecting One's Turf: Social Strategies for Maintaining Urban Neighborhoods* (Lanham, MD: University Press of America, 2005).

5. Kefalas, *Working Class Heroes*, 5.

6. Pinderhughes, *Race in the Hood*; Kefalas, *Working-Class Heroes*; Rieder, *Canarsie*; DeSena, *Protecting One's Turf*; Michael Patrick MacDonald, *All Souls: A Family Story from Southie* (Boston: Beacon, 1999).

7. Kefalas, *Working-Class Heroes*, 21.

8. Donald P. Green, Dara Z. Strolovitch, and Janelle S. Wong, "Defended Neighborhoods, Integration, and Racially Motivated Crime," *American Journal of Sociology* 104, no. 2 (September 1998): 379.

9. Ibid.

10. Ibid., 391.

11. Ryken Grattet, "The Urban Ecology of Bias Crime: A Study of Disorganized and Defended Neighborhoods," *Social Problems* 56, no. 1 (2009): 143.

12. Christopher J. Lyons, "Defending Turf: Racial Demographics and Hate Crime against Blacks and Whites," *Social Forces* 87, no. 1 (September 2008): 377.

13. Ibid., 378.

14. Ami Lynch, "Hating the Neighbors: The Role of Hate Crime in the Perpetuation of Black Residential Segregation," *International Journal of Conflict and Violence* 1 (2008): 18.

15. Ibid., 19.

16. Camille Zubrinsky Charles, *Won't You Be My Neighbor? Race, Class, and Residence in Los Angeles* (New York: Russell Sage, 2006), 46-48.

17. Green, Strolovitch, and Wong, "Defended Neighborhoods," 372.

18. Pinderhughes, *Race in the Hood*, 9; MacDonald, *All Souls*; DeSena, *Protecting One's Turf*.

19. Rogers Worthington, "Hate Flares as Iowa City Courts Blacks," *Chicago Tribune*, November 17, 1991.

20. Ibid.
21. Bryan Macquarie, "Amid Pain a Call for Action," *Boston Globe*, May 5, 1997.
22. Pinderhughes, *Race in the Hood*, 134.
23. Ibid., 34-35.
24. Carolyn Adams et al., *Philadelphia: Neighborhoods, Division, and Conflict in a Postindustrial City* (Philadelphia: Temple University Press, 1991), 73.
25. "Philadelphia Neighborhoods and Place Names, A-K," *City of Philadelphia*, 1998, http://www.phila.gov/phils/Docs/otherinfo/pname1.htm.
26. Michael A. Fletcher, "A Neighborhood Slams the Door: Racist Acts Drive Philadelphia Family out of White Area," *Washington Post*, May 18, 1996, A1.
27. Marianne Costantinou and Kurt Heine, "A Fairly Redneck Neighborhood," *Philadelphia Daily News*, September 27, 1994, 3.
28. Ibid.
29. "Black Woman, Son Assaulted, Four Are Jailed," *New York Times*, September 27, 1994, A4.
30. Ibid.
31. Joseph A. Slobodzian, "Neighbor Tells of Racial Vandalism," *Philadelphia Inquirer*, April 4, 1998, B1.
32. Adams et al., *Philadelphia*, 84.
33. Ibid., 81.
34. Ibid., 84.
35. These high-profile events include the beating of a sixteen-year-old white teenager by two black men in a Grays Ferry drugstore. For a discussion of some of these events, see Mike Newall, "A Prayer for Grays Ferry," *Philadelphia City Paper*, August 4–10, 2005, accessed March 13, 2011, http://archives.citypaper.net/articles/2005-08-04/cover.shtml.
36. Julie Stoiber, "Man Found Guilty, Again, in 1997 Grays Ferry Attack," *Philadelphia Inquirer*, September 18, 1999, B2.
37. Adams et al., *Philadelphia*, 24.
38. Ibid.
39. 984 F. Supp. 687, 714 (S.D.N.Y. 1997).
40. Lisa Belkin, *Show Me a Hero: A Tale of Murder, Suicide, Race, and Redemption* (Boston: Little, Brown, 1999), 32–34.
41. Ibid., 38–39.
42. Sasha Abramsky, "Yonkers Race Trap," *City Limits* 23 (September–October 1998): 24–29.
43. Ibid.
44. Patricia Leigh Brown, "Where Quiet Holds No Terror," *New York Times*, June 15, 1995, C1.
45. Fernanda Santos, "After 27 Years, Yonkers Housing Desegregation Battle Ends Quietly in Manhattan Court," *New York Times*, May 2, 2007.
46. Abramsky, "Yonkers Race Trap," 24–25.
47. Ibid., 28.

48. Xavier de Souza Briggs, Joe T. Darden, and Angela Aidala, "In the Wake of Desegregation: Early Impacts of Scattered Site Public Housing on Neighborhoods in Yonkers, New York," *Journal of the American Planning Association* 65, no. 1 (Winter 1999): 27–49.

49. Ibid., 27.

50. Abramsky, "Yonkers Race Trap," 28.

51. Ibid., 26.

52. J. Anthony Lukas, *Common Ground: A Turbulent Decade in the Lives of Three American Families* (New York: Knopf, 1985), 259.

53. Ibid., 241.

54. Daniel Golden and Donald Lowery, "Boston and the Postwar Racial Strain on Blacks and Whites in Boston, 1945–1982," *Boston Globe*, September 27, 1982.

55. JoAnne Ball, "A Look Back as South Boston Readies for Desegregation," *Boston Globe*, June 30, 1988; Peter J. Howe, "Former BHA Chief Says Base Was Laid for Desegregation," *Boston Globe*, August 15, 1988, 23.

56. Ball, "A Look Back."

57. Ibid.

58. M. E. Malone, "Echo of History over Race Issue in South Boston," *Boston Globe*, January 17, 1988.

59. Elizabeth Neuffer, "NAACP, City Sign Pact to Pay Victims of Housing Bias," *Boston Globe*, October 5, 1989, 56.

60. Michael Rezendes, "A Sense of Tolerance: Whites and Minorities Coexist in Boston Housing Projects," *Boston Globe*, May 20, 1990.

61. "Black Family to Flee Project: South Boston Shooting Probed," *Boston Globe*, October 13, 1989.

62. Michael Rezendes, "Tarnished Healer Mayor Flynn Invited Bostonians to Judge His Performance by His Ability to Maintain Racial Peace," *Boston Globe*, May 20, 1990.

63. Charles A. Reagan, "Public Housing Turns Back on Past Despite Trouble Spots: Many See Racial Tensions Easing at BHA Developments," *Boston Globe*, February 4, 1998.

64. Shelley Murphy and Georgina Hart, "More Tenants May Share BHA Funds: $350,000 from Settlements Earmarked for Additional Victims of Harassment," *Boston Globe*, July 30, 1999.

65. "Climate of Fear: Latino Immigrants in Suffolk County, New York," *Southern Poverty Law Center*, September 2009, http://www.splcenter.org/sites/default/files/downloads/publication/splc_suffolk_report.pdf., 10.

66. Ibid., 8.

67. Ibid., 14.

68. Ibid., 8.

69. Ibid.

70. Ibid., 21.

71. Ibid., 8.

72. Leonard S. Rubinowitz and James Rosenbaum, *Crossing the Class and Color Lines: From Public Housing to White Suburbia* (Chicago: University of Chicago Press, 2000), 104.

73. Charles Lamb, *Housing Segregation in Suburban America since 1960: Presidential and Judicial Politics* (New York: Cambridge University Press, 2005), 87.

74. Ibid.

75. Ibid.

76. Reynolds Farley et al., *Detroit Divided* (New York: Russell Sage, 1997).

77. Thomas J. Sugrue, *The Origins of the Urban Crisis: Race and Inequality in Postwar Detroit* (Princeton: Princeton University Press, 2005), 266.

78. Camille Zubrinsky Charles, "Processes of Racial Residential Segregation," in *Urban Inequality: Evidence from Four Cities,* ed. Alice O'Connor, Chris Tilly, and Lawrence D. Bobo (New York: Russell Sage, 2001), 233-265.

79. Reynolds Farley, Suzanne Bianchini, and Diane Colasanto, "Barriers to the Racial Integration of Neighborhoods: The Detroit Case Study," *Annals of the American Academy of Political Science* 441 (1979): 97–113, 105.

80. Ibid.

81. Charles, *Won't You Be My Neighbor?,* 183.

82. Keith R. Ihlanfeldt and Benjamin Scafidi, "Whites' Neighborhood Racial Preferences and Neighborhood Racial Composition in the United States: Evidence from the Multi-City Study of Urban Inequality," *Housing Studies* 19, no. 3 (May 2004): 325–59, 338.

83. Ingrid Gould Ellen, *Sharing America's Neighborhoods: The Prospects for Stable Racial Integration* (Cambridge: Harvard University Press, 2000), 153.

84. George Galster et al., *Why Not in My Backyard? Neighborhood Impacts of Deconcentrating Assisted Housing* (New Brunswick, NJ: Center for Urban Policy Research, 2003), 4.

85. Ibid.

86. Ibid.

87. Ibid.

88. Ibid., 1.

89. Alexander Polikoff, *Waiting for Gautreaux: A Story of Segregation, Housing, and the Black Ghetto* (Evanston, IL: Northwestern University Press, 2006), 203.

90. Laura S. Washington, "The Color of Fear: Blacks and Whites on Common Ground," *Chicago Tribune,* June 10, 1996.

91. Ibid.

92. Alexander Polikoff offers two explanations. First, this occurred because of a 1979 deal involving then Mayor Jane Byrne that allowed the CHA to match housing in white neighborhoods with housing in black neighborhoods. In addition, the 1969 court order allowed 25 percent of apartments in black neighborhoods. Polikoff, *Waiting for Gautreaux,* 213.

93. Ibid.

94. Ibid.

95. On Seattle, see Tammerlin Drummond, "Black Engineer Finds a Burning Cross on the Lawn," *New York Times*, July 19, 1991, B6; Darrell Glover, "The Hateful Truth: Racists Are Targeting Black Family," *Seattle Post-Intelligencer*, July 16, 1991, B1. On Boston, see Luz Delgado, "Black Family in North End Is Met with Racist Graffiti," *Boston Globe*, July 31, 1992. On Orange County, Florida, see Robert Perez, "KKK Warning Greets Biracial Couple," *Philadelphia Inquirer*, March 25, 1992, B1. On Chicago, see "Probation for Racial Slur," *Chicago Sun-Times*, February 15, 1996, 18; "Supporters Urge Berwyn Black to Rethink Move," *Chicago Sun-Times*, March 9, 1992, 5; Teresa Puente, "Increasingly Diverse Areas Face Hate Crimes," *Chicago Tribune*, July 1, 1996. On Philadelphia, see Stephanie Arnold, "Arrest Made in Gilbertsville: Attempted Cross Burning," *Philadelphia Inquirer*, February 10, 2005. On St. Petersburg, Florida, see Peggy Peterman, "Hate Has Become an Epidemic," *St. Petersburg (FL) Times*, May 28, 1991, 1D.

96. Arnold, "Arrest Made in Gilbertsville."

97. Gary Gately, "Pall of Racism Remains over Neighborhood Repaired after Arson," *New York Times*, October 6, 2005.

98. Nancy Marshall Genzer, "Arson Suspect Admits Racism Sparked Maryland Fires," *National Public Radio*, May 26, 2005, accessed March 17, 2011, http://www.NPR.org/templates/story/story.php?storyid=4667607.

99. DeSena, *Protecting One's Turf*, 86.

100. Ellen, *Sharing America's Neighborhoods*, 200.

101. Galster et al., *Why Not in My Backyard?*, 141.

CHAPTER 6

1. Viktora was a juvenile at the time of his arrest, so originally only his initials were given. His actual name has been widely published and is therefore offered here as well.

2. Laura J. Lederer, "The Case of the Cross Burning: An Interview with Russ and Laura Jones," in *The Price We Pay: The Case against Racist Speech, Hate Propaganda, and Pornography*, ed. Laura J. Lederer and Richard Delgado (New York: Hill and Wang, 1995), 27–28.

3. Richard L. Abel, *Speaking Respect, Respecting Speech* (Chicago: University of Chicago Press, 1999) 19.

4. Ibid.

5. United States v. J.H.H., 22 F.3d 821 (8th Cir. 1994).

6. Robert Kelly, *Bias Crime: American Law Enforcement and Legal Responses* (Chicago: University of Illinois at Chicago, 1993); Jack Levin and Jack McDevitt, *Hate Crimes Revisited: America's War on Those Who Are Different* (Boulder: Westview, 2002).

7. Lederer, "The Case of the Cross Burning," 29.

8. Ibid.

9. Jeannine Bell, *Policing Hatred: Law Enforcement, Civil Rights, and Hate Crime* (New York: New York University Press, 2004).

10. The actual name of the city has been disguised to protect the confidentiality of respondents. For more discussion of enforcing hate crime laws in Center City, see ibid.

11. Ibid.

12. The ways the community complicated police investigation are described in more detail in ibid., 83–112.

13. Southern Poverty Law Center, *Terror in Our Neighborhoods: Hate Crimes Law* (Montgomery: SPLC, 2006), 189.

14. Sections 242 and 245 of Title 18 are often described in the same breath as Section 241 and Section 3631 of the Fair Housing Act. Section 242 is designed to punish anti-integrationist violence that is committed "under color of law," that is, by law enforcement officials acting in their official capacity. 18 U.S.C. § 242 (1948). I have not dealt with it here because in the vast majority of cases, anti-integrationist violence is committed by the victim's neighbors. Section 245, the most specific of the federal legislation aimed at bias-motivated conduct, was enacted in 1968 in response to violence directed at blacks and other civil rights workers. It prohibits the use of "force or threat of force" to interfere with an individual's participation in federal or protected activities because of his or her "race, color, religion or national origin." 18 U.S.C. § 245(b)(2) (1968). Section 245 was enacted simultaneously with the Fair Housing Act. The sections that would be used to prosecute anti-integrationist violence are almost identical to Section 3631 of the Fair Housing Act. Thus, the notes to Section 245 indicate that it does not cover actions that could be reached under the Fair Housing Act of 1968, 82 Stat. 73 (codified at 42 U.S.C. §§ 3601–19, 3631 (1968)).

15. U.S.C. § 241 (1948).

16. United States v. Price, 383 U.S. 787 (1966).

17. See, e.g., United States v. McDermott, 29 F.3d 404 (8th Cir. 1994); United States v. Lee, 6 F.3d 1297 (8th Cir. 1993); United States v. Gresser, 935 F.2d 96 (6th Cir. 1991); United States v. Skillman, 922 F.2d 1370 (9th Cir. 1990); United States v. Stewart, 806 F.2d 64 (3d Cir. 1986); United States v. Wood, 780 F.2d 955 (11th Cir. 1986); United States v. Redwine, 715 F.2d 315 (7th Cir. 1983).

18. 18 U.S.C. § 241. The relevant text indicates that Section 241 protects "the free exercise or enjoyment of any right or privilege secured . . . by the Constitution or laws of the United States."

19. See, e.g., United States v. Allen, 341 U.S. F.3d 870 (9th Cir. 2003), *cert. denied*, 41 U.S. 975 (2004). In *Allen*, the court identified a local public park that had been a space for performances, exhibitions, and other sources of entertainment as a public accommodation for the purposes of 42 U.S.C. § 2000(a) in order to uphold the conviction of a neo-Nazi group for interfering with federal rights at the park.

20. 42 U.S.C. § 1982 (2000).

21. United States v. Callahan, 659 F. Supp. 80 (E.D. Pa. 1987).

22. "Fire Set in Philadelphia House Vacated by Blacks," *Los Angeles Times*, December 14, 1985, 16.

23. George Esper, "Racial Protest Splits Urban Neighborhood: Philadelphia Black Couple Forced to Move, Interracial Pair Plan to Stay Despite Threats," *Los Angeles Times*, December 29, 1985, 5. See also Callahan, 659 F. Supp. at 80.

24. See Fair Housing Act of 1968, Pub. L. No. 90-284, 82 Stat. 73 (codified at 42 U.S.C. §§ 3601–31, 3613 (1968)).

25. U.S.C. §§ 3617, 3631 (2000). For a discussion of the legislative history surrounding the Fair Housing Act, see Leonard S. Rubinowitz and Ismail Alsheik, "A Missing Piece: Fair Housing and the 1964 Civil Rights Act," *Howard Law Journal* 48 (2005): 841, 843–910; Aric Short, "Post-Acquisition Harassment and the Scope of the Fair Housing Act," *Alabama Law Review* 58 (2006): 203, 222–39; Robert Schwemm, "Cox, Halprin, and Discriminatory Municipal Services under the Federal Fair Housing Act," *Indiana Law Review* 41 (2008): 717.

26. *Hate Crimes Law* (New York: Clark Boardman Callaghan, 2007), 193.

27. See, e.g., United States v. May, 359 F.3d 683, 685 (4th Cir. 2004); United States v. Colvin, 353 F.3d 569, 571 (7th Cir. 2003) (en banc); United States v. Magleby, 241 F.3d 1306, 1308–9 (10th Cir. 2001); United States v. Whitney, 229 F.3d 1296, 1300 (10th Cir. 2000); United States v. Stewart, 65 F.3d 918, 921–22 (11th Cir. 1995); United States v. Montgomery, 23 F.3d 1130, 1131–32 (7th Cir. 1994); United States v. J.H.H., 22 F.3d 821, 823–24; United States v. Hayward, 6 F.3d 1241, 1243–44 (7th Cir. 1993), *overruled by* United States v. Colvin, 353 F.3d 569 (7th Cir. 2003).

28. See United States v. Lanza, 260 U.S. 377, 378 (1922). One prominent case of anti-integrationist violence in which state prosecution failed to punish the perpetrators was R.A.V. v. St. Paul, 505 U.S. 377 (1992). After the Supreme Court struck the Minnesota statute at issue, the Justice Department brought charges against one of the perpetrators in United States v. J.H.H., 22 F.3d 821, 823 (8th Cir. 1994).

29. See, e.g., United States v. Nichols, 149 F. App. 149, 150–51 (4th Cir. 2005); United States v. McInnis, 976 F.2d 1226, 1228–29 (9th Cir. 1992); United States v. Wood, 780 F.2d 955, 956–58 (11th Cir.), *cert. denied*, 476 U.S. 1184 (1986); United States v. Johns, 615 F.2d 672 (5th Cir. 1980).

30. United States v. Vartanian, 245 F.3d 609, 611–12 (6th Cir. 2001).

31. U.S.C. § 241 (1982).

32. United States v. Nix, 417 F. Supp.2d 1009 (N.D. Ill. 2006).

33. United States v. Gresser, 935 F.2d 96 (6th Cir. 1991).

34. United States v. Sharp, 81 F.3d 147 (Table), C.A.1 (N.H.), 1996; United States v. Wiegand, 45 F.3d 431 (Table), C.A.6 (Mich.), 1994; United States v. Craft, 484 F.3d 922 (7th Cir. 2007); United States v. Skillman, 922 F.2d 1370 (9th Cir. 1990); United States v. Bakenhus, 116 F.3d 1481 (Table), C.A.6 (Tenn.), 1997.

35. United States v. May, 359 F.3d 683 (4th Cir. 2004).

36. United States v. Mahan, 190 F.3d 416 (6th Cir. 1999).

37. Michael Selmi, "Race in the City: The Triumph of Diversity and the Loss of Integration," *Journal of Law and Politics* 22 (2006): 49, 58.

38. See, e.g., United States v. Redwine, 715 F.2d 315 (7th Cir. 1983); United States v. Hayward, 6 F.3d 1241 (7th Cir. 1993); United States v. Stewart, 806 F.2d 64 (3d Cir. 1986).
39. U.S.C. § 3617 (2000).
40. *Hate Crimes Law*, 203.
41. No. CV 04-06-3416, 2005 WL 5957624 (Ohio Ct. Com. Pl. Dec. 22, 2005), *rev'd*, 866 N.E.2d 1127 (Ohio St. App. 2006), *appeal allowed by* 825 N.E.2d 912 (Ohio 2007).
42. Lawrence v. Courtyards at Deerwood Ass'n, 318 F. Supp. 2d 1133, 1137 (S.D. Fla. 2004).
43. Ibid., 1143.
44. Ohio Civil Rights Comm'n v. Akron Metro. Hous. Auth., No. CV 04 06 3416, 2005 WL 5957624 (Ohio Com. Pl. Dec. 22, 2005).
45. Halprin v. Prairie Single Family Homes of Dearborn Park Ass'n, 388 F.3d 327, 330 (7th Cir. 2004).
46. Ibid., 329.
47. Ibid., 330.
48. United States v. Nicholson, 185 F. Supp. 2d 982 (E.D. Wis. 2002). See also United States v. Pospisil, 127 F. Supp. 2d 1059 (W.D. Mo. 2000).
49. Bloch v. Frischholz, 587 F.3d 771 (7th Cir. Nov. 13, 2009).
50. The Blochs owned and occupied three apartments in the building. "Mezuzot" or "mezuzah"—small rectangular boxes that house small scrolls of parchment inscribed with passages from the Torah, the holiest text in Judaism—were removed from outside each apartment.
51. Halprin, 388 F.3d at 330.
52. *Hate Crimes Law*, 193.
53. Jack Levin and Jack McDevitt, *Hate Crimes: The Rising Tide of Bigotry and Bloodshed* (New York: Plenum, 1993), 186.
54. Levin and McDevitt, *Hate Crimes*, 186, 252.
55. Ibid.
56. Cal. Penal Code §190.2(a)(16) (West 2007) (protecting race, color, religion, nationality or country of origin); Conn. Gen. Stat. Ann. § 46a-58 (West 2004) (protecting race, color, religion); Ariz. Rev. Stat. § 13-701 (2010) (aggravating factor for race, color, religion, national origin, sexual orientation, gender, or disability).
57. *Hate Crimes Law*, 265.
58. Ala. Code § 13A-5-13 (2005) (imposing additional penalties for bias-motivated offenses); Miss. Code Ann. § 99-19-307 (West 2006) (maximum penalty may be twice that authorized for the underlying offense if committed with bias); Neb. Rev. Stat. § 28-111 (Lexis Nexis 2006) (indicating that if bias is found, offenses shall be punished by imposition of the next higher penalty classification); Nev. Rev. Stat. Ann. § 207.185 (Lexis Nexis 2006) (reclassifying designated offenses as gross misdemeanors if bias is present).

59. Alaska Stat. §11.76.110 (2006); Conn. Gen. Stat. Ann. § 46a-58 (West 2004); Del. Code Ann. tit. 11, § 1304(a)(1) (2001); Iowa Code Ann. § 729.5.1 (West 2003); Me. Rev. Stat. Ann. tit. 17, § 2931 (West 2003); Mass. Gen. Laws Ann. ch. 265, § 37 (West 2003); Utah Code Ann. § 76-3-203.3 (2003).

60. *In re* Steven S., 31 Cal. Rptr. 2d 644 (Cal. Ct. App. 1994), 25 Cal. App. 4th 598 (1994); State v. Talley, 858 F.2d 217, 226 (Wash. 1993).

61. 505 U.S. 377 (1992). For discussion of the background facts in this case, see Jeannine Bell, "O Say, Can You See: Free Expression by the Light of Fiery Crosses," *Harvard Civil Rights–Civil Liberties Law Review* 39, no. 2 (Summer 2004): 335.

62. Wisconsin v. Mitchell, 508 U.S. 476 (1993).

63. Bell, *Policing Hatred*, 36.

64. Ibid.

65. Southern Poverty Law Center, *"Move-In" Violence: White Resistance to Neighborhood Integration in the 1980s* (Montgomery: Southern Poverty Law Center, 1987), 18.

66. Lederer, "The Case of the Cross Burning," 29.

67. Ibid.

68. Laura J. Lederer, "The Prosecutor's Dilemma: An Interview with Tom Foley," in *The Price We Pay: The Case against Racist Speech, Hate Propaganda, and Pornography*, ed. Laura J. Lederer and Richard Delgado (New York: Hill and Wang, 1995), 194-95.

69. Ibid., 195.

70. Ibid.

71. Ibid.

72. 720 ILCS 5/12-7.1.

73. M. Daniel Gibbard, "Skinhead Sued over Attack on Black Kids," *Chicago Tribune*, August 28, 2004, 16.

74. "$500,000 Awarded to Pal Beaten with Lenard Clark," *Chicago Tribune*, November 8, 2001, 3.

75. Matt O'Connor, "Huge Damages in Hate Crime: Jury Awards $720,000 in Cross Burning Case," *Chicago Tribune*, March 9, 1999.

76. Margaret O'Brien, "Prosecutors Being Added after Smith Shootings: Divine to Increase Focus on Hate Crimes," *Chicago Tribune*, August 2, 1999.

77. Chinta Strausberg, "Hate Crimes Down in City," *Chicago Defender*, July 21, 2001.

78. "William Press," interview with the author, October 23, 2006.

79. "Michael Weal," interview with the author, October 23, 2006.

80. Natalie Pardo, "Hate-Crime Patterns Highlight Parks," *Chicago Reporter*, December 1996.

81. Ibid.

82. Cal. Penal Code § 11411 (2007); D.C. Code Ann. § 22-3312.02 (2001); Vt. Stat. Ann. tit.13 § 1456 (1989).

83. Idaho Code Ann. § 18-7903 (1993); Mont. Code Ann. §45-5-221 (2003).

84. State v. Talley, 858 P.2d 217 (Wash. 1993).

85. State v. Sheldon, 629 A.2d 753 (Md. 1993) (striking down Maryland's cross burning statute); State v. Vawter, 642 A.2d 349, 354–55 (N.J. 1994) (striking down New Jersey's cross burning statute).

86. 538 U.S. 343 (2003).

87. For a list of cases involving drunken and joking cross burners, see Bell, "O Say, Can You See," 370.

88. Levin and McDevitt, *Hate Crimes*, 182.

89. Ibid.

90. "Hate Crime Data," *FBI Law Enforcement Bulletin* 4, no. 3 (1993): 4.

91. Rose Livingston, "Black Man Wishes He Hadn't Taken Klan Case to Court," *Birmingham News*, January 30, 1994, 18.

92. Ibid.

93. Michelle Campbell, "Silence Adds to Pain Left by Cross Burning: Some Neighbors Indifferent toward Victims," *Chicago Sun-Times*, June 18, 1996, 9.

94. Ibid.

95. U.S. Census Bureau, "Profile of General Demographic Characteristics: 2000", Zip Code Tabulation Area, 10710 (Northeast Yonkers), accessed November 5, 2012, http://factfinder2.census.gov/bkmk/table/1.0/en/DEC/00_SF1/DP1/8600000US10710.

96. Janny Scott, "The Census—A Region of Enclaves: Canarsie, Brooklyn, 'For Sale' Signs Greet Newcomers," *New York Times*, June 18, 2001.

97. Ibid.

98. Unpublished Disposition, United States of America, Appellee, v. Kenneth J. Lowery, Defendant-Appellant, United States Court of Appeals, Sixth Circuit, 885 F.2d 871 (6th Cir. Sept. 25, 1989).

99. Emily Miller and Jennifer Schofield, "Slavic Village: Incorporating Active Living into Community Development through Partnerships," *American Journal of Preventive Medicine* 37, no. 6, S2 (December 2009): S377–S385.

100. "Miguel Garcia," interview with the author, December 12, 2006. The respondent's name has been changed to protect his confidentiality.

101. Ibid. The respondent's son's name has also been changed.

102. John O. Calmore, "Spatial Equality and the Kerner Commission Report: A Back-to-the-Future Essay," *North Carolina Law Review* 71 (1993): 1487, 1514–15; Florence Wagman Roisman, "Long Overdue: Desegregation Litigation and the Next Steps to End Discrimination and Segregation in the Public Housing and Section 8 Existing Housing Programs," *Cityscape: A Journal of Policy Development and Research* 4, no. 3 (1999): 171.

103. Pub. L. No. 111-84, 123 Stat. 4701 (2009).

104. Federal Bureau of Investigation, Criminal Justice Information Services Division, Table 1: Incidents, Offenses, Victims, and Known Offenders by Bias Motivation (2010), accessed October 15, 2012, http://www.fbi.gov/about-us/cjis/ucr/hate-crime/2010/tables/

table-1-incidents-offenses-victims-and-known-offenders-by-bias-motiva-tion-2010.

105. Chris Branham, "Appeals Court Backs Hate Crime Conviction," *Northwest Arkansas Democrat-Gazette*, August 7, 2012, 7.

106. Federal Bureau of Investigation, Table 1: Incidents, Offenses, Victims, and Known Offenders by Bias Motivation (2010).

107. Levin and McDevitt, *Hate Crimes*, 246.

CONCLUSION

1. Bruce Tomaso, "Hard Ground: Desegregation Advocates Aren't Sure Battle Can Be Won against Town's Lingering Racism," *Dallas Morning News*, August 2, 1993, 1A.

2. "Death in Black and White: White Bigots Hounded Bill Simpson; Police Say Black Thugs Killed Him," *US News and World Report*, June 13, 1994, 34.

3. Sue Anne Pressley, "Racist Town's Last Black Resident Gunned Down Near His Home," *Charlotte Observer*, September 3, 1993, 1A.

4. Ibid.

5. Terri Langford, "Black Family Finds Open Arms in Vidor, Texas," *USA Today*, February 7, 1994, 3A.

6. Richard Stewart, "Vidor Prepares for New Wave of Desegregation," *Houston Chronicle*, January 2, 1994, 1; Henry G. Cisneros, "With Liberty and Justice for All: How America Can Provide Fair Housing for All Its People," *Hispanic Law Journal* 1 (1994): 70.

7. Michael Grazyck, "A 'Big Adjustment' for Vidor Housing," *Philadelphia Inquirer*, September 4, 1994, B8.

8. Pam Easton, "Vidor's Black Population Reaches Eight, Census Shows: Town Trying to Move Past Integration History," *Dallas Morning News*, July 16, 2001, 13A.

9. "Vidor (city), Texas," last revised January 31, 2012, http://quickfacts.census.gov/qfd/states/48/4875476.html.

10. Camille Zubrinsky Charles, *Won't You Be My Neighbor? Race, Class, and Residence in Los Angeles* (New York: Russell Sage, 2006), 164.

11. Xavier de Souza Briggs, Joe T. Darden, and Angela Aidala, "In the Wake of Desegregation: Early Impacts of Scattered Site Public Housing on Neighborhoods in Yonkers, New York," *Journal of the American Planning Association* 65, no. 1 (Winter 1999): 29.

12. "Letters to the Editor," posted March 23, 2011, http://www.philadelphiaweekly.com/news-and-opinion/letters/Letters-to-the-Editor3232011.html#ixzz1IZrkYWSQ.

13. Briggs, Darden, and Aidala, "In the Wake of Desegregation," 29.

14. David Ibata, "Couple Held at Gunpoint, Arrested After Buying Home," *Atlanta Journal Constitution*, April 20, 2012.

15. Frances Robles, "Shooter of Trayvon Martin a Habitual Caller to Cops," *Miami Herald*, March 21, 2012.

16. Zimmerman was later charged with second-degree murder after an investigation by an outside state's attorney following a national outcry.

17. Mary Pattillo, "Black Middle-Class Neighborhoods," *Annual Review of Sociology* 31 (2005): 320.

18. Camille Zubrinsky Charles, "Processes of Racial Residential Segregation," in *Urban Inequality: Evidence from Four Cities,* ed. Alice O'Connor, Chris Tilly, and Lawrence D. Bobo (New York: Russell Sage, 2001), 230.

19. John R. Logan and Brian J. Stults, "Racial and Ethnic Separation in the Neighborhoods: A First Look at Changes since 2000," Census Brief prepared for Project US2010, December 14, 2010, http://www.s4.brown.edu/us2010.

20. Ibid., 4.

21. Ibid.

22. Ibid., 6.

23. Greg J. Duncan and Anita Zuberi, "Mobility Lessons from *Gautreaux* and Moving to Opportunity," *Journal of Law and Social Policy* 1 (Summer 2006): 114.

24. Jennifer Comey, Susan J. Popkin, and Kaitlin Franks, "MTO: A Successful Housing Intervention," *Cityscape* 14, no. 2 (2012): 87-108.

25. Duncan and Zuberi, "Mobility Lessons from *Gautreaux*," 117.

26. Melvin L. Oliver and Thomas M. Shapiro, *Black Wealth/White Wealth: A New Perspective on Racial Inequality* (New York: Routledge, 1997), 17.

27. Ibid., 19.

28. Ibid., 23.

29. A Pew Research Center report based on government data from 2009 found that the median wealth of white households in America is twenty times that of black households. Rakes Kochhar, Richard Fry, and Paul Taylor, "Wealth Gaps Rise to Record Highs between Whites, Blacks and Hispanics," Pew Research Center Report, accessed November 4, 2012, http://www.pewsocialtrends.org/2011/07/26/wealth-gaps-rise-to-record-highs-between-whites-blacks-hispanics.

30. Sheryll Cashin, *The Failures of Integration: How Race and Class Are Undermining the American Dream* (New York: Public Affairs, 2004), 186.

31. Ibid.

32. Ibid., 192.

33. Ibid., 198.

34. "Our View: Racism, Vigilante Shootings," *Charleston Gazette,* December 28, 2008. Christina Loboguerrero, "Latinos on Edge in Pennsylvania Town," *La Prensa San Diego,* August 1, 2008, 1.

35. According to Ami Lynch, "When we ask why segregation persists, we must acknowledge the benefits whites believe it provides them. The opportunities associated with these neighborhoods are known by residents and non-residents alike, and as the population of racial minorities increases in the United States and they attempt to secure a 'piece of the pie,' whites may restrict access." Ami Lynch, "Hating the Neighbors: The Role of Hate Crime in the Perpetuation of

Black Residential Segregation," *International Journal of Conflict and Violence* 1 (2008): 11.

36. Easton, "Vidor's Black Population Reaches Eight."

37. David K. Shipler, *A Country of Strangers: Blacks and Whites in America* (New York: Knopf, 1997), 562.

38. Martin Luther King Jr., *A Testament of Hope: The Essential Writings and Speeches of Martin Luther King, Jr.*, ed. James Melvin Washington (San Francisco: Harper-Collins, 1986), 118.

39. Orlando Patterson, "The Last Race Problem," *New York Times,* December 30, 2006.

INDEX

Jeannine Bell is Professor of Law at Indiana University Maurer School of Law in Bloomington, Indiana. She is the author of *Policing Hatred: Law Enforcement, Civil Rights, and Hate Crime*; *Police and Policing Law*; and *Gaining Access to Research Sites: A Practical and Theoretical Guide for Qualitative Researchers* (with Martha Feldman and Michele Berger).